21 Siblings
Cheaper by the Two Dozen

HELEN MILLER

ISBN-13: 978-0-692-08928-6
ISBN-10: 0-692-08928-4

Contents

Foreword

To show how much she loved us, Mom cooked and baked with a passion. Always wearing a dress and apron, she spent much of her time in the kitchen, (the social center of our household, coincidentally half-way between the baby cribs and the washer/dryer). Several of my twenty-one siblings wanted their children to have the benefit of Mom's recipe collection, so I started gathering Mom's hand-written recipes and typing them in to my very first personal computer. I tried to imagine what it must have been like for Mom, teaching daughter after daughter how to cook, according to each girl's interest/ability, while juggling a dozen other priorities. How could I capture Mom's joy, her skill, and her zest for life, and pass it along to the next generation?

I prefer savoring the memories of meals our family ate back on the farm to memories of some pretty awesome five-star restaurants. I reminisce about a more intimate setting that made me feel insanely comfortable, happy, and satiated on multiple levels. I try to recreate that homey feeling where I enjoyed the comradery of many people seated around one table, animatedly chatting while enjoying simple but fabulous hearty Midwestern dishes.

To this day, I still don't feel completely "normal" unless a hubbub of friendship and hospitality surrounds me when I'm eating. Without a handful of my siblings, something is missing. While I treasure peace and quiet, I absolutely love having guests for dinner. Just like Dorothy in the Wizard of Oz, I traveled far and wide before I came to fully appreciate the fact that *there's no place like home.*

At the time my parents had twelve children, the movie "Cheaper by the Dozen" was playing in theaters. Mom and Dad sat down with my eldest sister who was about 15 at the time and asked, "Do you think we should go for an even two dozen? Things will be even Cheaper by the Two Dozen." As difficult as it is to fathom, they really did want a huge family!

Nearly thirty years ago, I started documenting Mom's recipes including stories about our family. When recipes became readily available on the internet, and people lost interest in hard-copy cookbooks, I put my project on hold. Now that organic food and sustainable gardening are all the rage, and huge families are a thing of the past, my nieces and nephews are more interested in the olden days. They want to hear more stories about life on the farm with twenty-two kids.

My eldest sister is fifteen years older than I, and my youngest brother is eleven years younger. Their experiences growing up were, no doubt, completely different from mine. Growing up as a middle child gave me a unique perspective to share our family story. I picked up where I had left off in hopes that readers will share my enthusiasm for a time when life was simpler. This memoir offers my two cents worth on what it was like growing up in a huge family on a farm in southern Minnesota thriving on locally-produced food.

"How do you feed all those kids, mister?"

"They come cheaper by the dozen, you know."

Frank Bunker Gilbreth, Jr., and Ernestine Gilbreth Cary in "Cheaper by the Dozen"

CHAPTER 1:

In the Beginning

I GREW UP the 13th of twenty-two children from one mother and one father, all born between December 21st, 1940 and January 13th, 1966. No twins, no triplets, and no fertility drugs. That's fifteen girls and seven boys, twenty-two natural-born single births in twenty-five years plus three weeks.

When their first child was born, Dad was twenty-three and Mom had just turned eighteen. Needless to say, my parents thrived on raising children. When asked why they had so many, and whether they were planned, Mom said, "I want all the children that God gives me." After she suffered a miscarriage on her 23rd pregnancy, Mom's doctor shocked her when he advised against additional pregnancies. Mom returned home with a heavy heart.

Because the U.S. census bureau doesn't keep statistics on family size, we can't prove we are the largest family in America. The Guinness Book of World Records declined my application for largest family in deference to a Russian woman who supposedly bore 69 children circa 1705. They also declined my application for the most single births in the least amount of time, stating that they did not want to start a new category. According to Wikipedia, our family holds the record for the largest living single-birth family in the U.S. in this century.

Given the way the birth rate is dropping, my parents' enduring legacy may go down in history as having raised the last huge family in America. Until 2013, seventy-three years after my eldest sibling was born, all twenty-two Miller siblings were alive and well.

In November, 1966, Earl Huneke from Huneke Studio took this photo at Tau Center in Winona, MN.
Back row: Rose Ann (1943), Jan Irene (1951), Bob (1946), Al (1942), Kathleen (1945), Ramona (born December, 1940), Marylu (1948), John (1950), Diane (1949), and Pat (1947)
Front row: Pauline (1960), Angi (1962), Lor (1957), Ginny (1954), Dad holding Damien (born January, 1966), Greg (1964), Mom holding Marcia (1963), Helen (1955), Linda (1953), wearing a dress I had sewed for her, Alice (1961), Marty (1959), and Art (1956)

People often ask: "How did they do it?" "How did they feed 22 children?" "How can anyone afford clothes for that many?" "How did your parents keep track of you?" "How did they get you to behave?" "How big was your house? Did you all sit at the same table and eat together?" "Did you have servants?" "How many bedrooms?" "How could you afford a college education?"

Hundreds of times throughout my life, inquiring minds have wanted to know. For all of you who so often encouraged me to write a book,

Lucille Kahnke Miller Family Tree

	John Meade	Jane Press	Elizabeth M. Rohenke	Albert John Kahnke
Born	Ireland	England		
Birth Date	5/1827 or 22	4/20/1818		
Died	10/22/1904	d.	2/12/1903 or 02	1/20/1904
Married			11/7/1842, emigrated to MN 1854	

	Bridget Philip Lynch	Sophia Rasberry Kimber		Johann Adam Amberg
Born		Ireland		
Birth date		3/24/1834		3/5/1820
Died		11/1/1918		6/20/1879

	Margaret Me-ade	James Lynch	Mary A. Amberg	George S. Kahnke
Born	2/7/1863	2/22/1858	2/10/1869	7/20/1861
Died	12/21/45	1/2/26	4/18/1934	12/3/1951
Married	4/29/1885		11/5/1889	

	Mary Hattie Lynch	Vincent John Kahnke
Born	2/3/1896	7/31/1891
Died	12/15/1970	1/29/1944
Married	1/27/1913	

Lucille Rose Kahnke

Born	12/16/1922
Died	08/28/2006
Married	4/16/1940

let me attempt to tell it like it was, or, at least, the way I remember it.

My Irish and German mother, Lucille Rose Kahnke Miller, was the third of seven Kahnke children raised on a farm in Janesville, MN. She came from humble beginnings where both boys and girls learned to milk cows by hand. *"We had plenty of work after school,"* Mom wrote in her memoir entitled "My Career," *"hauling in wood and water and feeding cows, horses, chickens, and hogs. For a few years, we also had sheep [ ] and about 15-20 cows to milk... Chores were a lot of work because there was no electricity or running water in those days."* She could harness and hitch her family's team of horses to work the barley, oats, corn, and alfalfa fields, including pulling a wagon while she hand-picked corn to feed their herd of hogs.

When Mom was still a young teenager, her father's health declined. Suddenly she found herself doing farm chores normally accomplished by a grown man. Without the help of her father, she and her siblings just barely kept their farm running.

As the country sunk further into the Great Depression, my mother's family posted a hand-carved face of a kitty by the railroad that ran past their farm. Drifters who noticed it while riding the train knew they would be welcome to exchange farm labor for a hot meal and a place to rest. It is entirely characteristic of my mother's incessant optimism that feeding these homeless drifters was the only anecdote Mom shared regarding the Great Depression.

At that time, Mom's younger sister, Marg, lived at home and helped run the family farm. Sixty some years later, Marg burst into tears all over again as she told the story of how *Grama Kahnke* (as we affectionately called her) asked her excited daughter what was needed for her upcoming wedding. Marg responded, "a dress, hat and shoes." They drove an hour to get to to

**1934: Mom and her siblings
Back row: Mom, Marian, Herb
Front Row; Dave, Therese, Vincent, Marg**

Mom and her sister Marg standing next to the load of corn they picked by hand the year before Mom got married

the store before Grama reached in her purse and pulled out her last two dollars. Handing it to Marg, she said, "This can help you with the shoes." Marg was devastated; her mother was her only source of income.

After Grandpa Kahnke developed cancer, Mom's mother learned to care for sick people in their homes in order to earn enough money to feed her family, while Mom's elder sister became a nun and a teacher. From this sister Mom learned to place high value on education. *"In*

1935-36 I started my last year in country school," Mom wrote. *"I had also been in the county spelling bee and was broken-hearted when I only took second place. In 1936 I graduated from eighth grade on the honor roll. The ceremonies were held at Central School with superintendent Arthur Spetstouser giving the Certificates. It was a big thrill for me as I had not been to many large gatherings such as that, having spent most of my life on or near the farm."*

My father, Alvin Joseph Miller, Sr., was born on a farm north of Waseca, MN, the third of six children.

The word Waseca derives from the native American word for fertile, and the area enjoys some of the best black-dirt farmland in the U.S. As a child, Dad learned to work the land and tend animals to make a living. At a young age, Dad learned that where there's work to be done,

1936: Dad and his siblings in front of their relatively new brick house. Francis, Leo, Dad, Gene, Mary, Irene

Alvin Joseph Miller, Sr. Family Tree

	Anna Mueller's parents	Maria Graf	Mathias Mueller
Born	From Konigsfeld, Austria	4/14/1816	5/23/1797
Died	Names and dates unknown	8/30/1846	7/23/1883
Married		7/21/1836	

	Johanna Weber	Franz (Frank) Schmidt	Barbara Spindler	Joseph Stangler
Born	6/24/1834	8/5/1832	6/10/1826	2/7/1817
Died	4/15/1896	d.7/5/1896	d.6/4/1906	d.6/27/1911
Married	1852?		1844?	

	Mary Schmidt	Frank Stangler	Anna Mueller	Joseph Mueller
Born	4/9/1862	7/28/1857	4/12/1839	4/14/1842
Died	11/6/1949	12/2/1929	12/2/1915	1/24/1930
Married	1/25/1883		12/4/1867	
	Edith Amelia Stangler		Peter John Miller	
Born	11/18/1889		3/8/1880	
Died	10/24/1977		11/8/1961	
Married	5/28/1912			

	Alvin Joseph Miller, Sr.
Born	4/26/1917
Died	4/26/2007
	4/16/1940

you don't sit around waiting for someone to let you know; you just DO it. During seventh and eighth grades, Dad was paid 15 cents a day to arrive by 8:10, put the kindling on, start the fire, then walk to the closest farm to draw a pail of drinking water. Whenever he described this, he didn't complain. He just said, "Yup, that's the way it was." Throughout his life, Dad placed high value on hard work.

Dad's rather stoic parents worked hard. Public displays of affection were virtually non-existent; Dad saw his parents kiss for the first time when he was a teenager. However, Dad's family took time to enjoy life. When my father was three, his parents took him to the circus. Some eighty-five years later he recalled, "*There was a clown running around there all day and I liked the clown. The clown took a rope 4-foot-long and he lassoed the horse and stopped the horse while the horse was running away. Then four horses came racing by and he threw the rope and lassoed all four horses at once.*"

According to Dad, "*It was always a busy time on [my childhood] farm but on Sundays or holidays we usually celebrated. With the old cars we had at that time it was nothing to go to West Bend, Iowa, Wisconsin Dells, or the State Fair. Families and friends got together for picnics and dinners much oftener than today.*"

Although Dad came of age during the Great Depression, I never once heard him talk about it. However, he shared this in his book entitled "Memoirs:"

"*I can remember the stock market crash of 1929. We were taking the St. Paul daily news at the time. A few days later Dad went to town and found that all the banks had closed but that only two had re-opened. Corn prices went down to $.10 a bushel and farmers started burning it for fuel. Hogs went down to $.25 a pound and other prices dropped accordingly. Farmers couldn't make the payments on their mortgages and they were losing their farms. To make it worse, a long-range drought set in about this time. For several years we had poor hay and grain crops and the corn ears were just nubbins. With the open winters we had several dust storms in March. The sky was murky for days and the dust blew through the locked windows and settled all over the house.*"

As with many people who survived the Great Depression, my father never used a credit card; he kept careful track of every penny he spent, and methodically cut corners so that he could save up for the world's most frugal vacations. In the mid-sixties, Dad had only been able to save up $278 to take Mom and seven kids all the way around Lake Superior in our van, and that included money for gas! Stretching his meager savings meant tents instead of hotels, sandwiches instead of restaurants, no fancy museums or movies, just a good ol' fashioned family vacation!

Dad penny-pinched on most things, but made an exception regarding the type and amount of food that was served when our family had company. He also made it a priority to give each of his children an "inheritance" when they

Mom, April 16th, 1940 photographed by Dad

Dad on their wedding day, likely photographed by his mother, Edith.

left home. In his old age, Dad donated money to every single charity that sent him a letter, even if only ten cents.

Unlike his two elder brothers, Dad had the benefit of a high school education. He recalled, "I went to [grade] school with Roy Nelson, my only classmate for 7 of the 8 years. One year a girl moved in, but she moved out the next year." Dad's parents sent him to live in town with his Grandma Stangler so he could attend high school. He was the first of the four boys in his family to graduate from high school. Dad's parents desperately hoped my father would join the priesthood; their wish faded after Dad met Mom at his cousin Ethyl's wedding dance.

Mom was the maid of honor at her eldest brother's wedding in November of 1936. Beautiful in her floor-length silk gown, she was a delightful and eager dance partner. In June of 1938, Dad showed up at her parents' house and asked if he could take Mom out for a strawberry soda. Grama Kahnke, thrilled that a boy from such a good, honest and forthright Catholic family would be interested in her daughter, immediately said, "Yes." Only after Dad fell in love did he find out that Mom was only thirteen when they first met!

Dad wrote: "1939 was one of the happiest years of my life. I had a steady girl friend and I had my own car. I had a good job, and most important, I was learning how to farm."

In September of 1939, Dad asked his parents for permission to get married. *Grama* and *Grampa* Miller preferred my mom and dad wait until Mom turned seventeen before they would support the young couple getting married. They were none too happy that Mom's family was struggling financially and that she had gone to school only through the eighth grade. They worried about her health and the health of any future grandchildren because of Irish immigrants' bad reputation for disease.

**Back row: Mom's sister Marg, Dad's brother Leo, Dad, his father Peter, mom's brother Herb
Middle row: Dad's sister Mary, Great Grandma Stangler, Herb's wife Ethel Miller Kahnke, Mom,
her father Vincent, Dad's mother Edith Stangler Miller,
Front row: Dad's sister Irene, Mom's brother Dave, Mom's sister Therese, Great-Grandma Lynch,
Mom's mother Mary Lynch Kahnke. Mom's brother Vince may have taken this photo.**

Another consideration was that Grampa Miller needed more time to save enough money to help Dad buy a farm. Grampa Miller almost always drove used cars to save money. In 1940, Grama and Grampa Miller were still boarding Sophie Chirp, the country school teacher, for $10 a month. "If he wouldn't have [driven used cars, boarded school teachers and lived frugally]," Dad told me many years later, "he couldn't afford to give $6,000.00 to each of his four sons." My father got $5500 instead of a full six thousand because he went to high school. His father "had it all planned out."

Grampa Miller did not want his sons to raise families in Waseca's Sacred Heart parish because the Catholic priest there believed in tithing. The priest even had carpet chains put across the pews (no entry for people who did not pay "pew rent"). The country was still recovering from the Great Depression, much of the world was at war, and Grampa insisted that strict ten percent tithing would put too much of a financial burden on young farm families.

Grampa Miller had already helped his first and second sons buy farms in New Richland, MN, thirteen miles south of his "home place." All of my parents' siblings lived their entire adult lives within an hour or so of where they were born. Describing the real estate situation in the late 30's, Dad wrote, "*Land was a lot cheaper south of Waseca, mostly because at that time it was a sort of gumbo that wasn't tiled, and it was hard to plow.*" In the summer of 1939, Dad worked threshing hay in South Dakota. It was during this trip that he decided he no longer wanted to work for other people. Instead, he wanted his own farm and the opportunity to earn money while having a good time.

"*I spent all my free time at home hunting. A man's threshing wages at that time were a dollar a day and I could make that much hunting and enjoy myself. 22 shells were $.15 a box or two for a quarter. We sold our rabbits for $.15 and jack rabbits were $.25. I also did a little trapping.*"

In the fall of '39 Dad and his brother, Leo, sat down with a Montgomery Ward's catalog and bought equipment for their farms: hammers, saws, chisels, etc. They went to every auction sale to buy equipment, beds, furniture, etc. and they got some things from their parents including Grama Kahnke's dishes, and her treadle sewing machine.

As soon as Mom and Dad received their parents' approval to get married, Dad gifted Mom an engagement ring for Christmas in 1939 and Grampa Miller bought a house on 158.5 acres of farm land for $36 an acre, and rented it to Dad and Mom. "The Hartland farm" was not far from Dad's two elder brothers' farms. The house itself was brand new, built in November of '39. An old bachelor named Iwald Hanson lived there, and had not painted it yet. Dad moved in March 4th, 1940 and painted the house in the weeks before

Mom came. Dad built a wooden sink with a slop pail (wash basin under). Then he bought linoleum and had a helluva time getting it under the stove and even years later didn't know how he could have succeeded. Mom helped paint, and made curtains with Grama's treadle machine.

With the support of both families, Mom and Dad celebrated their 8AM wedding at St. Anne's Catholic Church in Mom's home town of Janesville, MN on April 16th, 1940 , followed by a simple reception at her parents' home. Because it was the custom for Catholics to fast from midnight on before receiving communion, weddings in those days were often held first thing in the morning.

Instead of honeymooning, Mom and Dad immediately started farming. *"I was a farm girl,"* Mom wrote in her memoir, *"and had no adjustments to make being married to a farmer."*

To increase the amount of tillable land, Dad dynamited huge rocks; together he and Mom picked up pieces and used a team of horses to haul them away. "Many of the stones were used in the foundation of the barn which was just being built." With help from Dad's brother and a hired hand, my father cleared the trees with a cross-cut saw. They hired a portable saw miller and were super-excited to get planks for constructing buildings on their very own farm. White Rock

capons (neutered roosters) ran all over the yard. They built picket fences with two wooden gates so chickens could not go on the lawn.

Two months after their wedding, they were down to their very last dollar. Because Mom's parents had once borrowed money from a bank, the newlyweds felt confident they would be able to get a loan. They spent that dollar going to a dance and ordering a hamburger. The next day, they went to Albert Lea to borrow money. The banker asked, "Are you farmers?"

"Yes."

"Then go borrow money from the Production Credit Association (PCA)." The PCA would see what you own and lend money for 5%. Mom and Dad borrowed $1,000 that day, of which Mom's memoir states $700 was for the "Farmall H" tractor, and Dad's notes show $970 for that same tractor. When it comes to arithmetic, I definitely trust Dad's recollection!

In 1940 Dad raised certified oats, and certified flax. State-tested flax and oats sold for what Dad considered "big money." Overall though, income was scarce because there was a blizzard the fall of 1940, and they couldn't pick corn 'til spring. Dad and Mom survived eating squash, the one plant that had produced a bountiful harvest in their new garden. Mom was pregnant with her first child, and had difficulty keeping down anything but soda crackers and pickles, a diet she stuck to during many pregnancies.

My father was a gifted story-teller; he quite frequently told one story after another without stopping, whether or not some of us had heard it before. As Mom lay confined to her bed in the Janesville Nursing Home at age 83, I documented some of Dad's ramblings as he tried to keep Mom cheered up. About a month before Mom passed away, Dad and Mom regaled me with this story:

Five days after her eighteenth birthday, Mom told Dad, "It's time to go to the hospital," even though it was seven or eight weeks prior to her due date. She remembers being excited, "and some scare." Dad replied that he wanted to finish milking the cows before they left. They didn't have a phone to call anyone, so they started for town about 8PM after he finished milking. They dashed over the frozen roads. Mom told him, "You gotta drive faster..."

Dad grinned as he said, "Going over those rutty frozen roads must have been a thrill for you." He looked sheepishly at Mom while he told the story, "It probably hastened the baby's birth."

"My water broke between Hartland and Albert Lea in the car; that's how I knew," Mom said.

"We just got to the hospital and got to the bed and the first baby was born," said Dad.

Mom had a puzzled look on her face, and mentioned she thought it took a couple hours, but Dad remembered how the baby came while he parked the car.

Mom said she was ready for her (Ramona), to be "out." "When she was born, Ramona weighed six pounds - pretty big for being early."

Dad ended this story with a piece of advice. "She almost had the baby before we got there... So now I tell new fathers: Don't stop to milk the cows!"

Only because her doctor considered Mom's first pregnancy risky, Mom delivered the baby in the local hospital (instead of at home as generations before her had done). After that, each of Mom's children were born in a hospital.

Throughout her life, my mother epitomized going with the flow. You know the poem that starts, "Go placidly amid the noise and haste?" That was my mom. Nothing ruffled her feathers. For Mom, it was a big show of emotion to use expressions like "Dear Me!" "Mercy me!" or "Oh my heavens!" Where other people might have sworn, my mom would say, "Heavens to mercatroy!" Typical of 1950's matriarchs, Mom's career was being a full-time mother. She cooked, cleaned, and raised a family. She shared her talents and her energy with her community, and helped Dad with outdoor chores when time permitted.

Mom was humble, kind, generous and religious. She almost never got sick and did not complain about being tired. My mother didn't express love verbally, but she exuded it. She maintained close friendships with her siblings, and craved time to chat with her three sisters. She wrote to her elder sister once a week for years. She replicated her own mother's generosity and created a similarly trusting household within our family. She was joyful to the point of being eternally optimistic, but not unrealistically so.

She helped our family develop an appreciation for the joy of life, and of mothering. She was a very good cook who managed the organized chaos of raising a large family while maintaining a gentle voice and a loving attitude. She tolerated messiness as long as everyone was happy. In her leisure time, she did what she called "fancy work" (mostly embroidery). Like many of her Irish ancestors, Mom loved music. For two years, her father took her to Mankato by horse for weekly violin lessons. *"The violin? It belonged to Grandpa Kahnke, could have come from Germany, I'm not sure."*

She played violin as a hobby, and very much liked to dance. A favorite moment was when she entertained the crowd with a tap dance routine at my sister Kathleen's wedding dance, August 10th, 1974. Asked about when she learned to dance, Mom replied; *"I taught myself from a book I took out of the library when I was a girl."*

Our parents taught us inclusiveness, compassion, and overcoming adversity. They emphasized that it was our duty to use our God-given talents to the best of our ability. It was clear that Mom and Dad were ALWAYS too busy; those of us in the middle of the family grew up trying not to bother them. My Irish heritage cautions that idle hands are prone to getting into trouble. My German heritage taught me to stay busy and to work hard, in order to be rewarded.

As a child, I never felt certain that all was well; I felt I had to DO something to make things better. Sometimes the weight of all that responsibility burdens my siblings and me but considering my siblings' accomplishments, it's clear that the duty to use our talents was a lesson well-learned.

My dad almost never used emotional words, but he showed his pride by puffing out his chest whenever he was photographed with his family. He was quick to smile and enjoyed a good joke. Dad complemented Mom's easy-going Irish disposition; he ran a very tight ship. With so many people under one roof, Dad had to do whatever it took to prevent mass chaos. Outsiders might have viewed the way our household ran as "organized confusion" or what my first employer referred to as "scramble management;" Dad was a stickler for getting things done the way he wanted. "How many times do I have to tell you?" was one of his favorite expressions of frustration.

When it came to straight rows in his fields, my father was an absolute perfectionist, but the rest of the time his rule of thumb was "Good enough is good enough." From my father's German ancestry, we inherited discipline, a sense of duty and determination, a fierce independence, a phenomenal work ethic (with a focus on efficiency and productivity); there was no rest for the weary. Dad also gifted us with a spirit of wanderlust, and plenty of motivation to reap the rewards of success.

When I was young, my father read whatever he could find about fishing and big game hunting all over the world, and excitedly re-told these stories, planting seeds of adventure in our young minds. His budget restricted his early vacations to going hunting and fishing in northern Minnesota and across the border into Canada. However, in middle-age, my parents traveled as much and as often as they could afford, both throughout the United States as well as to Europe a few times, Mexico for a cheap winter break (many years in a row), to Yugoslavia, to Panama, and to the Holy Land.

From my mother's Irish roots, we benefitted from a cultural heritage of joy, sensitivity, generosity, celebration, and community building. My mother taught us patience and showed us what it meant to listen more than we spoke. My mother was more interested in happy children and continuous education than in a spotless home. She had been trained to "make do" with whatever was available, and she was an expert at that.

Dad was as strong as an ox and he worked harder than anyone I have ever met. He never got sick; he worked happily to provide for our family, often whistling a merry-go-round tune as he went through his day. An expert hunter, fisherman, and accomplished trapper, Dad was also an excellent marksman. When given the chance, my father could talk, literally non-stop, about his hunting and fishing adventures, his childhood memories, and entertain us with stories of distant places to visit. Typical of men of his era, my dad did not often talk about his feelings, but it was pretty darn clear to us when he was happy and when he was mad. Whenever Dad had leisure time, he enjoyed fishing, hunting, trapping, telling stories of his own adventures, and reading about other peoples' adventures.

The only time I ever heard my dad raise his voice with Mom, I must have been about six or eight years old. Dad often shouted at us kids to get us to behave, but the mere possibility that Dad was yelling at Mom one night woke up the whole family. Such a thing had never happened before!

The girls' bedroom sat directly over our dining room and had an air vent with a metal grate so heat could rise; we called that vent "the register." If you laid on the floor, and looked down through the eight by eight-inch register with slanted grates, you could catch a glimpse of what was going on near the kitchen table.

My parents had just returned from a wedding where Mom had danced the last dance with Dad's cousin, Milt. In the kitchen beneath us, my parents sat drinking coffee.

"You're supposed to dance the last dance with me!" Dad bellowed. His booming voice instantly awakened me and my sisters. Six little girls, me included, quietly hustled toward the register.

"But I didn't realize it was the last dance," Mom said. We laid in shock on our bedroom floor, heads squeezed together, eyes and ears glued to the register, desperately trying to peek through the grates to see what was happening.

"But you should have!" His blaring voice carried clearly. He continued, "They *always* announce the last dance."

My sisters and I had never before heard my parents argue. That was the first time I had ever heard my dad even *raise his voice* in disagreement with my mom. My sisters and I were in shock. Mom probably realized at least six children were watching from above to see how she handled the situation.

As was her nature, Mom stayed calm and self-deprecatingly apologized profusely for something that was clearly not her fault, then passively served Dad more coffee and something to eat while she waited for him to relax and move on.

That incident was indicative of my mom's nature. Mom never argued; she didn't even stand up for herself when she was dead right. Mom was willing to give you the shirt off her back; she treated others better than she treated herself, and sacrificed her desires for her children's. Our mom lived in service to others; that is her enduring legacy. For the next forty-five years of Mom's life, I never again heard my parents quarrel.

We were raised Catholic on a farm where we enjoyed both a happy and a healthy childhood. Together Mom and Dad raised a family of people who are happiest being around other people. Following in my parents' footsteps, our family has developed a well-deserved reputation for engaging with those around us to make the world a better place for all, each in his or her own way.

Children of Lucille Kahnke Miller and Alvin Miller, Sr.	
Name	Date of Birth
1. Ramona Mary, aka Sister Perpetua, Sister Ramona	December 21, 1940
2. Alvin Joseph, aka Al, or Junior	September 15, 1942
3. Rose Ann, aka Rosie	December 10, 1943, (mentally challenged)
4. Kathleen Edith, aka Katie, Sister Elvira	June 3rd, 1945
5. Robert Vincent, aka Bob, Bobert	June 17, 1946, (mentally challenged)
6. Patricia Jean, aka Pat, Patty	July 21, 1947
7. Mary Lucille, aka Marylu	August 15, 1948
8. Diane Margaret	August 24, 1949
9. John Charles	August 22, 1950
10. Janet Irene aka Jan, Jan Irene	December 4, 1951
11. Linda Louise	February 4, 1953
12. Virginia Therese, aka Ginny	March 21, 1954
13. Helen Rita	May 26, 1955
14. Arthur Lawrence, aka Art	September 12, 1956
15. Dolores Maria, aka Lor	September 24, 1957
16. Martin Peter, aka Marty	June 22, 1959, (mentally challenged)
17. Pauline Carmel	May 23, 1960
18. Alice Callista	October 14, 1961
19. Angela Mary, aka Angi	October 6, 1962
20. Marcia Marie	September 21, 1963
21. Gregory Eugene, aka Greg	October 18, 1964
22. Damien Francis	January 13, 1966

CHAPTER 2:

Our Burgeoning Household

ALTHOUGH DAD NEVER spoke about WWII, he wrote: *"In 1942, with Hitler taking over Europe and our war with Japan, following the Pearl Harbor bombing, our government urged the farmers to produce more food with less fuel and machinery. We went to meetings and were taught all the labor-saving ideas. Gasoline, tires, sugar and coffee were rationed. There was a shortage of rope and a hemp factory was built at New Richland [MN]."*

Fortunately, Dad did not have to join the army; instead he helped the war effort by growing hemp used for ropes. Mom got pregnant with her second child around the time that the US entered WWII.

In September of 1942, Mom and Dad drove little Ramona to Grama Kahnke's, then

Al and Ramona, all dressed up for a photo shoot

proceeded to the Waseca hospital where Alvin Joseph (Junior) was born. He was known simply as "Junior" for his entire childhood. My father spoke of the early forties as amongst the best days of his life. Happy to have a beautiful wife who was willing to help him manage the farm, and two healthy and adorable children, he could work hard for himself and his family instead of for someone else's benefit. Overall, he felt very, very lucky.

Grama Kahnke lived about 30 miles away. When Mom delivered each of the first two grandchildren, Grama came by horse and buggy to assist. While she helped whenever she could, it was still difficult for Mom because Grama lived so far away, and because Grama was also caring for her husband whose health was rapidly deteriorating. Grampa Kahnke succumbed to bone cancer in January of 1943.

Rose Ann, aka Rosie, was born the month before Grampa died, the first of our family's three Intellectually Disabled children. While Mom and Dad grieved Grampa's passing and struggled to raise their third child, WWII was at its peak; this was just before the Germans surrendered in Stalingrad and the Axis troops in North Africa. My mother never spoke about the war, but she inserted the following poem into her memoir.

"Quiet Please! Forget your headlines

Of Hitler screaming at the Poles,

Of starving refugees in breadlines,

Of latest strikes and Gallup polls.

Let politicians air their views,

Let Japs ignore stern British warning

Listen to more important news;

Junior took two steps this morning."

— **Author unknown**

Dad wrote: "*There was no large school in Hartland, no doctor or hospital. We both longed for the Waseca area, where our parents and most of our relatives lived. I missed the good hunting and the many lakes for fishing. Ceil [nickname for my mom] missed her family even more so, now that we needed a baby-sitter more often, and hints on housekeeping, child-raising, sewing, and all the other needs.*" Mom and Dad decided to move back to Waseca even though "*it was something that people just didn't do at that time, to build up a farm, clear the fields, put up cattle fences, lawn fences, put up new buildings and then move away.*"

Including newborn Kathleen, the Millers had become a six-person family. Taking advantage

of equity from selling their Hartland property, they could afford to trade up. September
16th, 1943, they bought the Fell family's farm
in Waseca, right next door to where Dad was
raised. Their new home was rented out for the
season, so they rented "the Armstrong place" as
of February 25th, 1944. Dad often told stories of
the joy of moving to their new home. My brother,
Al (who was only three at the time), mostly just
remembers moving the sheep in an old "pick-up"
truck.

This small farm community where I grew
up exemplified "Minnesota Nice." Neighbors
all knew each other and helped each other out,
whether that involved lending someone a cup of
sugar until they went to town shopping, pulling
a vehicle out of a snowbank, or helping fix farm
machinery. At that time, Waseca had a population of just over four thousand and each township had a journalist wannabe who published
the events of the week in the local paper, e.g.,
"Mrs. Alvin Miller hosted the Blooming Grove
Beautiful Girls Club (neighbor ladies who got together monthly to swap recipes and child-rear-
ing stories) for a luncheon on Thursday."

Waseca enjoyed fifteen minutes of fame when
Dairy Queen chose to shoot a TV commercial
on main street in the mid-sixties. Waseca is the
kind of wholesome all-American town where, as

**1944: Ramona standing in front of Mom hold-
ing Rose Ann, and Dad holding Al. This picture captures the rickety steps of their humble farmhouse, Mom's interminable smile,
and hints of stress on Dad's face.
This photo was likely taken by Grama Edith
Miller on her little brownie camera.**

1945: Mom holding Kathleen, Dad holding Rose Ann, Ramona, and Al

Garrison Keillor might say, "All the women are strong and the men are good-looking."

Mom and Dad didn't care as much about good-looking as they did about raising "good" children. They fervently prayed that some of their children would enter religious life. They hoped the others would marry a "good Catholic," preferably from our parish, and raise children on farms nearby, just like they, and their parents before them, had done in previous generations.

The farmhouse they moved into on October 30th, 1944 contained a kitchen and living room on the first floor. At the entry to the house stood a small pantry where they hung clothes to dry. Mom decorated this modest farmhouse in shades of green, her favorite color. *"The rest room was a house with a path." "The outhouse was by the hog-house, down by the old oak tree. We used it for about a year. It was already there... that far (about 50 yards) from the house."*

As I was collecting information from elder siblings about their impressions from those days, Al described the downstairs: "The ice box was in the pantry, tight against the wall; there was no fridge. The kitchen had a range: a green wood stove with two burners over the oven, and two warming bins up top. It burned wood or coal. Someone had to fetch corncobs from the porch to start this range, or else use the sled to haul in a fresh sack of corncobs. A cement floor basement held a wood furnace. While this

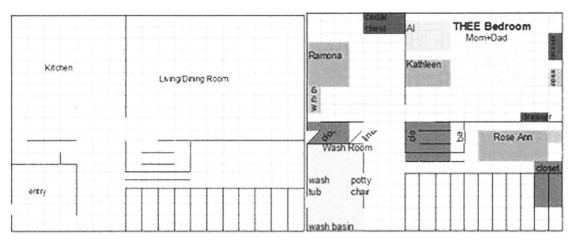

farmhouse was quite rudimentary, amazingly, it had a party-line phone!"

The upstairs consisted of a short hallway with an oversized storage room on one side and a "wash room" on the other. The hallway opened up into what Mom called the "fat hall," (five-by-twelve-foot of open hallway space adjacent a walled bedroom). The wash room contained a wash basin, a wash tub, a potty chair for toddlers and a white ceramic-coated tin chamber pot for the others to use at night. During the day, everyone used the outhouse. Although they had jet pump electricity put in the first year they lived there, they had no running water nor bathroom until after they hired a new 240-feet-deep well dug.

All six people slept upstairs; our growing family had to squeeze into a relatively tiny space: Mom and Dad slept in the twelve-by-twelve-foot bedroom alongside two cribs, one for little Al and the other for baby Kathleen, while Ramona slept in the fat hall. Even though it had no bathroom, Mom and Dad called their bedroom a master bedroom. Rose Ann slept in the oversized storage room. It was just barely big enough for one single bed, but because it had both a window and a closet, it could technically be called a second bedroom, and Mom called it "the little room."

Year after year, the young couple's household kept growing. Baby number five, Bob, was born in June of 1946. At birth, the umbilical cord was wrapped around Bob's neck; afterward, he had trouble breathing and grew up mentally challenged. Mom used to talk about taking turns with Dad to stay awake (to make sure Bob was still alive). To accommodate all five children, they needed to add a bed in the fat hall. They kept two cribs in the master bedroom, and a single bed in the little bedroom.

Mom wrote: *"Throughout the years, Alvin was good at playing games with the children in the evening so I could get a bit of a break. At the time that I had five, and when the children became a bit noisy or quarrelsome, I learned to start singing. One by one they would leave their noise and quarreling to sing with mother, the youngest perhaps beating out the rhythm on an old pie pan with spoon. Their troubles were soon forgotten and it would become peaceful again. I haven't got a very good voice myself; the children do somewhat better. But a good song beats a spanking anytime."*

When their sixth child, Patricia, was born that summer, an additional crib was needed. This time they decided it needed to go in the master bedroom. Now three babies slept in the master bedroom, two youngsters in the fat hall, and still one in the little bedroom. To keep up with the growing workload, Mom needed more arms and legs, or more minutes in the day.

Up until this time, Grama Kahnke had helped Mom with each new baby. With so many to care for, Mom hired Elsie Hart as a nanny, and, of course, Elsie needed her own bed. There was no space for more "real" beds, so my parents added a rollaway bed in the fat hall. The bed could be folded and stored in the corner during the day to allow more room to move.

Elsie was Mom's first hired helper. When Elsie left, Mom hired seventeen-year-old Aggie Pete full-time. Aggie assisted with housework and tending babies for a few years until my eldest siblings could act as backup for Mom. Mom recalled her toughest year was when she had seven children under the age of eight. "After seven," she said, "it's all the same [workload], because the eldest ones take care of the younger ones."

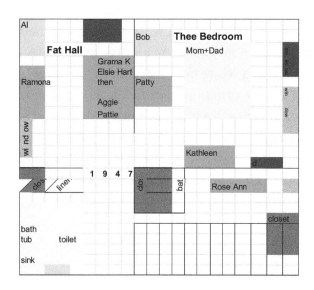

Number seven, Marylu, was born in August of 1948. I try to imagine dressing seven preschool children in time for 7AM Catholic Mass every Sunday morning, each outfitted in their fancy clothes; Mom must have been a saint! At that time, babies wore only cloth diapers. Mom's daily chores included using a wash bucket to do laundry by hand, and then hanging clothes outdoors to dry. Without a dryer, if it was below freezing, she hung clothes on a wooden rack indoors.

Between monitoring Bob's breathing day and night, nursing Marylu, feeding the family and doing laundry, Mom wasn't getting enough sleep. Contributing to Mom's workload was the lack of indoor plumbing and raising children with special needs. To be politically correct, I could use the term "Intellectually Disabled" to describe siblings with an IQ less than seventy-five. Throughout our childhood, our family used the word retarded without malice, but I prefer the use of the term "mentally challenged."

The house was bursting at the seams. Three beds completely filled the fat hall. The master bedroom had become somewhat of a nursery; it now slept Mom and Dad plus four babies! Trying to have everyone sleep in such a small space wasn't easy. To prevent Mom from collapsing

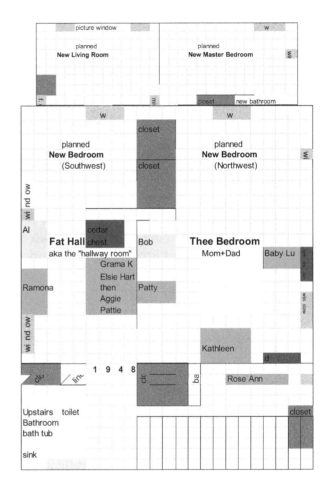

from exhaustion/sleep deprivation, something had to change.

Dad drew up plans to add a two-story addition on the west side, which would provide two more sorely needed bedrooms upstairs, a "real" master bedroom and bathroom downstairs, and a new living room. This would nearly double the

1948: Ramona holding Patricia, Al, Rose Ann, Kathleen, Robert
Before the expansion, the house had only two bedrooms, and no picture window in the living room.

Our house after 1948. On the left side of the house sits the new living room with a big picture window. Next to it stands the master bedroom. Above those two stand the two new bedrooms.

space in the house, from 840 to 1600 square feet, and give everyone room to breathe.

The addition included plans for a separate sixteen-by-thirty-foot room in the basement which, once built, became known simply as "the new part." The original basement included a bench attached to a makeshift wooden coat rack. Boots belonged under the bench, and hats/coats/jackets hung on nails directly above each kid's boots. Along the south wall stood a freezer and a wood pile. A sink, a well-water tank, and an egg-washing equipment lined the east wall. An antique cast iron wood-burning stove stood in the middle of the basement not far from the wood-burning furnace. The new part was a welcome addition for storing canned goods to feed our growing family.

At about the same time, my parents installed running water and indoor plumbing, quite an improvement over using an outhouse! Once they had running water, Grampa Kahnke gifted Mom the ultimate luxury of that era: a wringer washing machine! These improvements reduced Mom's workload in a very substantial way.

Marylu's birth came in the midst of that first major house extension project. *"It was terribly hot that summer,"* Mom wrote, *"and the house was wide open for construction, so flies were coming*

1947 in front of Grama Kahnke's house. Back row: Mom holding Robert
Front row: Ramona, Al, Rose Ann, Kathleen

in." That was the year Dad bought her what he thought of as an extravagant gift: an oscillating fan with four six-inch rubber blades. The fan was likely Mom's first electrical appliance. Under the circumstances, it was considered a delightful improvement.

As construction proceeded, which child slept in which room was a function of steering clear of the construction mess. Everyone knew they would have a bed; they just didn't know where it would be. Before the newly constructed rooms were painted and assigned, everyone waited impatiently to move into their new bedrooms. Our cousin, Matt Kahnke, practiced his artistic skills by drawing a mural of a big pig and a big cow in the northwest bedroom upstairs. Mom and Dad were so proud of their nephew's artistry they left the drawing there for years before they reluctantly painted over it. The next person to do a mural in our house was when Lor created a painting on her bedroom ceiling in the mid-70's.

Finally, in December, heating ducts were installed in the new addition, and beds were moved to their permanent

1950: The first eight children
Back Row: Kathleen, Rose Ann, Alvin Jr, Ramona, holding Diane
Front Row: Marylu, Patricia, Robert

1951 Mom, Dad and nine children, dressed for church
Back Row: Ramona holding Diane, Dad, Mom holding John
Front Row: Robert, Pat, Marylu, Kathleen, Rose Ann

location. Ramona slept in the newly added room in the northwest corner, and Al slept in the new southwest corner bedroom. Rose Ann stayed in the little bedroom. Aggie Pete continued to sleep in the fat hall. Kathleen had the luxury of her own room at age four (what had been known as the master bedroom upstairs, thereafter known as the middle room) until two-year old Patty moved in.

Post-expansion, Mom and Dad's master bedroom stood downstairs in the northwest corner of the house. Windows on two sides allowed a nice breeze. They installed a sturdy and beautiful white oak bedroom set including a tall dresser and a vanity with a big half-moon mirror. Pre-school children and my parents were the only ones allowed to use the master bathroom with its easy-to-clean Formica wainscoting and sheet-rock walls. Mom rinsed cotton diapers in the toilet and set them in the diaper pail right next to the toilet. She kept a potty chamber for the youngest kids. Back then, diapers were not throw-away. In the context of the war-rationing, Mom reminisced, "In those days, we didn't think of throw-away *anything*!"

Diane, #8, was born in August of 1949. Mom, Dad, Diane and Marylu moved into the new master bedroom downstairs. Starting with Diane, "only" two babies slept in the master bedroom. They arranged the bassinet on Dad's side of the bed, and the baby crib on Mom's side. Keeping the baby close by made it easier for Mom to nurse. Dad always took night duty for fussy babies who were not nursing; he rocked, changed, and fed them so that Mom could get her rest. Considering that two babies slept in Mom and Dad's room most years, it's a wonder how any children were conceived!

When Mom and Dad drafted plans for the extension, they had intended for two babies to remain in their new master bedroom downstairs and for the rest of the children to sleep upstairs. Bob was planned to have slept upstairs. However, before Bob could sleep on a different floor from Mom, he needed to outgrow his congenital breathing difficulty. Since that had not yet happened, Mom and Dad had no choice but to set Bob's crib just outside their room so that they could monitor his breathing. That meant placing a crib in the new living room! Thus began a new and unforeseen tradition: toddler cribs in the living room. Once a baby outgrew the little crib in the master bedroom, that baby moved to a regular size crib in the living room. As soon as a three-year-old toddler was old

Dad's younger sister, Sister Iria, and Ramona in front of our family's first station wagon, a 1951 Pontiac.

enough to sleep comfortably without expecting their mommy or daddy to get up, they were bumped upstairs.

Finally, the house felt quite comfortable for a family of ten. As part of the expansion, the range was replaced by an electric stove and the old living room became a dining room, perfect for entertaining cousins at mealtime. The living room had a "picture window" and the new front entryway faced south, complete with ample closet space and a handy deer-antler hat rack.

1952: Ten Miller Kids
Back Row: Al, Rose Ann, Ramona, holding Janet. Middle Row: Robert, Patricia, Kathleen Front Row: Diane, John, Marylu

John, #9, arrived in August of 1950, the third August baby in as many years. By the time Bob moved in to Al's bedroom that year, Aggie had moved on and Ramona became Mom's primary helper. At ten, Ramona quickly became proficient at cooking, cleaning, and babysitting. From then until Mom passed away, Mom relied heavily on her eldest daughter.

The fat hall was now used exclusively for storage, mostly just storm windows and off-season clothing. Mom's hand-made cedar "hope chest" stored winter coats in moth balls, and what had been the fat hall became known as the "cedar chest room."

Mom wrote that the low point of her career was when *"All the children had chicken pox and measles. From Thanksgiving until Easter they were sick. We had nine children then, and it seemed a long time because they did not get sick all at once but just kept getting sick one that a time."*

The blue baby bassinet was painted pink, awaiting Janet, #10, to arrive home from the hospital in early December, 1951. Marylu moved upstairs in 1952 resulting in seven kids upstairs and three downstairs.

Linda was born in February of 1953. Mom and Dad now had eleven children who were twelve years old and younger. Whew! And to think that this was only half of the children they would end up with!

Dad wrote that he and Mom had Blue Cross insurance for many years. *"It paid all the hospital bill but the $25 deductible. It paid $60 to the doctor for delivery but Dr. Ben Gallagher only charged $35, so the remainder was credited to our account. Dr. Gallagher delivered twelve of our babies, and when he retired, at this testimonial dinner we were featured for being his, should I say, best customer!"*

After Linda was born, it was Diane's turn to move upstairs. Whenever the number of beds in either the boys' or girls' room were insufficient to accommodate the newest youngster's move upstairs, it triggered a cascade of moves for the

other children. This developed into a disruptive tradition of rotating beds and sometimes bedrooms.

Only many years later did I realize that Mom rearranged our assigned beds without warning in order to make room for the arrival of a new baby downstairs. Mom tried to make sure the toddler who was moving upstairs had been potty-trained beforehand. Most of the time she succeeded.

Over the years, a conflict would occasionally develop between roommates. If the conflict was significant enough, we would come home from school to find that Mom and Dad had switched around bed assignments without warning. Moving one person meant displacing another, so at least two people at a time had been abruptly assigned new roommates.

These unannounced changes would proceed without notice for many, many years to come. If anyone ever did have the nerve to say out loud that they didn't like it, I certainly never heard a peep. So long as we each had a blanket, a pillow, and a horizontal surface, we slept soundly.

When I interviewed my siblings to get their recollections, there were, naturally, a few contradictions. Most of us remember the good times in our childhood in a general way, and remember rather specific facts about disappointments. Such deep-seated memories anchored various recollections of where we slept in any given year. One of Diane's first memories was of sleeping in the northwest room with Marylu. "Lu wet the red quilt," she recalled, and, "It made me mad." About that same time, Pat remembers that Ramona needed her own room because of the "smelly stuff" she used; perfume was no doubt new to Pat at that age.

Around this time, Mom began formally assigning each of the older siblings a youngster to care for, to help out in whatever way was needed. Mom and Dad called the younger one your "charge," a term that was borrowed from the military. *"As the size of the family grew,"* Dad wrote, *"we relied quite heavily on the buddy system. This covered everything from personal hygiene like bathing and dressing to more important issues like swimming or hiking."* Marylu took care of Linda; Patty took care of Ginny, and so on.

1954: Cheaper by the Dozen
Back Row: Patricia, Kathleen, Rose Ann, Ramona, Alvin Jr., Robert
Front Row: Janet, Marylu, Dad holding Linda, Mom holding Virginia, Diane, John

Mom disliked having her picture taken when she was pregnant. Since she was pregnant for roughly sixteen and a half years, we don't have nearly as many photos of her as of other family members. She made an exception on Mother's Day, 1955. Just a few weeks before my birth, when she won Mother of the Year, she posed for this portrait.

Mom was concerned about how her large family looked to the outside world, careful about anything that might reflect poorly on her as a mom, no doubt still striving to counteract Grama Miller's early concerns as to whether my under-educated Irish mother could become a good wife and parent. While Mom was concerned about this, it was obvious that over the years she became one of Grama's favorite daughters-in-law. When I was a teenager, Grama confided to me that Mom was the best mother of the bunch.

Mom taught the surrogate parents well, and everyone took this duty seriously, endlessly craving approval of our parents. Getting ready for church on Sunday, for example, the responsible sibling made sure their charge was awakened, dressed, had their face washed, hair combed, their prayer book in hand, and their collection-box donation-envelope prepared. The surrogate parent accounted for their charge's whereabouts, making sure they made it into the car before it was time to leave. Everyone had better be ready to go by the time Dad backed the car out of the garage (or else)!

Before taking on surrogate parent type responsibility for Pauline as part of the new buddy system, Kathleen had enjoyed holding her breath underwater whenever she went swimming; she prided herself that she could do so longer than other siblings. Around the time she was assigned responsibility for Pauline, she was also given the task of frequently counting heads to make sure no sibling had drowned. She said,

1955: Thirteen Miller Kids at Grama and Grampa Miller's house, our first colored photo
Back Row: Ramona, holding Helen, Kathleen, Rose Ann, Al
Middle Row: Robert, Pat, Diane, Marylu
Front Row: Janet, John, Virginia, Linda

"After that, I never went underwater again. I was afraid that someone would drown, and I would catch hell. I feared Dad's wrath. Looking back, it was simply too much responsibility."

Ginny, #12, was born on the first day of spring, 1954. John became Kathleen's charge. He wasn't considered old enough to sleep in his near-teenage brother's room, so he had to sleep in the girls' room for a few months. Later that year, Janet moved upstairs and shared a room with Ramona until Ramona left for college.

I was born "Lucky number thirteen" in May 1955. Lucky, that is, until I developed bronchitis as an infant and had extreme difficulty breathing. Ramona recently told me that when I was six weeks old, I actually quit breathing, and

Spring 1956: Thirteen Miller Kids in front of our tree strip
Back Row: Ramona with Helen, Rose Ann, Robert, Kathleen, Al
Middle Row: Marylu, John, Diane, Pat
Front Row: Janet, Linda, Virginia

turned blue. Because Mom thought I was dead, she rushed toward her bedroom, sobbing. My siblings vividly recall how Dad picked me up by the feet and whacked me on the back until, luckily, I "came to."

I became Diane's charge. I remember her brushing my long, thick, hair, giving me a bath, covering me up at night, and later, teaching me how to make a bed and how to tie my shoes. From my sister I absorbed the notion that everybody should be able to sing and play guitar.

Before I old enough to go to school, she taught me how to play the ukulele; she encouraged me to sing "In Old Shanty Town" at the county fair. I was too chicken. Besides, I was not gifted with rhythm nor a beautiful singing voice like hers.

Diane had more influence on my early childhood than either of my parents. It was from my sister Diane that I learned that two plus two equals four, and came to believe that being smart was an important goal. Whereas Dad hid my report card full of A's while he praised my

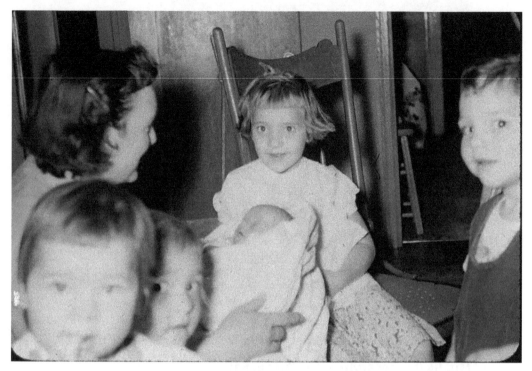

Mom showing Art to his next older siblings who could not wait to hold him. Clockwise from the top: Janet, Virginia, Linda, and Helen

older sister's report card with B's and C's because that's the best she was capable of, Diane took pride in my accomplishments and inspired me to keep up the good work.

When I broke off my front teeth in third grade, Diane instructed me to close my mouth so my jagged tooth would not show. It's no surprise that there are no photos of me with a smile; I obeyed Diane to a T. I remember Diane advising me not to talk back Dad (it had not worked

for our older sister), and to steer clear of siblings when they were mad. From Diane's influence, I learned to avoid conflict with authority. I was usually the first one to tattle on my sisters for jumping on the bed.

After the 1948 extension, our upstairs contained three legitimate bedrooms, the little room and the fat hall. By 1955, with ten children upstairs, and three downstairs, the enlarged house was once again filling up. We desperately

Fall 1956, Fourteen Children
Back Row: Ramona, holding Art, Al, Rose Ann, Kathleen, Robert
Middle Row: Pat, Marylu, Diane, John
Front Row: Helen, Virginia, Linda, Janet

needed more storage space. Dad added a "sweater chest," and installed floor-to-ceiling cabinets in the fat hall.

Depending on the age of the sibling you ask, each of the rooms in our house had different names. The twelve by twelve middle room became known as "the little girls' room" when five girls slept in two double beds and one single bed. To add room for a sixth girl, Dad replaced the single bed with a white wooden bunk bed. He also bought an army surplus bunk bed to replace the double bed he had moved to our precious new rustic cabin so we could sleep there overnight. More on that later.

I don't know what year doctors started doing routine ultra-sounds, but by the time I can remember, Mom was pretty confident about whether her next child would be a boy or a girl based on how high she carried it. In 1956, the same bassinet used for all twenty-two infants was given a coat of blue paint; that's pretty much how the family first learned that Mom was

1957: Fifteen Children, fourteen happy Millers plus one crying infant in front of our family's altar
Back Row: Ramona holding Dolores, Al holding Art, Rose Ann, Kathleen
Middle Row: Diane, John, Marylu, Patricia, Robert
Front Row: Janet, Linda, Helen, Virginia

planning for the arrival of a baby boy. I wonder how many coats of paint that old wooden basket eventually held! Art, #14, was born in September. Including him, our family now consisted of four boys and ten girls.

In August of '57, nearly eight months pregnant, Mom suffered from headaches and fever; she became sicker than she had ever been. The doctor tested her for Asian flu and for polio before diagnosing her with meningitis. Thankfully, Grama Kahnke came to help. My siblings pitched in to do what they could to make life easier for Mom and Grama. Thankfully, within a year, Mom recovered. The doctors never really knew what had caused the meningitis-like symptoms.

1957: Diane's First Communion, the year of the chimney fire

The bassinet got a color change once again before Dolores, #15, was born in September of 1957. At that point, Ginny moved upstairs leaving me, Art, and Dolores downstairs. That meant there were three boys and nine girls upstairs. Marylu, recently told me that: "With two of the bigger bedrooms used for girls, one was called the little girls' room, or simply, the girls' room, and the other was called "the other room."

Normally at night there were no night lights upstairs. Diane recalls caring for Ginny when she first moved upstairs. When Mom was sick and Grama Kahnke was babysitting: "Grama traded off between me and Lu to help her calm toddlers who were not quite ready to sleep in the dark." Much to John's dismay (he preferred to sleep in darkness), in 1958 our family began a new tradition of leaving the upstairs hall light on at night.

For many of us, memories of our childhood are a blur. When trying to remember, we start by trying to figure out which room we slept in and who our roommates were in order to anchor our memories. Due to frequent re-arranging, it is difficult to remember who slept where. With all the comings and goings in and out of various rooms, how could anyone keep track!

Diane knows she slept in the little room the year of her first communion because she has a clear recollection of the chimney fire there that wrecked her violet coat. Al clearly recalls that boys slept in the middle room around this time; in particular, he remembers shooting a gun out the middle room window, and he knows he surely would not have been shooting at grackles or crows from someone else's room!

In spring of '58, Ramona recalled, "The girls slept in the *big* room," also known by various family members as the girls' room, the little girls' room, or the middle room, depending on which era that person grew up in. "The northwest room was the boys' room at that time." Ramona remembers that I had already moved upstairs when Lor outgrew the bassinet that spring.

1958: Mom, Dad and fifteen children lined up in reverse birth order next to our freshly painted white fence
Dad holding baby Dolores, Art, Helen, Virginia, Linda, Janet, John, Diane, Marylu, Patricia, Robert, Kathleen, Rose Ann, Alvin Jr., Ramona

1960: Fifteen of the sixteen children (Ramona had left for college.)
Back Two Rows: Marylu, Al, Pat, Bob, Rose Ann, Diane, Marty held by Kathleen, John
Front Row: Art, Lor, Helen, Janet, Virginia, Linda,

When Ramona left for college in September of 1958, the first of the Miller clan to do so, Kathleen moved into Ramona's room. Thus began another new annual tradition: changing bedroom assignments in the fall when the eldest child left for college. Janet remembered Ramona's leaving home as traumatic because she was moved into the middle room after having lived with her eldest sister. At that time, the middle room had two bunks and a double bed.

If Mom's sixteenth pregnancy had gone full-term, there would have been a two-year break between Dolores and Martin. As it turned out, Marty was born prematurely in June of '59; he weighed less than five pounds and was severely developmentally delayed. Mom wrote, *"I had to leave him in the hospital ten days 'til he was big enough to take home, and while he was there I had to express my milk and take it in each day... He was so frail we didn't know if he was going to make it. He could only take in less than an ounce at a time. He had to be fed so often I could hardly get anything else done. [It seemed like forever but it was only a month] until he started getting strong."*

At that time, I slept in the little girls' room along with Marylu, Diane, Janet, Linda, and Virginia. Al slept down the hall by himself. John remembers fighting with Bob over blankets when they slept in the double bed in the boys' room. Finally, John rolled up a flour-sack dish towel and laid it down the middle as a border between the two of them. Using two sets of covers, one on either side of the makeshift border, they could both stay warm *and* get some sleep!

As a four-year-old, when I lost a blanket tug-of-war during the night, I wandered downstairs because I was cold, hoping to snuggle with Mom and Dad. To prevent this pattern, Mom sewed me a new orange quilt (my favorite color) with extra-warm wool batting. I loved that quilt! Not long after that, I craved having my own warm covers instead of sharing that quilt in a double bed. Mom re-assigned me to a bunk bed;

1957: Delivering eggs for sale before the addition of the back porch.

sadly, the orange quilt had to stay on the bed for which it fit. In retrospect, my desire for a beautiful twin size wool quilt may have been my first awareness of my life-long love of sewing, as well as my appreciation of quilts and of quilting.

Just after Linda started first grade, she had her appendix removed. In the hospital, Linda received new pajamas and a teddy bear that was nearly as tall as she was. During her convalescence, she got a lot of special attention, including being allowed to sleep downstairs and to drink as much pop as she wanted. Boy, was I jealous!

Every once in a while, "one of the little girls would go up to the big girls' room while they were gone to school and she would come downstairs like you've never seen. She would look like a clown. There would be some scolding after school!"

Considering how many children slept upstairs, keeping each person content with temperature and sleep hours worked remarkably well. Dresser drawers for clothing were not usually too constrained; we didn't have enough clothes to need any more than that. As an example, each of the six pre-teenage girls who slept in the little girls' room was assigned one specific drawer in the only dresser in that room.

Closet space was not quite as simple. We shared two wooden dowel rods in a three-by-four-foot closet for each of us to hang one Sunday dress and three or four school dresses. We each had two pairs of shoes, one pair for Sunday and school, and the other for everything else. Sunday coats were jammed into the front entryway closet; all other coats and boots got put away "down the basement."

To keep the six youngest girls from arguing over limited closet space, the eldest four were each assigned one specific quarter of the already-small closet. The two youngest girls' Sunday dresses were normally hung downstairs on Mom's over-the-closet-door-hanger to free up closet space upstairs.

Dad hired a local carpenter, Erv Sanders, to build the second major extension on to our home. Erv extended the east side of our house by adding a back porch. Up until this time, Dad hauled eggs to town in the back of our 1956 red and white Pontiac station wagon. Dad wanted the "egg man" to have access to our basement to pick up twenty cases of eggs twice a week and haul them to town. The porch added an entrance which could be used for this purpose.

Most people would probably think of our new back porch as more of a mud room. Coat hooks

Who else but our family hung an Indian arrow head collection on the porch wall?

for Dad's many hats lined one wall. As a farmer, he needed a straw hat for driving tractor, a mosquito net/hat for dealing with beehives, a camo cap for duck hunting, an orange cap and an orange stocking cap for deer hunting, a warm hat for Minnesota winters, and at least half a dozen seed corn hats (baseball caps, each monogrammed with a different seed corn company logo) to wear when riding a tractor.

Over time, the porch assumed a myriad of functions. It was not unusual to see trophy size deer antlers mounted in Minnesota farmers' entryways. But who else mounted deer feet on a plaque in their porch (to hang horse bridles or to store bow and arrows)? Who else stored a

three-gallon bucket, a two-gallon kettle and a huge funnel strainer on a metal tea cart on their porch with which to strain raw cow's milk? Who else lined shelving above mud room windows with plants? And who else covered half the cement floor of a porch with newspaper (instead of rugs) to catch dirt and dung from barnyard overshoes?

Even more unusual, who hung a telephone on the wall of a porch? The porch phone made it easy for Dad to take a phone call without having to take off his work boots. It also offered relative privacy for teenagers' phone conversations, even though for years we still had a party-line. One kitchen chair sat against that wall, doubling as a place to sit while chatting or while putting on overshoes. Honestly, when I think about all the functions that new porch served, I don't know how our family managed without it!

Another construction project followed the back-porch extension. Dad replaced all our wooden windows with metal combination windows. From then on, he no longer needed to store twenty bulky storm windows upstairs. He converted the window storage room to a bedroom for Rose Ann. Patty moved into Rose Ann's former room. Marylu roomed with *just* Kathleen for a couple years, memorable because it was quite a treat to have one roommate instead of five!

Pauline, #17, arrived in May of 1960 and Al left for the army in September of that year. After he left, Bob and John slept in the southwest room by themselves for a short time. Not long thereafter, Art moved in. After our two eldest siblings left home, three boys and nine girls slept upstairs. Mom wrote:

"Since Marty was only eleven months old when Pauline was born, and because he was behind in his development, the two of them learned to walk within a few days of each other. They were just like caring for twins. One day they decided to paint our new green car blue. When I found them in the garage they had dark blue paint on one side of the car and they were paint from head to toe. I took a washtub and stood them in it over by "the gas barrel", and washed them in gasoline, hair and all. After a soap and water bath they were again two little blonds."

Around that time, our family kept using the phrases "big kids," and "little kids," and began using the term "middle kids." Marty became known as the eldest of the "little kids." As far back as I can remember, our family used the term "kids" instead of "children." My New York boss occasionally reminded me that kids are

1961: Seventeen Children
This photo was taken in Grama Miller's new house on Loon Lake after Ramona had joined the convent.

goats that get raised, not to be confused with children who get reared; I had to tidy up my word choices and grammar at the office, but reverted back to old habits when speaking with my siblings.

Our family differentiated all twenty-two of us by grouping us into "*little* kids," "*middle* kids," and "*big* kids." Big kids had three different meanings, depending on the context:

1. Big kids included the first eight kids in the family, (vs. the seven youngest "little kids," and the rest of us were simply called "middle kids.")

2. Big kids meant school kids, versus little kids who had to stay home from school.

Bob filling the double corncrib with ears of corn before Dad had a drying bin built.

[Note: "*had to*" stay home; we all *loved* school and couldn't wait to go.]

3.   When Mom or Dad needed help, a big kid meant the oldest person capable of, and immediately available, for helping out.

Other people sometimes sent their children to live with our family. After Elsie Hart and Aggie Pete lived with us as nannies, our family took in one child at a time for a variety of reasons. They weren't technically foster children, but we considered each of them part of our family. One such child was Gayle Thissen. Gayle needed medical care to help reduce the frequency of her epileptic grand mal seizures. Mom assisted a local family by taking in Gayle and helping find specialized healthcare for her.

When Gayle was having a good day, she expertly embroidered and/or knitted (even better than what my mom could do, which is saying a lot). Gayle embroidered intricate patterns to create the most beautiful dish towels, and she knitted stunning matching sweaters for Mom and Dad. In her later years, she also knit an afghan for Mom as a birthday present.

Gayle slept in the little bedroom when Marylu was in seventh grade and was roughly the same age as Gayle. When Gayle came downstairs each morning, Marylu said she could tell by looking at her eyes and/or her bruises whether Gayle had suffered a grand mal seizure with convulsions the night prior. "That was SO stressful!" Marylu recalled. Diane agreed: "I was in charge of putting a stick in Gayle's mouth so she wouldn't swallow her tongue when she vomited."

Normally, my siblings and I were well-behaved, but Gayle's seizures frightened us. As immature children, my siblings and I sometimes teased Gayle that she stunk, or had germs. We taunted each other: "Thissen's germs, no returns!" Poor Gayle. Sometimes we were awful to her.

One day, Gayle got so frustrated she literally ran away. She went out to the double corncrib next to our barn in sub-zero weather at night

1961: Erv Sanders adding a Family Room to our crowded home.

and hid in a wooden box the size of a coffin that sat in the half-empty corn crib. Dad had built this "winter freezer" to store frozen food when our "regular freezers" were too full following a successful hunting trip.

We couldn't find Gayle anywhere. After searching high and low, Dad called the cops. Using a dog, they located this vulnerable teenager in a place we *never* would have looked. That was the end of our makeshift freezer. It also brought an abrupt end to our bullying Gayle, or, for that matter, anyone else. It also lends credence to the authors' comment in the book "Cheaper by the Dozen," *"Experience has established the fact that a person cannot move from a small peaceful home into a family of a dozen without having something finally snap."*

When Gayle moved out a year or two later, we replaced her single bed with a bunk bed and turned that room into John's room.

By this time, Mom and Dad had seventeen children and our home was once again bursting at the seams, a perennial issue with growing families. By this time, Dad had plenty of experience thinking through what size of addition to build, how many windows to request, etc., etc. In 1961, Erv Sanders extended the house for the third time, adding a twenty-by-fifteen-foot family room on the north side of the house. The furnace could not keep up so the new addition had its own natural gas heater; a large propane tank was installed in the yard solely for that room.

Despite our large new family room, to say that our house was overflowing would still be an understatement. It's hard for me to imagine now, but when I started school, eighteen of us lived quite happily in our jam-packed space. In fact, it did not seem too much different than our cousins' crowded homes.

On the first day of school, 1961, Mom exchanged the girls' room with the boys' room without notice in preparation for a new baby.

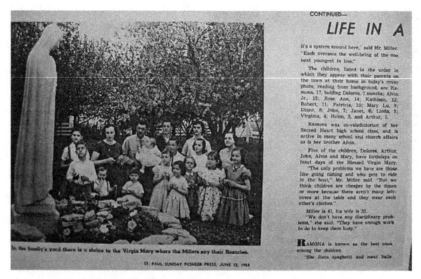

CONTINUED—
LIFE IN A

It's a system around here," said Mr. Miller. "Each oversees the well-being of the one next youngest in line."

The children, listed in the order in which they appear with their parents on the lawn at their home in today's cover photo, reading from background, are Ramona, 17, holding Dolores, 7 months; Alvin Jr., 15; Rose Ann, 14; Kathleen, 12; Robert, 11; Patricia, 10; Mary Lu, 9; Diane, 8; John, 7; Janet, 6; Linda, 5; Virginia, 4; Helen, 3, and Arthur, 1.

Ramona was co-valedictorian of her Sacred Heart high school class, and is active in many school and church affairs as is her brother Alvin.

Five of the children, Dolores, Arthur, John, Alvin and Mary, have birthdays on feast days of the Blessed Virgin Mary.

"The only problems we have are those like going fishing and who gets to ride in the boat," Mr. Miller said. "But we think children are cheaper by the dozen or more because there aren't many leftovers at the table and they wear each other's clothes."

Miller is 41, his wife is 35.

"We don't have any disciplinary problems," she said. "They have enough work to do to keep them busy."

RAMONA is known as the best cook among the children.

"She fixes spaghetti and meat balls

In the family's yard there is a shrine to the Virgin Mary where the Millers say their Rosaries.

ST. PAUL SUNDAY PIONEER PRESS, JUNE 22, 1958

Through six sliding glass window panes, we could view our shrine of the Blessed Virgin in front of a poplar and evergreen tree strip my parents had planted in 1945. We could also see one plum and one crabapple tree, and our huge vegetable garden, right next to our hog yard.

Jet-black haired Alice was born in October. Art and Dolores now both slept upstairs, while Marty, Pauline, and Alice slept downstairs. Ginny remembered she slept in the northwest room at age four or five. "When I got the chicken pox, I slept on the couch in the living room. Patty was babysitting, Aunt Mary brought me mints and Aunt Marg brought [me] cosmetics."

By 1962, we had a whopping nineteen hundred square feet of usable space. Our eleven hundred square foot downstairs included a kitchen, dining room, master bedroom/bathroom, the old living room and the new family room complete with built-in shelving for Books of Knowledge and a World Book encyclopedia set, and an entire cupboard plus a deep drawer for storing board games. We were thrilled with what we considered a huge home.

We moved the couch from the old living room to the new family room. We moved the piano from the dining room to the old living room which became known as "the baby room," the nursery, the piano practice room, and/or the sewing room, depending on who was using that room for what. Primarily because this was the only room downstairs that had doors, it was

1962: Alice was the baby when Al was in the army. This photo was taken on the College of St. Teresa campus where Ramona lived after she was given her Franciscan name, Sister Perpetua. Hats were required for visiting Catholic chapels; we all wore our Easter outfits, including our bonnets.

where each of us practiced our respective musical instruments. The absurdity of combining such varied activity into a single small space still humors me, but, believe it or not, it all worked!

After finishing the new family room, Erv totally overhauled the downstairs bathroom. Marty was still in diapers, as were Pauline and Alice. For the first time, Mom had three kids still in diapers. Since Mom used only cloth diapers, the downstairs bathroom needed space for a bigger diaper pail. Enlarging the bathroom

and upgrading it with green and white tile became the first goal. Installing a shower in the master bathroom became a secondary objective. Erv achieved both.

Dad and Erv also installed a showerhead above the upstairs bathtub, and added sliding shower doors. Prior to this, the basement had been the only option for taking a shower instead of a bath. What a pleasure! No more washing hair in the laundry room sink. No more shivering while standing on the cold basement cement under a bare shower head. No more showering next to an antique wood stove (right in between the egg washer, the water pressure tank, a dozen pails of dirty eggs, and two upright freezers), without a privacy curtain or wall.

This also meant Dad needed to put in a commercial size water-heater and a water softener. Even though we had strict time limits in the bathroom, a family our size used a lot of hot water, and it was not unusual for the last few people to be stuck taking cold showers!

During this renovation phase, Dad replaced our wood-burning furnace with a modern fuel oil furnace, and installed its tank where the wood pile used to sit. Even though the wood-burning furnace was gone, he kept the antique wood-burning range in the basement to use for rendering lard, processing honey, and in case the power went out.

Dad must have had a good harvest because when Alice outgrew her bassinet, Mom bought new baby cribs. Angela was born in October of

1963: Nineteen and Counting
Back row: Patricia, Rose Ann, Robert, Al, Kathleen, Marylu, John, Diane, Janet
Front Row: Marty, Dolores, Mom holding Angela, Dad holding Alice, Art, Sister Perpetua, Pauline, Helen, Virginia, Linda

1962, child number nineteen. I was in college before I became aware that there had been a Cuban missile crisis that month. I was completely oblivious to the fact that my eldest brother was an army parachute packer at that time and that his unit was training for night landings in case our country went to war.

What was front and center on my mind at that time was that three children needed to be spoon-fed, and I was the designated feeder (much to my chagrin). Marty needed lots of extra help; he didn't learn to walk until age four. Mom kept Marty, Pauline, Alice, and Angi downstairs. For the first time, four children slept downstairs, two in the master bedroom and two in the baby room.

Kathleen recalled that in '62, Pauline sometimes slept upstairs in the same room with her. She particularly remembers her girlfriend, Carol Schimek's, amazement that six girls slept in the middle room, with two doubles and a white bunk bed, later two bunk beds and one double. Including Pauline, Kathleen sometimes babysat three little girls sleeping in one double bed.

By comparison to the little girls' room, the northwest bedroom, aka the big girls' room, was luxurious; it was more like ten by fifteen feet, with two full-size beds, *two* dressers, and only

April, 1965
Mom and Dad celebrate their 25th Anniversary. By that time, we had our second blue van, this time light blue.

four girls instead of six. And no one ever wet the bed! When one of the big girls went off to college, one of the little girls got the privilege of being promoted to the big girls' room.

Marcia was born in late September of 1963, the youngest girl in our family. Mom preferred more space and less noise in the baby room so she moved the piano out to the dining room and kept more children downstairs. For the first time in many years, no one moved upstairs following the birth of a new sibling even though Kathleen had just left to join the convent so there would have been enough room upstairs.

When Al came home from serving three years in the army, he was a grown man. This was the first of many years of big kids returning home. To accommodate college kids during the summer months, we often had to re-arrange beds and bedrooms so that there would be the right combination of girls' beds versus boys' beds.

In Al's case, his roommates included: Bob, age 17, John, age 13, and Art, age 8. Can you imagine any four boys those ages trying to get along in one bedroom? How about four boys including a mentally challenged 17-year-old? Unsurprisingly, Marylu remembers these four boys fighting with one another. The girls in our family virtually never wrestled or fist-fought, and even boys tussling with each other was new to us. Marylu was not the only one who was upset by all that fighting. Al recalled, "A month after I returned home, Dad kicked me out." Tough lesson!

In the little girl's room, our white wooden bunk beds wobbled and the double beds were just plain old. Our mattresses routinely fell off their frames, sometimes in the middle of the night. After Ginny tumbled and hurt herself on the brass bed post, Dad moved that bed to our

1962: Happy hunters David Ostendorf, Marylu, Diane, and John in front of our first blue van.
From the smile on their faces, they must have succeeded in bringing home a sack of either walnuts or hazelnuts.

cabin. He replaced the beds with three WWII army-surplus cot-style bunk beds standing side-by-side against the west wall, with just enough room for a little tiker to squeeze in between them to crawl into bed. The cots were a welcome improvement; no more crashing to the floor in the middle of the night when someone rolled over too fast!

When I started school, I couldn't understand why boys and girls had to use separate

April 16, 1965 Mom and Dad's 25th Anniversary with 21 children
Back Row: Janet, John, Pat, Rose Ann, Mom, Dad, Al, Robert, Marylu, Diane, Linda
Seated: Virginia holding Marcia, Dolores holding Gregory, Sister Elvira, Sister Perpetua, Pauline, Helen
Front Row: Marty, Art, Angi, and Alice

bathrooms; after all, we all used the same bathroom at home. One day, I put on my dress for school and forgot to take off my shorty bloomer-style pajama bottoms. I worried that I would be laughed at if anyone noticed them pulled down around my shoes while I was peeing, so I tried hard not to pee for a whole day. It didn't work; I wet my pants. After that, my teacher said if I really had to go, I didn't have to raise my hand, and in case of emergency I could use the boys' bathroom (adjacent the first-grade classroom). No more emergencies; I had learned my lesson.

Around that time, one of my younger sisters wet the bed every single night in the middle of the night. One roommate would start yelling at the bed-wetter, and the next person would yell at the loudmouth, and so on, until everyone in that bedroom was wide awake. The lights would get turned on, and all six girls would be annoyed until wet pajamas and sheets were replaced. Because the beds were less than a foot apart, changing sheets in the middle of the night was no easy thing to do.

David Ostendorf came to live with us after his family's house burned down in 1963. David liked to ice skate, so John built a makeshift ice rink in the middle of our hog yard. Marylu remembers David as a wild man, "but I'm glad he taught us how to skate backward."

Gregory was born in October of '64. He was the sixth boy and had fifteen sisters. Normally, that would have meant a three-year-old would be moving upstairs. However, Pauline stayed downstairs until she started school. For the first time, the little girls' room had an empty bed. Unheard of! The only moving around that happened that year was when Marylu broke her arm on the last day of school; Mom switched around the beds so that Lu could be propped up in a single bed in the southwest room.

We didn't have a guest bedroom. My friends and relatives had anywhere between four and eighteen children. Nobody I met as a youngster had a guest bedroom in their house; I wasn't even familiar with the concept. Whenever one of us invited company overnight (a privilege allowed only on birthdays), Mom let us sleep either on the family room floor or in a tent outdoors. She hauled a couple of feather ticks out of the fifty-gallon cardboard drum in the so-called new part, and laid them on a tarp as a mattress. We covered up with warm quilts sewn from scraps of worn-out wool suits or coats, and used pillows stuffed with feathers plucked from ducks and geese we had eaten. As we got more experience sleeping outdoors, we used cement blocks and a set of coiled wire springs to hold up the featherbeds in our tent.

A few nights a year when it was particularly hot and humid, Mom let us bring a blanket and pillow downstairs to sleep on the floor in the new family room. During the "dog days of summer," it gets up to 100 degrees in Minnesota with high humidity. The breeze coming through five-foot-high sliding glass windows and Mom's small, rubber-bladed fan kept us cool enough to sleep comfortably.

When Pauline moved upstairs in 1965, I was assigned to sleep on the top bunk in the little girls' room. One muggy night, I fell asleep on the family room floor and sleep-walked up the stairs to my top bunk bed. When I awoke, I had a sprained ankle and no recollection of what had transpired. Because I could no longer get in and out of bed, Mom re-assigned me to a single bed in the big girls' room.

Each of us little girls stored a cardboard box under our bed with our name across the side in black magic marker. That's where we stuffed any clothes that did not fit in our one and only dresser drawer, our library books, and our precious treasures, such as a secret diary, a doll, or a souvenir we had received as a present. Most of us also saved at least one special stone, agate or arrowhead that we had found while out walking with Dad. I had so much stuff I needed more than one cardboard box, but because the springs under the middle of the mattress caught on the boxes, there was never enough room under my bed.

I was really excited to move into the big girls' room with Marylu and Diane. That southwest bedroom was sometimes used as a girls' room, and sometimes as a boys' room. It was maybe ten by ten feet and housed one double bed, one single bed, and one dresser. The second-best part of moving in with big sisters was listening to teenage chatter about boys and dating. Especially when they whispered that if Dad saw a [boyfriend's] car parked out by our woods, he'd get out his shotgun and shoot at it! I was too young to fully understand the implications of a parked car near the woods; however, the consequence was fully understood. But for me at that time, the very best part of moving in with my big sisters was that with only three girls in a room, I got lots of under-bed storage space so I could have multiple cardboard boxes!

Marylu and Diane and I got bumped from our bedroom to a tent the following summer when Ramona, aka Sister Perpetua, came home from the convent for a long-awaited two-week visit. For the first five years of a Franciscan's religious life, she is a postulant, a candidate for admission to the order, and is not allowed to go home to visit. Mom wanted our eldest sister to have her old bedroom all to herself. Because the tent had no mosquito netting, I endured just two nights before Mom took pity on me and let me come back in the house. Unfortunately for the big girls, they didn't get a choice.

Little did Sister Perpetua know that a couple of us little kids were trying to spy on her to *finally* find out whether nuns actually had hair. No luck! However, Ginny "caught" her pressing her veil between two boards tucked under a bedpost. She also discovered that Sister Perpetua used the towel rack for panty hose, and also for her rosary. That sent the rest of us girls into a full-on giggling fit.

Many years later, Ginny recalled: "Sister Perpetua encouraged everyone to say the Rosary in bed; we would just fall asleep while pretending to pray." It turns out Sister Perpetua was equally unhappy sleeping alone in her old room. Many years later she reminisced: "I longed to be in the same room with all the giggling girls."

Depending on how many boys' vs. girls' beds we needed at any one point in time, the little room held either a single bed or a bunk bed. In 1965, Patty, slept there until she left for Winona State. At that point, Diane and Marylu moved into Pat's old room. Marylu is positive that she and Diane slept there in bunk beds because she has a specific recollection of getting chapped hands from doing chicken chores the year that she slept in that room. It's funny the little things we remember!

Once Marty was old enough to move upstairs, the little room was needed for a boys' room. John took it over when five-year-old Marty moved in with Bob and Art. At that point, the southwest room where I had slept with two big sisters transitioned from the big girls' room to the boys' room.

Lor's very first memory was getting nauseous one night the year she slept on the top bunk in the little girls' room. That's the same incident where Mom was pregnant and got food poisoning; no wonder Dad took her to the hospital right away. Damien was born on January 13th, 1966. The Waseca Journal wrote: "Damien joined 18 of his brothers and sisters in regular family life in a 10-room farm home." Mom was quoted saying: "Ramona had entered the convent, and Al was married [so] we had *only* 18 at home." Yup, they really did quote her correctly as saying *only* 18, as ONLY she could do.

I was assigned baby Damien for a charge. Since no more children were delivered after Damien, Mom had more time to spend with the baby of the family. Also, my siblings stood in line to cherish the youngest sibling who was, as they say, cute as a button and sharp as a whip. Because Damien was *such* a pleasure to care for, everybody wanted to help. I honestly don't remember spending much time caring for him before I left home to live with Grama Miller when Damien was five.

After Grampa Miller had died in 1961, a couple of my sisters had lived at Grama Miller's house during the summer so they could make money working at the canning factory without needing their own vehicle, and, as we used to

Huneke Studio - Waseca

1969: Twenty-two Children celebrate Pat's Wedding
Back Row: Helen, Diane, Robert, Sister Ramona, Pat, Marylu, Al, John, Janet, Virginia
Middle Row: Pauline, Dolores, Kathleen, Rose Ann, Linda, Art
Front Row: Gregory, Marcia, Dad, Damien, Mom, Alice, Marty, Angi

say, "keep Grama company." By the time I was in high school, Grama Miller's eldest son, Francis, had begun to worry that Grama might forget to turn off a gas burner and should, therefore, have someone stay with her full-time. I was absolutely thrilled to be given the opportunity to live in town during my last years of high school. I had a bedroom and bathroom all to myself, (awesome!) I had the opportunity to make money working from three to eleven at the canning factory a few days a week (yippee), and I also had the flexibility to attend extra-curricular events (what a blast)!

Grama Miller spent her days playing scrabble and having tea with her friends, gardening, crocheting, and watching TV. Seeing the ease with which she passed her days informed my choices and aspirations. Grama lived on dividend checks because Grampa had invested in such successful companies as AT&T, General Electric, and Greyhound Bus. I had never heard of dividend checks before, and that lesson was not lost on me. I promised myself I would go to college and then get a good job.

In the fall of 1966, Marylu graduated from high school and left for the College of St. Teresa. After John enrolled in a boarding school for high school farm kids, the little room once again became a girls' room. Janet and Diane slept there in bunk beds. Because that room went back and forth between boys' and girls' so many times, maybe we should have simply called that room the "swing room."

As usual, our house was filled to capacity; when college kids and their friends came home on weekends, our house overflowed. We were living life to the fullest, and loving every minute of it. Our house bustled with children's games to play, toys to pick up, pets to fuss over, laundry to wash, wild animals to skin, eggs to pack, homework to do, science projects to experiment on, piano and violin and recorder to practice, hit records to play on our phonograph, friends and neighbors stopping by to buy our farm's honey, strawberries and/or eggs, hungry mouths to feed, diapers to change, and plenty of messes to clean up. Never lacking for things to do and people to do them with, we worked hard, played hard and slept hard.

Diane moved in with the big girls to make room. Angi recalled that five little kids slept downstairs in the baby room. That was also the peak year for children who slept downstairs. I can't imagine how we ever fit five beds in the very same room where we kept our sewing machine, sewing supplies, toys, and school books. After Pauline started school, Alice moved upstairs leaving four children in the baby room.

Uncle Dave, Aunt Ev, and at least four of their children were visiting the farm when the 1966 blizzard struck. When we lost power for four days, we had no furnace for the very first time (prior to that we had had a wood-burning furnace). The antique wood range in our basement saved twenty-five of us from freezing to death. For three nights, the babies, my parents, and my aunt and uncle slept next to it on the cement floor. The basement stayed warm, the

1969: Fifteen girls   Back Row: Rose Ann, Linda, Helen, Marylu, Dolores, Pat, Diane, Sister Ramona, Kathleen, Virginia, Janet
Front row: Alice, Marcia, Pauline, Angi

downstairs stayed just above freezing, and the upstairs was cold enough that we scraped frost off the northwest bedroom wall.

Dad moved baby Damien's crib to the basement. Dad put five of us giddy girls in a double bed upstairs, three heads facing one way and two the opposite way, all covered with multiple quilts. Dad laid his heaviest parka (with fur around the hood), on top of the only blankets we had left. He knew that with five children in a bed, we'd giggle all night and wouldn't get a wink of sleep, but we'd stay alive. It worked.

That was the only time I can remember where Dad put anyone over three years old to bed.

The driving and blowing snow made it so hard to see that Dad had to string ropes from the house to the other buildings to make sure he could make it back after feeding the animals. No one else was allowed to go outdoors. As far as cooking and eating without electricity, Mom didn't skip a beat. She cooked meals using the wood stove; she even baked bread during the blizzard, just like she had done as a child. For her, life without electricity was business as usual!

The blizzard left many of us with head colds and runny noses. Whenever kids caught a cold, Mom applied Vick's vapo-rub, then wrapped a soft cotton diaper around the child's neck at bedtime, using a diaper-style safety pin to hold it in place, and served us hot lemonade or chicken broth.

Mom's home remedies were insufficient to heal Greg from his breathing difficulty. On the recommendation of the doctor, Mom bought a vaporizer... still no success. When the doctor injected Greg with penicillin, Greg developed a life-threatening reaction. That day, our family doctor made his first and only house-call to the farm. He constructed a clear plastic tent over Greg's crib, and Greg lived in his bubble for a few weeks until he recovered.

When Damien, the baby of the family, was eleven months old, Mom wanted to get all twenty-two children in the same room for the very first time. At that time, Sister Perpetua worked at St. Mary's parish in Winona, MN while Kathleen, now known by her Franciscan name, Sister Elvira, lived at Tau Center in Winona, MN. Nuns were rarely allowed to travel, so if our family wanted to visit these two siblings, we needed to make the drive. With gas at twenty-five cents a gallon, it was doable to charter a bus to Winona so that twenty of us could travel together from Waseca without anyone sitting on someone else's lap. That way, we could keep our "good clothes" from getting wrinkled during the three-hour ride.

"Good clothes" was synonymous with "Sunday clothes," as opposed to "everyday" clothes. We shortened our made-up word, "everyday" (*EV-ree-day*), to only three syllables, and used it to describe clothing, tables, chairs, dishes, etc. For example, good dishes meant china, usually only used when we had company, while everyday dishes were plastic.

My parents hired the local photography studio to take a photo of twenty-two happy and healthy children dressed in our good clothes, one exceedingly proud father and one equally humble mother. Mom sent our very first "whole family photo" as her 1966 Christmas card.

When Damien moved from the newborn crib into the baby room, Alice, Angi, Marcia, and Greg still slept downstairs. Shortly thereafter, Alice moved upstairs and was assigned as my charge. She was cute with beautiful black wavy hair; dressing her was much more fun than dressing dolls!

Kathleen left the convent and moved home for the summer. As Catholic children, we were taught to do the will of God. As Miller kids, we strived to please our parents. After five years as a Postulant, Kathleen realized she was not happy, that convent life wasn't necessarily God's will for her. She chose to leave the convent knowing full well that her decision would disappoint our religious parents.

That summer was when we had the most girls, and also the highest number of children (18 including a foster kid) living under one roof at one time. For the first time that I can remember, our parents told us they were expecting another baby. Having another baby was almost an annual event, so it didn't get much fanfare; it was just expected. No baby showers. No rubbing Mom's belly to feel the baby kicking. No reading books to little kids about becoming a big brother or big sister. But, us kids looked forward to sharing the news with our friends and relatives. For this particular baby, Mom did not feel comfortable committing as to whether she was expecting a boy or a girl. My parents agreed to let me paint the bassinet yellow in excited anticipation, awaiting baby number 23. Unfortunately, Mom miscarried on November 2nd, 1967.

Dad kept my big sisters home from school that morning; I was the eldest one to board the school bus. I was in seventh grade with no clue what the word "miscarriage" meant. Since Dad told us Mom was in the hospital, I assumed miscarriage was some kind of disease.

When my cousin got on the bus, she asked, "Where's the rest of your family?"

"Mom had a miscarriage, so Dad said they had to stay home and help out," I told her.

"I didn't know she was pregnant," said my cousin.

"What does that mean?" I asked. She wouldn't tell me, and I never looked it up.

In our family, we almost never talked about pregnancy, and if we did, we only used the word "expecting." The word pregnancy was in the same zone as sex, i.e., off limits for family conversation.

"I came back from Faribault after that day," Patty recalled; "Mom just stared out the window, absolutely depressed." After twenty-two successful deliveries, Mom was totally devastated to have lost a child and to be told by her doctor that she would never again experience the miracle of a bringing a new baby into the world. For several years after that, Mom still kept the newborn crib in their bedroom, longing for infant grandchildren who needed a quiet place to nap.

CHAPTER 3:

Growing up Catholic

To say my mother and father were religious is a colossal understatement. Besides the pope, my parents were the most religious people I have ever met. They taught us that God made the world in seven days, that Mary was a virgin, and that Jesus rose from the dead. My parents taught us to adhere to the ten commandments. More importantly, they lived their Christian values of honesty, integrity, kindness, tolerance, and service to others.

1950: Al's first communion
Pat, Rose Ann sitting on our "new" front steps, Kathleen, and Al

Our family upheld Catholic traditions with gusto. We attended Catholic Mass every single Sunday. In addition, we went to Mass on the six Holy Days of Obligation: New Year's Day-Feast of the Holy Family, Assumption of the Blessed Virgin, Ascension of Jesus, The Feast of the Immaculate Conception, All Saints' Day, and Christmas. We attended Mass all forty days of Lent, plus certain saints' Feast Days, and many, many weekdays.

We celebrated the sacraments that marked milestones in our and our cousins' lives: Baptisms, weddings, funerals, First Communions, First Confessions, Confirmations, and Last Rites, aka Anointing of the Sick. Whereas many families run their calendar around their children's sports schedule or the breadwinner's work schedule, our family prioritized church-related events, and everything else came second.

When I had chicken chores to complete before school, I hated having to get up early enough to attend Mass. It wasn't that I was tired; I just didn't like having to rush, and detested smelling like a farmyard (normally we took showers only once a week) and having kids at school make fun of my stinky shoes after I rushed to feed chickens without taking time to put boots on. Often, Mom would drive us to church before school and Dad would stay home with the babies and then, mercifully, he would do all the chicken chores.

Lent was onerous; Mass every morning plus Stations of the Cross on Friday nights. While many of my siblings were very religious, I found weekday Mass pretty boring (no singing). However, when I lived with Grama, I enjoyed talking with her as I walked her to church every day before school, so I didn't mind.

We celebrated Angela's Baptism at the home of her godparents, Lawrence and Leta Clemons.

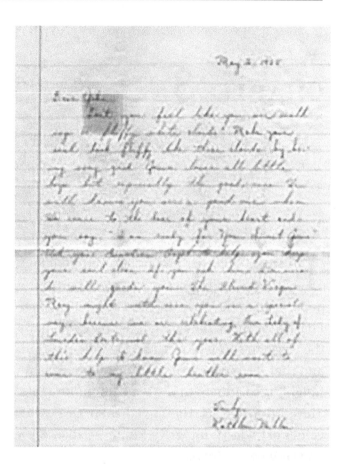

1958: Letter to John, for his 1st Communion: "Don't you feel like you are walking on fluffy clouds? Make your soul look like fluffy clouds by being good. Jesus loves all little boys but especially the good ones. He will know you are a good one when He comes to the door of your heart and you say, "I am ready for You, Sweet Jesus." Ask your guardian angel to help you keep your soul clean. If you ask him I'm sure he will guide you. The Blessed Virgin Mary might watch over you in a special way, because we are celebrating Our Lady of Lourdes Centennial this year. With all of this help I know Jesus will want to come to my little brother soon." Truly, Kathleen Miller

1962:
Back row: Al, Dad, Robert, Mom, Kathleen holding Alice
Middle Row: John, Rose Ann, Pat holding Marty
Next Row: Diane, Janet, Linda, Marylu holding Angela wearing
the Baptismal gown Mom had embroidered.
Front row: Art, Helen monitoring Pauline, Virginia, Dolores

Interestingly, Angi raised her family in a house that is a near-replica of her godparents' home.

My parents named almost every child after a canonized saint, being careful not to duplicate names of our first cousins; they never called us by nicknames. Six daughters were born on a feast day of the Blessed Virgin, and Mom insisted they have Mary, Margaret or Marie as either a first or middle name: Ramona Mary, Mary Lucille, Diane Margaret, Dolores Maria, Angela Mary, and Marcia Marie.

We attended Sacred Heart grade school and high school where Franciscan nuns taught us. Although this was a private school, there was no tuition. To fund the schools, the parish received state and federal aid for parochial schools, and collected the difference in Sunday Mass donations. Almost all the teachers were nuns and priests, so that kept expenses down. The nuns shared my parents' beliefs and values; it would not be a stretch to say they helped raise us. The nuns prayed that their students would join a religious order. In 2011, Sister Ramona celebrated her Golden Jubilee, her fiftieth anniversary as a Franciscan nun.

Mom and Dad prayed with us morning, noon, and night, and always counted their blessings. We prayed together as a family before every meal, and said the Rosary together most nights after our evening meal, which we called supper. Every single night, we ended our bedtime prayers with "God bless: Dad, Mom, Mona, Jr., Rose Ann, Kathleen, Robert, Patricia, Marylu, Diane, John, Janet, Linda, Virginia, Helen, Arthur, Dolores, Martin, Pauline, Alice, Angela, Marcia, Gregory, and Damien."

Having so often recited all 22 names in birth order (even when we were over-tired and anxious to sleep), most of my siblings can rattle off the names of all twenty-two siblings in birth order sequence in less than ten seconds. However, don't ask *any* of us to list them from youngest to oldest; that's way too difficult!

In 2006, after Mom had passed, Dad confided to me, "When I asked your mother what she wanted before she would commit to marriage, she responded, 'a gaggle of kids and a white picket fence.'" The picket fence was the easy part; a gaggle of kids took a lifetime.

Dad had not fully understood what Mom meant when she first requested a gaggle of kids. He was shocked when Mom wanted another child so soon after the first two. As the years went by, Mom said she wanted "as many babies as God would give her," and Dad wanted whatever Mom wanted. They raised a huge family prior to the availability of birth control. Even if birth control had been easily accessible, I trust that Mom's Irish Catholic frame of mind together with her "more the merrier" attitude would still have ruled the day.

Some of Mom and Dad's ancestors also had large families. Mom's father, Vincent Kahnke, was the second of 16 children but was raised as a first-born because the eldest child had died at birth. Mom's mother was the sixth of nine children, the first two of whom died at birth, possibly due to the fact that both parents were deaf,

1963: Helen's, First Communion
Mom always invited the godparents, the grandparents and often one
set of cousins to celebrate First Communion
Back row: Rosemary Grubish, Dolores, Kate Wesley, Helen
Front row: Jim Grubish, Pauline, Richelle Wesley

one from birth and the other either from spinal meningitis or from a lightning bolt, depending on the information source.

Mom's paternal great grandparents on her grandmother's side, Sophia Rasberry Kimber and John Amberg, raised eleven children. Mom wrote: *"Alvin's grandfather's sister, Susanna [Miller Seberger] lived [in Schereville, IL] many years ago and many of her descendants live in this area. She married a man with eleven children who had lost his wife. Together they had fourteen more. She and her husband are both buried in the cemetery where her father is also buried; that would be Alvin's great-grandfather."*

Mom's brother Herb and his wife raised ten children. Dad's brother Francis and his wife raised eight children. Our community also included several large families. A local family from whom Dad bought land had sixteen children. Their parents were away for a few weeks and

Mom decided we should take them Christmas gifts. Visiting them was the closest thing in my life to experiencing what it would have been like to visit our home. The night about 16 of us visited them, they wasted no time in determining it was too cold for everyone to go outside, and that the big kids couldn't play outside leaving only little kids in the house. They also instinctively knew there were too many people to play cards or hide and seek, so they taught us how to play "Spoons."

About thirty people sat or stood around their big kitchen table. When the music stopped, everyone tried to grab a spoon from the middle of the table. There's always one less spoon than there are participants, and that person is "out." We had a BLAST! That night felt like a family reunion, lots of kids from big families that played well together.

The notion of birth control was against the Catholic religion, and talking about sex was off limits. To put this in perspective, allow me to share what I learned from very intelligent Catholic mother of three who is fifteen years older than I. Her doctor advised her to slow down after having delivered three babies back to back. She honestly did not know what caused her to get pregnant, so innocently asked, "How would I do that?"

I often wondered how other staunch Catholic parents managed their family planning. Did they let God decide for the first half dozen kids, and then realize they had a choice between disobeying their religious beliefs and feeling overwhelmed contemplating raising more children?

One night when I was in ninth grade, I asked Mom to help me with my Algebra homework. I had never before asked for help with homework. I didn't know Mom wasn't handy with numbers, so when she said she was too busy with the younger kids, I blurted out, "Then you shouldn't have had so many kids!" Thinking that we all loved each other dearly, she replied, "Which of them would you not want to have?" I had no trouble brashly telling her a specific sibling that, at that time, I'd rather not have had. "Don't SAY such things!" she admonished, and that was the end of that conversation. Forever.

I grew up with dozens of first cousins; in fact, I had five female first cousins the same age as I! Knowing there were forty-four Miller first cousins and fifty Kahnke first cousins, I honestly did not think of our big family as terribly unusual. When I stayed overnight at my friend Susie's house in seventh grade, her dad knew my name and remembered what things I liked to talk about. Wow. What a nice guy. As a teenager, I began to realize that people with less kids knew their children better and also knew their kids' friends, and I liked that.

In 1974, when I started college at St. Ben's in St. Joseph, MN, the average number of siblings for each of my classmates was seven, and I thought nothing of it. My college girlfriend, Christina Aamodt, came from thirteen. I had been forewarned about the size of her family so I had fun with it. When we were introduced, I started right in: "How many boys and how many girls? How big was your house? How many bathrooms did you have?" Not until I had exhausted the "typical question list" did I tell her that I was the 13th of 22. We both had a good laugh. When I moved to New York at age twenty-six, I started meeting people who had never heard of families of more than eight or ten, and whose jaw dropped at the mere thought of so many children in one family.

I grew up in an era with a low divorce rate where I had the benefit of living with both my birth parents, knowing three of my four natural grandparents, and twenty-some aunts and uncles, almost all of whom lived within twenty minutes of us. The exceptions were two aunts who became nuns and lived further away. My parents, grandparents, cousins, aunts and uncles were all loving, thoughtful, and generous. We lived the adage, "It's never wrong to do the right thing." Our Christian values were strengthened in private school and reinforced by our faith community. We believed that families who prayed together stayed together.

In August of 1958, eighteen years after their wedding, Mom and Dad took their exceedingly belated honeymoon. Mom and Dad worked with a travel agent to plan a pilgrimage to two Marian apparition sites in Europe. Over a three-week vacation, they visited Lourdes and Fatima, and also toured Barcelona, Paris, Rome, and the Swiss Alps. Grama Kahnke was supposed to babysit while our parents were gone. On July 21st, after "the honeymooners" left the country, Grama's brother in Omaha died, and Grama immediately took the train to attend his funeral. She had no qualms about leaving seventeen-year-old Ramona in charge, and Ramona had no qualms either, so Grama stayed away the entire time.

While my parents traveled, Ramona and two babies slept downstairs and the other twelve kids slept upstairs, nine girls and three boys. Ramona rose to the occasion and took on the incredible responsibility of babysitting fourteen siblings, including managing farm work, driving, cooking, cleaning, laundry, changing diapers, etc... Dad wrote:

"Ramona hauled feed for our 300 hogs, and she did a super job, as we never had a finer bunch of pigs, or that large of a check in the fall, as we did that year. Bob and Rita Korteum took us up to St. Paul to the airport and picked us up at Rochester [MN] on our return."

A year or so later, Ramona decided to join the Sisters of St. Francis. Does anyone think it's a coincidence that she decided against getting married and raising a family after having taken care of that many kids for so long???

The year after the Civil Rights Act allowed inter-racial education, about fifteen students and a faculty member from St. Teresa's (women's, white college) in Winona, Minnesota went to Spelman (women's, black college) in Atlanta, Georgia and vice versa. The two college presidents "had engineered this after being at a College Presidents' Conference the year before," recalled Marylu. Pat took time off from her job at the Faribault State Hospital to babysit fifteen siblings while Mom and Dad drove Marylu to Atlanta to participate in the exchange program. Years later, when Mom wrote her memoir, she included the babysitting log she had asked Patty to keep for what my mother thought of as a "typical week."

*"**Monday, September 9th, 1968**

5:00 AM Parents and Marylu left for Atlanta, Georgia*

7:20 Pat got up. Woke school kids. Got breakfast.

8:05 School kids left. Little ones ate breakfast.

9:00 Pat laid down for an hour, feverish and sore throat.

10:00 Rosie got the mail.

11:30 Dinner. [Sister-in-law] Donna called, wanted to know how we were doing.

12:15 Angela left for school.

1:00 Dishes done. Pat made bread. Started washing. Little ones aren't taking naps this afternoon.

4:00 School kids home.

5:30 Supper [note: making and serving meals for sixteen barely merited a mention!]

6:45 Janet's classmates come out to load papers in Lawrence Clemon's semi-truck.

8:30 Babies to bed.

9:00 School kids in bed.

10:00 Everything peaceful and quiet.

Tuesday, September 10th

7:30 School kids up. Breakfast

8:10 School kids to school.

10:00 Rosie got mail.

11:30 Dinner

12:15 Angela left for school.

1:00 Junior came over to pick load of corn.

4:00 Angela home from school.

4:30 Kids home from school. Forgot Virginia; had to go back and get her.

6:00 Supper

8:30 Babies to bed.

9:00 Everyone else to bed.

10:15 Was awakened by cows mooing outside my window. Anything can happen around here. Called Chuckie [the next-door neighbor]. Said they might be his. Linda and Virginia got dressed, took a flashlight out to chase them. They were making shambles of the garden. Chuckie's coming up to make sure they're theirs.

10:45 Chuckie and the girls got the cows in. Maybe we can all settle down for the night now.

Wednesday, September 11th

7:00 Pat got up and got the little kids ready to go to church. The school kids went to church too.

9:00 Ate breakfast

10:00 Rosie got the mail.

11:45 Dinner

12:15 Angie left for school.

1:00 Pat started in cleaning. Got the family room and dining room scrubbed and waxed.

3:30 School kids home.

3:45 Angela home from school.

6:00 Supper

7:00 School kids got homework finished. Dishes done.

8:30 Babies to bed.

9:00 Everyone except high school kids to bed.

Thursday, September 12th

7:00 Everyone up. Ate breakfast. Arthur opened his [birthday] gifts.

8:10 Kids off to school. Bob got the chores done.

9:00 Little kids and Patty went to town. Bought groceries, school supplies for Dolores, and Patty got some new things. Stopped to visit Grandma Miller.

11:30 came home, got dinner on.

12:15 Angela left for school.

1:00 Babies took naps. Jr. came and picked load of corn. Patty made birthday cake for Artie. Cleaned kitchen floor.

5:00 Ate supper.

6:00 Mom called from Atlanta.

7:30 Linda and [neighbor] Shari went to sing at Catholic Daughter Style Show.

9:30 Linda home. Everyone in bed.

Friday, September 13th

7:30 Kids up, ate breakfast

7:45 School kids went to Mass.

9:00 Did some ironing. Washed bedding.

10:00 Rosie got the mail. Dolores called. She left her music books at home. [more typically, there was a problem of one kid inadvertently having picked up the other one's books.]

11:30 Dinner

12:15 Angela went to school.

1:30 Went to town. Gave Dolores her music books. Pat got her new car tire from Dave.

2:30 Dairy man came.

3:45 Angie home from school.

5:30 Ate supper. Dishes done. Some of the kids did homework. Others outside to play."

We really missed Mom and Dad when they traveled, especially when they traveled to Europe for three weeks. We must have been super lonesome because virtually all of us remember in which room (and in exactly which bed) we slept during their trip.

Ramona visualizes two doubles and one bunk in the girls' room. I slept in the middle room in a double bed with Diane. While my parents were on their pilgrimage, I specifically remember being allowed the privilege of sleeping downstairs on the couch in the living room after being traumatized by a thunderstorm. Sleeping downstairs felt safer, even though Mom and Dad were not home. Besides, anyone who slept downstairs got extra attention, whether that meant snacks before bed, or the opportunity to use the bathroom without having to wait.

Diane remembers having high fevers and running around delirious in the night while our parents were away. Janet remembers sleeping in the bottom bunk by the window and getting up in the night to help Diane who slept in the other bottom bunk. Ginny was especially lonesome for our parents. After she got stung by a bee, she sat on her single bed in the southwest room for several days, staring out the window, hoping to see Mom and Dad coming home. Kathleen recalls, "Ramona tried hard to console Ginny.

Finally, she let her sleep downstairs in the living room. Thankfully, Ginny got some comfort when Mom sent her a post card from Barcelona."

Mom and Dad returned home with magnificent photos of snowcapped mountains, gorgeous cathedrals, and lots of exciting stories. Dad took most of our family's photos until the mid-60's when he gifted Mom a Polaroid camera and she started shooting pictures as well. Practically every Saturday night for months after their European trip, my parents entertained group after group of cousins or friends with their slide show, regaling the same stories over and over. The incident I remember best occurred when they were in Paris.

Mom and Dad had an outdated copy of their itinerary and missed their plane from Paris to Lucerne. They couldn't afford a commercial flight to catch up with their schedule, and it was difficult to find someone who spoke enough

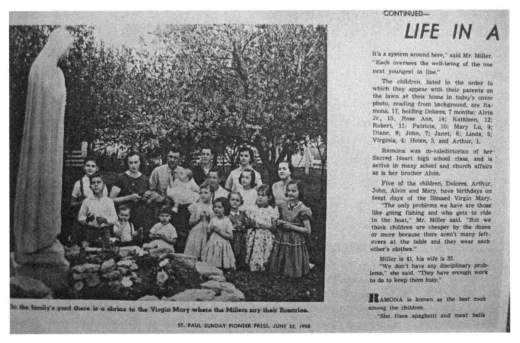

CONTINUED—
LIFE IN A

it's a system around here," said Mr. Miller. "Each oversees the well-being of the one next youngest in line."

The children, listed in the order in which they appear with their parents on the lawn at their home in today's cover photo, reading from background, are Ramona, 17, holding Dolores, 7 months; Alvin Jr., 15; Rose Ann, 14; Kathleen, 12; Robert, 11; Patricia, 10; Mary Lu, 9; Diane, 8; John, 7; Janet, 6; Linda, 5; Virginia, 4; Helen, 3, and Arthur, 1.

Ramona was co-valedictorian of her Sacred Heart high school class, and is active in many school and church affairs as is her brother Alvin.

Five of the children, Dolores, Arthur, John, Alvin and Mary, have birthdays on feast days of the Blessed Virgin Mary.

"The only problems we have are those like going fishing and who gets to ride in the boat," Mr. Miller said. "But we think children are cheaper by the dozen or more because there aren't many leftovers at the table and they wear each other's clothes."

Miller is 41, his wife is 35. "We don't have any disciplinary problems," she said. "They have enough work to do to keep them busy."

RAMONA is known as the best cook among the children.

"She fixes spaghetti and meat balls

In the family's yard there is a shrine to the Virgin Mary where the Millers say their Rosaries.

ST. PAUL SUNDAY PIONEER PRESS, JUNE 22, 1958

To say the rosary, we knelt in our living room or in front of a statue of the Virgin Mary representing the Marian apparition at Fatima. We prayed fifty-three Hail Mary's and the rest of the prayers that make up a rosary. I'm the one staring at the camera instead of praying. 1958 Photo from St. Paul Pioneer Press

English to book them a train ride to Switzerland. An eleven-year-old Swiss girl who was learning English in school came to their rescue; Suzanne Dexter translated for them and rode the train with them to her native Switzerland. Thus began a life-long friendship.

Whenever Mom and Dad traveled, they brought home a souvenir for each child; from Europe, each of us received a rosary blessed by the Pope Pius XII just a few months prior to his death. Each of the girls also got a scarf with Swiss flowers. I started a collection of pennants from the places Mom and Dad traveled. After each trip, they told wonderful tales. I never tired of hearing my parents describe their honeymoon; the thrill of their European travels influenced me to spend one college semester in Germany and another in Switzerland, where I took the opportunity to meet the gal who had helped them find their tour group so many years ago. Their adventures inspired my lifelong love of traveling. Several of us inherited both my parents' travel bug as well as Dad's propensity for collecting stuff.

We kept our rosary beads blessed by the pope on our family's altar. The altar was a sacred place containing a crucifix, a picture of the Sacred Heart, statues of Mary and Joseph, candles Mom lit whenever we prayed, and a music

1951: Dressed up for Easter
Back Row: Al, Kathleen, Rose Ann, Ramona holding John
Front Row: Bob, Marylu, Pat, Diane

box from Fatima with the three little children who had seen an apparition of Mary. We also kept holy water blessed by Pope Pius XII on the altar; Mom gave a vial of blessed water to our relatives whenever someone got deathly sick.

Mom always knew to which saint we should pray for special requests. We prayed to St. Christopher for safe passage when we traveled, and to St. Thomas to strengthen our faith. If we lost something, we prayed to St. Anthony to help us find it. To help keep us safe, Mom pinned medals on young girls' tutu-like can-can slips as well as on cotton undershirts and gave the teenagers Sacred Heart scapulars to wear around our necks.

I was four when Mom bought matching green and red jumpers for Ginny and me. That jumper was my first store-bought outfit; it was one of only two store-bought dresses purchased for me from the time I can remember until I left home to attend college. All the others were hand-me-downs, or homemade. For some of my siblings, especially those most interested in plants and animals, not having new clothes was no big deal. For others, it created resentment, "No, I don't want to wear her First Communion dress for my First Communion!" [Tough luck; deal with it...] For others, it created sufficient motivation to start sewing.

As a special treat, Mom hung Ginny's green jumper and my matching red jumper upstairs in our bedroom closet (instead of in her bedroom) so that we could admire them more easily until the day of the party. She must have needed to buy nice clothes for us when she did not have time to sew dresses. Some time after my uncle Dick Wesley lost his life in a tractor accident in June of 1957, his mom, Rowene Wesley, hosted a get together. I vividly remember the jumpers we wore while sitting on little chairs, eating cake served on the folded down writing area of Rowene's antique secretary desk. I had to be extra careful not to soil my new jumper.

Most of my other memories of dressing up occurred around Easter, because Easter week is the most important week of the Catholic Church Calendar. During the forty days preceding Easter, we fasted: we "gave up" candy as an act of penitence, a way to prepare our bodies for the Easter celebration. Our Catholic tradition involved abstaining from meat on Ash Wednesday and on Fridays in Lent. Our family

Easter 1954:
Back row: Rose Ann, Al, Ramona holding Virginia
Middle row: Pat, Marylu, Robert, Kathleen,
Front row: John, Janet, Diane
Seated by the white Easter bunny pulling an Easter basket on wheels: Linda

went the extra mile, observing the pre-Vatican II recommendation of foregoing meat on Fridays.

Two weeks before Easter, Mom would gather up a couple dozen Easter bonnets from the built-in storage cupboards in Rosie's bedroom. Then she'd open up the 10'x4'x4' cedar hope chest (a traditional gift from her father that could be handed down in the next generation), and bring out the spring coats that smelled like moth balls. We'd dance around with excitement as we tried on the coats and hats we had worn the prior year, and the next bigger one until, finally, each of us had a "new" Easter coat and an Easter bonnet that fit.

Once coats and bonnets were finalized, Mom would bring out the change-of-season dresses and the kids would go through the same process all over again. *"I always disliked the changing of the seasons because it was so much work to get all the clothes out of storage and to see what fit whom, and to see if I had to buy anything new. The oldest one would usually be the one to get something new and the rest would be handed down. This worked quite well for everything except shoes. That's the one thing that never fits anyone else."* It didn't help that most of us inherited my mother's long feet and my dad's wide feet and therefore have a difficult time finding shoes that fit well even when we are buying them new.

Easter Morning, 1961
Ginny, Helen, Art, Linda, Lor, Janet, holding Marty,
We were told to "sit nice" on the couch (and not eat any Easter candy until after church). Looks like I had a malted milk ball in my cheek. Busted!

Most of our clothing was washable, even the woolen coats, hats and mittens, but Mom took the "new" coats to the dry cleaners. Easter was the only time of year that Mom would pay for the luxury of dry cleaning. Dad found it extravagantly expensive that in 1954, *"We must have been well dressed for Easter that spring as I see a bill in the ledger for $11 for dry cleaning 11 coats!"*

Mom also used Easter as an excuse to buy everyone new underpants and socks, the only time of year when that happened.

On Palm Sunday, the Sunday before Easter, we brought palm branches from church and put one behind each crucifix throughout our house. We had a saint's picture and/or a crucifix in every room. The following Thursday, Holy Thursday, aka Passover, Mom always invited another family to join us to celebrate the Last Supper, usually one of our first cousins.

We put on our good clothes, (quite unusual for days other than Sundays), used our best linen tablecloth, and hosted our version of a traditional Jewish Exodus meal: leg of lamb with mint jelly (in memory of how the Jews slaughtered their best calf as an offering to the gods), horseradish sauce (for their bitter treatment), unleavened bread (because they left in such a hurry), raisin/apple chutney "mortar" (to re-build), and wine (served on extremely rare occasions).

The following day, Good Friday, before going to church from noon until three PM, we planted potatoes. To plant potatoes as the first item in the garden on the Friday before Easter was an invocation for a successful gardening season. When Easter landed in March and the ground was considered too chilly for planting, we simply planted less potatoes at that time. Every spring, the parish priest came to our farm to bless the fields and pray for a plentiful harvest. My exceedingly-religious parents prayed a traditional prayer:

Lord Jesus,

Sower of all the good that is in the world,

Place in us the seeds of goodness and justice

Let our land yield a harvest of human love

and sheaves of joy for eternal life.

Remember us, O Lord,

in your loving care!

To create Easter "baskets," we painted two-pound coffee cans in pastel colors, or picked up branches from the weeping willow tree and wove our own. On Holy Saturday, we set out our

Easter baskets, dyed Easter eggs, baked hot cross buns (decorated with a white powdered sugar frosting and a chocolate cross to commemorate Jesus' death on the cross), and attended Easter Vigil services. That night, the Easter Bunny magically arrived, and we ended our Lenten fast.

On Easter morning, we celebrated the Resurrection by attending Mass/sunrise service. We felt very pretty all dressed up in our Easter outfits. The Easter Bunny brought each person a colored hard-boiled egg with their name in wax, one cream-filled chocolate egg, plus a few pastel-colored malted milk balls, a dozen or so jelly beans, and sometimes, a three-inch hollow chocolate bunny. After fasting for the forty days of Lent, finally, we could dive in to our Easter baskets and eat candy again. Yeah!

One year, my two-year old sister got up early and ate all the cream-filled chocolate eggs, and she never even got sick! The rest of us pouted for a week, to no avail. The Easter Bunny comes but once a year. That was one of many life lessons in the category of "life's not fair!"

We ate hot-cross buns once a year, for Easter Sunday breakfast. We each peeled and ate our own colored Easter egg, along with our usual Sunday treats: bacon, orange wedges or orange juice, and, of course, lots and lots of toast.

Easter 1962
Helen, Diane, Janet, and Linda
Janet re-painted the Easter cart for her pet bunny.

The traditional menu for Easter Dinner included delicious roasted whole ham topped with pineapple and cloves and served with mushy apple sauce, our favorite, Ambrosia (which we called overnight salad) with coconut, mandarin oranges, and sour cream and mandarin oranges, and Easter bunny cake with jellybean eyes, sticky white frosting, and coconut fur.

We decorated our table with at least one Easter lily, pastel colored candles with ribbons on them and an Easter Candle. This special candle had been blessed as part of the Easter service; we used it to celebrate Baptisms and First Communions. The rest of the year it sat on our

In 1963, Mom's sister, Therese, and her four children joined us for Easter dinner, along with Grama Kahnke.
Clockwise: Aunt Therese, Lor, Grama Kahnke, Kate Wesley, Helen, Linda, Al, Marylu, (behind the lily), Diane, Pat, Janet, Sylvester Wesley, John, Steve Wesley, Mom

altar near where we prayed the Rosary every night.

Although Easter marks the most important occasion in the church calendar, for our family, Christmas was a far bigger celebration. When I was a teenager, we set the Christmas Eve table for about forty people. We connected our kitchen table and our dining room table to make one long table to accommodate everybody.

In winter, decorations consisted of asking Mom to buy two new candles, draping four strands of the right color of crepe paper from the light fixture to the corners of the dining room, pasting construction paper artwork on our family room sliding-glass windows, and/or, decorating a cake.

Having "everybody" home for our traditional Christmas Eve feast included Mom (the happy chef), Dad (the contented boss), as many of the daughters and sons as could come, spouses, grandchildren, and usually at least one of our unofficial foster children. We typically had at least two college friends whose parents lived too far away, and one or more of our pre-teen neighbors. Christmas was all about family. To me, Christmas still means extended family time, it requires serving lots of good food to a big crowd, and it involves tons of people sipping on something yummy while munching on nuts, candy, and Christmas cookies.

Before Christmas, Mom's Aunt Rosie brought us a big grocery bag full of fruit and mixed nuts with the shells still on. We put the nuts in our nut bowl with two nutcrackers and two picks. All through Christmas vacation, we'd work our way through hazelnuts, pecans, peanuts, English walnuts and what we innocently called "nigger toes." Honestly, I never learned they were actually called Brazil nuts until I was in college.

My dad had a rather limited palate. If it were up to him, he would eat Wheaties and toast for breakfast, fried potatoes and eggs for lunch, and meat and potatoes and dessert every weekday of the year. On Sunday, he would add bacon and eggs and oranges to his boring menu. Christmas Eve offered a one-day-a-year opportunity for our family to really splurge.

Christmas Eve supper started with oyster stew. Dad would shop for however many fresh oysters he could afford, usually half a pint-size cardboard container from the butcher shop. Mom would heat them with milk, onion, salt and pepper. She served oyster stew in her china chafing dish because it had a candle under it to keep the stew just the right temperature; it was the only time of the year that container was used. Not very many kids liked oysters, so we drank homemade eggnog (with plenty of nutmeg) while impatiently waiting for the oyster stew to be gone so we could start feasting.

The question, "What would you like to eat?" was something I normally heard only at other peoples' homes. At our house, kids could request specific foods only twice a year, once on their birthday and again on Christmas Eve. To celebrate the night before baby Jesus' birth day, Mom served "restaurant style," each child had the privilege of requesting an entrée and my mother cooked *all* of them for our Christmas Eve feast.

Christmas Eve was the only day of the year when Mom served steak for the whole family, and it was always Swiss steak. For this holiday tradition of feasting on whatever we wanted, Swiss steak was tenderized by thoroughly pounding it with a meat mallet, and served with whipped potatoes and gravy. The other dependable main

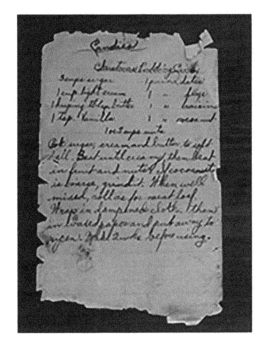

Even if us kids don't really like to eat Christmas Pudding Candy, it's still such a holiday tradition that in 2005 Marylu, John, and Helen reminisced over fruitcake and Christmas Candy... just like our mother, and her mother before her.

course was deep-fried shrimp with store-bought cocktail sauce. Almost all of us loved shrimp; we waited all year long to be able to feast on breaded shrimp. We didn't know about lobster and crab or we surely would have requested them. Inevitably one kid would request a hamburger, and another one would request noodles. Mom would try her very best to please all of us, and almost always succeeded.

To begin the meal, Mom served a basic iceberg lettuce salad and her yummy homemade rolls. She also served homemade French fries AND tater tots, sweet corn, lots of different Christmas cookies along with hard ribbon candy and plum cream pie for dessert. Plum cream pie was one of Mom's specialties. We had two Toka plum trees in our front yard. Mom would can the plums in a light syrup, and add tapioca and cream to make a pie filling. There were never enough plums to have this type of pie very often, so we saved this treat for our Christmas celebration.

Christmas Eve always included far more food than we could eat, which, with so many of us, was a pretty rare occasion. One Christmas Eve, Sister Ramona brought twelve dozen Spritz (pressed cookies) that she had baked herself. We shocked the heck out of her by polishing off every last Spritz cookie, that very night, *after* the Christmas feast we had just eaten.

On a different Christmas Eve in the early sixties, Mom was cooking up a storm; all four burners were going, both ovens were full, and the L'Ectra Maid (electric skillet) had Swiss steak simmering. A storm came through and suddenly, the farm lost power. Panic gave way to thrills as we quickly brought out the antique kerosene lamp and an assortment of candles, and excitedly improvised some menu items. That year we simply ate whatever was cooked "good enough," enjoyed a more old-fashioned Christmas, sans electricity, and created a memory none of us would soon forget.

As far back as I can remember, Mom put names of whichever siblings planned to be home for Christmas into a hat, and our family exchanged presents. Depending on who drew whose name, the amount spent on a gift varied widely. To flatten out the jealousy factor, Mom started setting a spending limit. When I was in fifth grade, the limit was one dollar per gift; this

After our Christmas Eve feast, we re-enacted a full Christmas pageant, singing religious songs throughout the pageant before switching to secular holiday music.
Back row: Alice, Damien, guest one, guest two
Front Row: Marty, Greg, Marcia

forced all of us to get super-creative and hand-make our gifts. The subsequent year, Mom upped the limit to five dollars. If someone no-showed, or if, by mistake, someone didn't get a gift, Mom filled in with candy, a pair of gloves or a spare pair of new socks that she kept hidden in her top dresser drawer for just such emergencies.

I can't think about Christmas without mentioning the old-fashioned Christmas candy that Mom made six weeks ahead of time and stored in wax paper and newspaper so the flavors could meld. It contained red, green and gold candied fruit, coconut, figs and dates, kind of like an unbaked fruitcake. Mom's siblings absolutely loved it. They also liked Mom's dark, heavy fruitcake. At every single meal for two weeks before and after Christmas, Mom served her Christmas pudding candy in her ever-present blue glass candy dish with the silver cover, as if more kids would eventually like it if we saw it often enough.

After our Christmas Eve feast, we set out our "costume box" (a three by four-foot cardboard box left-over from emptying a case of Wheaties) filled with hand-me-downs and assorted fabrics, and assigned roles for the annual Christmas Pageant. We needed youngsters to play the parts of Mary, Joseph, baby Jesus, the shepherds, the angels, and the three kings. Typically, everyone younger than sixteen took part, and the older ones served as the chorus.

1970 Christmas Pageant
Continuing from one generation to the next:
My devout youngest sister Marcia, played Mary. My youngest brother, Damien, played Joseph. Marty, and Greg played shepherds. The angels include Angi and our two eldest nieces, Jennifer and Rebecca.

We used the same couple yards of light blue fabric each year for Mary's veil, an old bathrobe and a walking stick for Joseph, some white nightgowns for angels, and so forth. I can remember only one year where we didn't have a baby who was young enough to play Jesus, and we were forced to pretend using a doll. Kings' crowns never seemed to last from one year to the next. Every year, each of the three kings had to quickly shape their own new tin foil crowns in time for the pageant, and find gift boxes to represent frankincense and myrrh.

We set out the empty baby cradle and sang "Oh, Little Town of Bethlehem" or "Silent Night" while Mary and baby Jesus entered the "stage."

Next came Joseph, to "Away in a Manger." Then came the shepherds while the chorus sang, "Do You Hear What I Hear?" The angels arrived to the tune of "Hark the Herald" and "Angels We Have Heard on High," and finally, "We Three Kings."

Following the Christmas pageant, we sang "Jingle Bells," "Rudolf the Red-Nosed Reindeer," "White Christmas," and ended with "We Wish You a Merry Christmas." The little kids giggled

The big kids ended Christmas Eve by attending midnight Mass. After coming home, Dad placed the wooden baby Jesus into the life-size 2D wooden manger on our front lawn. Then he shoveled any snow away from the spotlight on the life-size Virgin Mary shrine in our back yard, decorated for Christmas with a string of blue lights.

as they silently mouthed "Jingle bells, shotgun shells, Santa Claus is dead..." The gifts from our family gift exchange sat under the tree until we finished singing. Then, pretty much all at the same time, we ripped them open to squeals of laughter and Christmas joy.

After we cleaned up the ribbon and wrapping paper, we ran upstairs to find one Sunday knee-high sock. Each of us used a diaper pin to attach a knee-high to the back of our couch as our "Christmas stocking," hoping to get more from Santa than if we had hung an ankle-length sock. By the time the stockings were hung, it was time to change clothes and get dressed up for Midnight Mass.

When Dad arrived home from midnight Mass, he enthusiastically brought down any packages he had hidden in the rafters of the freezing-cold detached garage. Santa quietly wrapped and labeled twenty-two gifts and arranged them around the Christmas tree, double-checking to make sure everyone got something.

Santa brought each of us one present. In first grade, Santa brought me a black doll with an Afro hair-do. I had never seen a black person, and since we didn't have a TV, I didn't even know there was "such a thing." I figured that Santa

Christmas, 1968: Damien, wearing an SJU T-shirt, and Greg, having just received his first bow and arrow

had acquired the doll second-hand and that it was simply dirty.

Mom insisted we always wash everything we bought before we used it, a smart rule when much of our new stuff came from second hand stores or the dump. I took my new doll upstairs to the bathroom, got out bath tub cleanser and a stiff brush, and scratched the heck out of my new doll's face and hands. Then I took my little paper scissors and cut off all the hair that I could not comb, (just like Mom had said she would do to my hair if I got bubblegum caught

in it). I brought the ruined doll downstairs to show Mom. I told her how I had tried *really* hard to clean the doll and comb its hair, but it just wasn't working. I don't remember exactly what she said, but she soothed my hard feelings without laughing, and without reprimanding me.

If my present was a new game, I needed to scramble to find other kids who wanted to play *my* game, and then I'd have to agree to play *theirs*. We sometimes stood in line to play each other's new game.

In third grade, each of us got our own set of deer-hide mittens lined with red felt. Prior to that, Grama Kahnke had knitted most of our mittens and they were, of course, not waterproof. What a joy to be able to have leather mittens that actually kept us warm! In fourth grade, Santa's gift for me was a tan ski hat with blue decorations; it was so long it went down to my waistline. In fifth grade, I got a hot pink sweater and some matching tights, the nicest gift I had ever received. Dad must have made money that year.

Santa also brought an orange or an apple in each knee-high sock, plus coloring books and a set of crayons, colored pencils or something like that, and toys for the whole family to share. One year we were given a new toboggan, a different

A new driver learning to use our new snowmobile... tugging a toboggan full of happy kids.

year we received Parcheesi and Crocinole, another year the game Twister and a red plastic sled. One year we got a flying saucer, but then Dad decided that was too dangerous.

When I was in second grade, Santa surprised us with a Polaris snowmobile that Dad would use to pull us UP the sledding hill so we could slide down over and over. It was one of the very first snowmobile models, and was advertised to reach a breath-taking speed of twenty-five miles per hour. Our snowmobile tugged us along at one tenth of that. Before Minnesota outlawed hunting with a snowmobile, Dad liked to use it for pulling his ice-house onto the frozen lake and for checking his mink, muskrat and fox traps. Fox pelts were worth about twenty-five dollars apiece at that time; mink was worth fifty. When eggs were selling for 25 cents a dozen, Dad could trap one fox or raise enough chickens to produce a hundred dozen eggs. It's easy to understand why trapping became a not insignificant income source.

After Christmas Day Mass, we ate our oranges and apples for breakfast. As a child, I was so busy playing with my present (and checking out everyone else's) that I have no specific memories of Christmas Day meals except for Mom's famous plum cream pie. In my teenage years, Mom roasted ducks or a goose with plum dressing, served potatoes and gravy and a green vegetable, an iceberg lettuce salad, a variety of homemade pickles, her special Christmas Candy, fudge, plenty of Christmas cookies and, of course, a relish tray.

On Christmas Day in 1975, Dad called a family meeting (a rare event, occurring only for extremely important reasons), sat us all down and told us Mom had developed rheumatoid arthritis, and lectured us about being more helpful without being asked. Probably for the first time in his married life, that day he diligently attempted to set a good example by helping clean up the kitchen so Mom could lay down for a few minutes.

1967: standing in front of our garage displaying that season's fox pelts: Alice, Pauline, Art, Marty, and Angela

Mom normally warmed a metal coffee pot on the electric stove throughout the day, and re-filled it as necessary. However, when we had company, Mom used a newly invented insulated coffee carafe we called a "coffee saver." Trying hard to be helpful that Christmas day, when no one was paying attention, Dad set the plastic coffee saver on the back burner of the electric cooktop and turned the burner on warm. No one noticed, and we all went to the living room to play.

Suddenly, someone smelled smoke and warned Dad that something was burning. Dad thought the unusual smell might have come from our furnace (the hot air register from the basement was right near our kitchen stove). Without being asked, we *all* dutifully followed him down the basement *to help him out,* as discussed that morning in the family meeting.

Meanwhile, Mom couldn't stand the stench. She got out of bed to check and see what was burning, (even though she was in pain). She immediately found the melted plastic coffee saver and cleaned up the smoldering mess, not realizing all of us were down the basement still frantically looking for the source of the smell of something burning. Afterward, we all had a good laugh.

Before the Christmas holidays, my mother sometimes went "on retreat" with other Catholic moms. Mom valued education as a way to rise out of poverty, and she prided herself that all of her children would be given the opportunity to receive a good education. Mom had wanted to attend high school as a teenager but did not have the chance. As a busy mother, she continued her education through the County Home Extension program, Toastmasters, Catholic Daughters of America and Winona diocese Council of Catholic Women. She also served in on the Board of the Day Activity Center.

Whenever she went to a meeting, she put one of the teenagers "in charge." We were taught to "Do as you are told" by anyone who was older. Occasionally, Mom put someone in charge that was not the eldest person. She knew the person in charge would not likely bully a younger kid knowing that he or she might have to take orders from that younger sibling the following week.

When my parents became empty nesters, and most of the grandchildren no longer needed babysitting, Mom wrote in her memoir, *"The highlight of my career to date has been to have given birth to so many healthy babies. My greatest accomplishment was after I had my family, I still had the yearning for further education; in 1989 through community education I studied and earned my high school diploma. What a thrill!"*

People often ask me how my parents could afford to send so many of us to Catholic college. The best answer is, "They couldn't, but that didn't stop us from going." Dad announced that if we attended a Catholic college instead of a public university, he would give us cash that was equivalent to what he had gifted his first son when he was starting his farm. When Al got married and left home, Al's $2,500 "inheritance" bought his first milk-cows.

By the time I started at the College of St. Benedict in 1974, Dad adjusted inheritance

In 1977, Art graduated from Airframe and Powerplant Mechanics School, and I marched in the College of St. Benedict's graduation ceremony even though I was missing one required physical education credit and didn't formally get my diploma until I completed a PE course shortly before I retired.

amounts for inflation, so he gave me $4,000. His tax returns showed he wasn't making much money that year, so he had to borrow money to fund my first semester of college. The silver lining of Dad's low income was that, like most of my siblings, I received a lot of scholarship money, took a work/study grant, and was able to borrow from the federal government's student loan program. Even though I spent two semesters abroad and two summers studying in Vermont, I finished my undergraduate degree only eight thousand dollars in debt.

My first job paid $13,000 a year. Within about three years, my school loans were paid off and I had already bought my first house and a brand-new car. Mom was absolutely right; college was an excellent investment.

Growing up Catholic meant that Sunday was a day of rest. Of course, we had to feed chickens, gather eggs, and milk our sole cow, Bossie, but other than that, Sunday was a day of prayer and leisure. Saturday was ironing day. We sprinkled distilled water on our Sunday dresses and rolled them up in a ball and set them in a specific clothes basket known as the "ironing basket." One teenage girl was assigned to do the ironing so that everyone could have their good clothes ready for church.

On Saturday nights, in preparation for going to Mass on Sunday morning, we each took our weekly bath, washed our hair in the laundry room sink, and stood in line for Dad to clip our finger and toe nails. Mom bathed the children younger than three downstairs. A teenager was assigned to scrub the three, the four and the five-year-old together in the bathtub upstairs. We used about three inches of water in the bath tub, no more! To save on hot water, we re-used that muddy bath water for the six-year-old, unless it was truly filthy. School age children were allowed to take a bath alone, as long as they didn't use too much hot water. Because we considered swimming at Reed's Lake a substitute for taking a bath, bath time was much shorter in the summer.

Wearing our good clothes meant girls putting on clean, starched can-can slips and crisply pressed dresses, and boys wearing shirts and ties, all wearing freshly polished shoes. No one in our family wore overalls in those days. Just jeans, regular pants, or for the men, coveralls. It was always difficult to finish barn chores, clean up, change from smelly coveralls or other everyday clothes into good clothes, and still be ready to leave in time for early Mass (7AM) on Sunday.

1962: Marylu, Linda, Art, Helen in front of our new blue van

On rare occasions, we even went to 6AM Mass. We had better not get caught wearing Sunday shoes out to the barn to quickly feed the hens before church, not even with rubber overshoes, or else!

It was frustrating that Dad wouldn't let us just slip boots over our Sunday shoes because it would have saved a lot of time, but now I totally understand why he didn't... the smell. If you have never been in a stinky 1950's chicken coop, just imagine dirty diaper smell mixed with the stench of ammonia so strong it's capable of burning your nostrils and throat.

To get to Mass every Sunday morning, fifteen or so of us would sit on each other's laps in our station wagon, and later, in our then-current van. In 1962, our family had thoroughly outgrown our station wagon, so Dad bought the first of four less-than-luxurious vans; it was royal blue and had zero insulation; in winter we shivered, and in the summer, we baked. That van was designed with the motor positioned between the driver and the passenger seat. The motor cover was black steel, and made a handy (and warm!) extra seat. Occasionally, however, the motor caught fire, so that first van didn't last long with our family.

Once we got the van, about fifteen of us could squish into the van and attend early Mass together. We filled the same two church pews every week. Mom and Dad made sure we looked our best, including wearing hats or chapel veils until I was in about sixth grade. Mom and Dad prided themselves on how well we behaved. If Mom raised an eyebrow at one of us in church, all of us would immediately straighten up and act like little angels. We did not want Mom to be unhappy with us as that often translated into more housework. The risk of getting spanked by an older sibling once we got home also helped keep us in line.

One teenager stayed home to babysit the baby and the youngest toddler; whoever babysat during 8:30AM Mass drove Mom's (smaller) car to ten o'clock Mass. Prior to 1962, Catholics who wanted to receive communion were required to fast before Mass. By the time we arrived home on Sundays around 9:15AM, we had hunger pangs. To make Sundays special, Mom served one can of Hi-C orange juice, or three oranges cut into eight wedges each. Sundays were the only day of the week that we drank juice or ate oranges. Once a month or so, Mom took time to, as she used to say, "whip up" sweet rolls for Sunday breakfast. Mom baked the world's best cinnamon/raisin rolls, sticky caramel rolls with

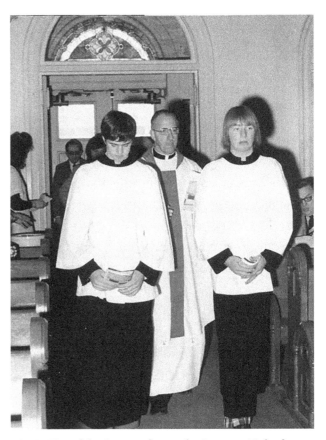

1975: Humble Art and cousin Duane Kahnke, serving as altar boys for Father Kunz.

black walnuts, poppy seed rolls, and Kolackies, usually with prune or apricot filling.

Twice a year Mom would bake four or five batches of various pastries and rolls to donate to the Catholic Daughter Bake Sale. When Dad saw these, he would usually pull out his wallet to give her his donation on the spot. He insisted she keep her best baking at home for us to enjoy.

He was willing to donate to their cause, but he had no interest whatsoever in buying someone else's cooking at a bake sale.

To stretch our food budget, we reserved such treats as store-bought bacon or breakfast sausage for Sunday mornings, a limit of two pounds of either, never both. When the good stuff (bacon or sausage, sweet rolls and orange juice) was gone, (instantly), we ate lots of eggs, and toast with tons of butter and jam. We washed it down with plenty of milk, fresh from our cow.

The L'ectra Maid allowed us to easily fry eight eggs at a time. We thought nothing of putting a half cup of pure pork fat into the pan before we cracked the eggs into it. Dad liked his eggs sunny-side up, with bacon grease splashed over the top until a white coating appeared, then add extra salt! For cooking, we used a salt shaker that was four inches in diameter with relatively large holes. My dad and I shared a love of anything hot, salty, and greasy. Fortunately, our family is blessed with low cholesterol.

Occasionally, Mom made pancakes for Sunday breakfast. If milk had begun to sour, Mom could use it up making golden buttermilk pancakes, served with loads of butter and syrup. Homemade syrup consisted of one cup of white sugar plus half a cup of brown sugar boiled in half a kettle of water, and flavored with vanilla and/or maple. It cost half as much, tasted great, and, because we could quickly cook up another batch, we never worried about running out.

When I was in sixth grade, pancakes suddenly changed from a rare treat to a weekly meal. A train carrying dry pancake mix got damaged in a local railroad accident. While the insurance companies did battle with each other, weevils infested a train car's worth of merchandise. Months later, when the owner of the pancake mix gave it away, our family was thrilled to accept easy-to-make, free food! We simply sifted out the bugs and thought nothing of it. We wondered why other people didn't do the same, and marveled at how no one else wanted it! The train accident that brought us a year's worth of pancake mix happened in the same place where a far more serious accident had happened roughly seven or eight years prior.

At that time, there were no automatic gates to prevent a car from crossing the tracks when a train was coming. Sometimes the flashing signals would stay on for a full hour while trains attached and detached railroad cars in the rail yard next to the school. On the day of the tragic accident, the eldest Zimmerman daughter, Kathy, lived just long enough to suggest that a school boy had waved the driver across the

My Dad's youngest sister, Irene Miller Zimmerman, and her six children: Kathy, Mike, Connie, Timmy, Barbara, and Jan, were tragically killed when a train broadsided their station wagon while they were on their way to Sacred Heart school the morning of September 11, 1959.

tracks without having seen the oncoming train. Little did anyone know how much sorrow the date 9/11 would bring in years to come.

The Zimmerman train accident occurred just over two years after my uncle Dick passed away. Because of these tragedies, fear and grief shadowed my formative years. Unconsciously, it was as if my family continuously worried that another shoe would drop. Following the death of my uncle, my aunt and her children, my already very religious parents took further solace in their Catholic faith. It was under this veil of

grief that I grew up a rather serious child. We had fun, but I don't recall a single thing in my early childhood that was funny.

Prior to 9/11/1959, I had never seen my mother cry. For days thereafter, she couldn't stop sobbing. Our six Zimmerman first cousins and their parents had visited our family just days before the tragic accident. We spent that afternoon climbing up our big metal slide, then sliding down, over and over and over. Dad had built us a slide with a wooden ladder that was more than twice as high as the little-kid-slide attached to our swing set; it was even higher than the slide at the local park. Besides softballs, a football, and a basketball, our family had precious few outdoor toys. Our slide was a big hit with our neighbors and cousins.

We used wax paper from empty cold cereal boxes to make our metal slide extra slippery. For waxing the slide, Kix liners worked better than the Cheerios liners, and much better than regular wax paper. I had promised my cousins that I would save up wax paper for the next time they came over. Because of how much fun we had had, I was anxious to play with them again, and asked my mother, "When can Timmy come over?"

Mom put me up on her lap and tried to explain.

"Timmy is dead. You won't see him again until you go to heaven," she said.

The only thing my four-year-old mind could compare this to was when Mom had kept us home during a measles outbreak, and she wouldn't let cousins come to visit.

"Is *dead* worse than the measles?" I asked.

"Yes," Mom replied.

After several tries, she still couldn't get through to me what *dead* meant. To help me understand, Mom took me along to my cousins' wake. Seven caskets lined my widowed uncle's small living room. The house was jam-packed with relatives and flowers. Everybody was sobbing or bawling. I ran straight up to Timmy's casket and touched his hand, wanting him to get up and play. His hand was cold; it felt like the green snakes in our garden. I bolted back to Mom. Between the fright of feeling Timmy's hand and the intense smell of roses, I felt suffocated, and couldn't wait to get out of there. To this day, roses remind me of death, and cause me to gag.

As I mentioned earlier, uncle Dick had also been killed in a tragic accident, just two years prior. His widow, my mother's youngest sister Therese, had three small children, and was pregnant when her husband died. In September of '59, our extended family was still mourning our young uncle's passing. Mom and Dad spent a lot of time trying to help Aunt Therese's family recover from their loss. The shock of losing a whole family of first cousins was more than any of us could handle, especially considering it was layered on top of the still-raw bereavement of our uncle's passing.

22 Kids
Grade School Pictures in birth order
starting from the upper left corner

Ramona recalls a veil of grief descended over our family that year, lingering throughout our household. It cast a shadow over everything and radically changed the family dynamic from happy-go-lucky Irish humor to a more somber, almost stoic mood. We found ourselves needing to find ways to try to celebrate life.

May Day was a special day. Besides the traditional May Day baskets, each of us kids picked flowers, lilacs, or branches from a blossoming fruit tree to take to "May Crowning." Students of our Catholic school formed a big parade from the school to the church, then presented bouquets to the Virgin Mary as we sang, "Bring flowers of the fairest, bring flowers of the rarest..."

For students of Sacred Heart grade school and high school, St. Patrick's Day was a school holiday. St. Patrick was said to have driven the snakes out of Ireland and converted the Irish to Catholicism using a simple clover to educate people on the Holy Trinity: God the Father, God the Son, and God the Holy Spirit. Many of the families in our parish were Irish, and Waseca celebrated our Irish Catholic heritage with gusto.

As with any Catholic celebration, the day starts by going to church. After Mass, volunteers served a traditional Irish feast of Mulligan stew, corned beef and cabbage, boiled potatoes and Irish soda bread. The year that I ran for Irish Queen by singing "When Irish Eyes are Smiling," Katie O'Grady was crowned Miss St. Patrick. No surprise there. She's cute, talented, and a heck-uva lot more Irish than I am! The Queen rode in a convertible leading the big parade, followed by a bazaar in the school gym.

Each of us was given a ticket to try at least one game: bean bag toss, the cake-walk, or fishing over a curtain for prizes. We also got a little money from Mom so we could buy homemade cookies or fudge at the bazaar.

When Ginny was in about fifth grade, she won the cake walk game right after the church ladies had run out of donated cakes. For a prize, they gave her a black puppy named Pepper. Ginny had been afraid of dogs, but because she was excited to have won a prize, she learned to like Pepper (at least for a little while), until taking care of a dog became more work than play.

Dad built a really fun game for the St. Paddy's Day bazaar; it worked like a horizontal roulette wheel. He painted various colors on the perimeter of a plywood circle five feet in diameter. Each color had a hole in the middle and was labeled with its odds to win. Blue paid five to one, red paid three to one, and so on. Before Dad spun the wheel, people placed bets as to which color of hole a live mouse would choose. The winner would then get a prize. It was the highlight of our parish bazaar!

Prior to 1965, private school students were not eligible to ride the [public school only] bus to school. Like our cousins who died in the train accident, a mom or dad drove their kids to and from Catholic school. When one of my parents picked us up from Sacred Heart, someone usually counted heads to make sure everyone was in the car. Every once in a while, we neglected to count.

"If there wasn't some humor in raising a large family, I don't think Ceil and I would have made it. We were coming home from a visit to Dave Kahnke's one afternoon, and a rabbit ran across the road. Now John was especially interested in wild life, and I called his attention to it. It was very quiet in the back of the station wagon and someone said, "We don't have John along." He didn't get in the car, and nobody missed him."

I missed my ride home one afternoon when I was in first grade. I patiently stood at the school's front door for an hour or two until the principal left for the day. She directed me to walk to my Grama Miller's and call home from there. Whenever someone got left somewhere, the rest of us were more diligent with our counting heads, at least for a while, but, inevitably, we slacked off, and someone else got left behind once again.

Prior to free bussing, neither I, nor any of my siblings, attended kindergarten. It would have been too time-consuming for my parents to drive one child back and forth to a half-day session at the public school.

After my aunt and my cousins were killed in the train accident, my uncle and his sister spearheaded the passage of a law entitling parochial school children to also receive free bussing. Marty and Pauline were my first siblings to attend kindergarten. Mom wrote: *"They were shy, and with some learning disabilities, they needed that extra start."*

They were also the first ones of our family to ride the bus to school; they started on the same day.

Reading was completely foreign to me and my siblings when we first started school. I don't remember any books for preschoolers in our home. My Dad loved to read, but he was much too busy to read to us. Instead, Dad often had little quizzes for us, challenging us to learn new things. "How much is one plus one?" he would ask a toddler. "Does DDT stay in the ground year after year?" he asked a teenager. His favorite prize for a correct answer was a third or half a piece of Juicy Fruit gum.

No one read to us at bedtime, and no one kissed us goodnight. Following in my German father's cultural tradition, hugs and kisses in general were exceedingly rare. Instead of listening to a bedtime story followed by getting tucked in by a parent, we simply kept playing with each other. When we felt tired, we hopped in our beds, declared "lights out," and instantly fell asleep, exhausted from another day of working hard and playing hard.

At the beginning of first grade, my teacher, Sister Conall, wrote each student's name on a construction-paper airplane. She pinned them to her bulletin board below paper clouds and above a picture of an airplane garage; the word "hangar" was not yet in our vocabulary… Whenever a student correctly read aloud a sentence such as "See Dick run," Sister Conall pinned that student's airplane up near the clouds. Unfortunately, my airplane sat in the airplane garage for what seemed like an eternity before my reading skills caught up to my classmates. Even though I had a slow start, from then on, I was a top student, as were most of my siblings.

In my mid-fifties, I flew from NY to Minnesota to attend my uncle Leo's funeral. Coming out of church, Sister Conall recognized me and greeted me as if we were old friends:

"Hi, Helen."

"Do I know you?" I asked.

"I'm Sister Conall. I taught you in first grade."

"You must have had thousands of students in your teaching career. How *in the world* did you recognize me?" I asked, remembering the countless times my aunts, uncles, teachers, and sometimes even my dad called me by the wrong name.

"Oh, that's simple," she responded. "You are the only student I ever had who didn't like recess!"

OMG. *I* didn't even remember that I didn't like recess. I do remember that I had been terribly embarrassed by my ignorance when I started first grade, and I remember wanting to learn to read far worse than wanting to play outside and, also, I hated going outside when it was cold out. However, I didn't realize what a pain it must have been for a first-grade teacher to spend her break time babysitting me in the classroom while all the other children played outdoors. Oops!

It still shocks me that a lady who I did not recognize actually remembered my name... fifty years later! The only adult who consistently called all of us by our correct names was my mom. Our teachers would often call us by the names of an elder sibling they had taught. Even my dad would say, "Hey, you!" or "You little tiker," or, "One of you kids, get over here and help me."

My aunts and uncles would often call us by the name of one of our siblings, (any which one), and then apologize that they couldn't tell us apart. When local people didn't know

our names, they would rhetorically say, "You look like one of the Miller kids," as if we were the only Miller family in our town. Several of us inherited my dad's very dark eyes, and that distinguished us as a family by comparison to his brother's family who lived next door and who had light-colored eyes.

On occasion, Dad used far less complimentary terms, like dummy, or "You numb skull," "You nincompoop!" or "You blithering idiot!" My father was capable of being what one sibling called "brutally disrespectful." One of our so-called foster kids swears my dad had as many as thirteen different idiot names. Thankfully, I can only remember him using a couple of them on me.

Living in fear of being reprimanded by parents or by elder siblings, it was a rare occasion when any of us would pull a prank on someone at home. Short-sheeting a bed was about as far as we were willing to go. In town, however was a different matter. On one sleep-over, a half dozen of us rang about 30 doorbells at three o'clock in the morning without any of us getting caught.

On a different occasion, I was very fortunate that Dad closed his eyes to my teenage prank. Our town's new high school building was put into use before the heating, ventilation and air conditioning had been properly installed. My classmates and I hated the new school because we were always either way too hot or way too cold. One evening, my friends and I picked up about a hundred real estate "for sale" signs from peoples' yards, and posted them around the new school.

The next night, the cops called our house at suppertime, a no-no with my dad. He believed everyone ate supper promptly at six, and no one should be using a phone at supper time.

"Who's on the phone?" Dad asked.

"It's the police department."

"What do they want?"

"They want to talk to you." Cussing under his breath, my dad took the phone.

"What do you want?" groused my father, annoyed that anyone would interrupt supper. We were all listening intently, and could hear the sheriff on the other end of the line.

"It's been reported that a light blue van bearing license plates M-I-L-L-E-R was seen picking up real estate signs and posting them around the new high school."

Without turning around to talk to any of us about this incident, Dad practically shouts into the receiver: "None of my kids would have done that!" and slammed down the phone. Case closed. We never heard another word about it.

My siblings and I were not perfect angels, but we acted like goody-two-shoes most of the time. Having watched some of my teenage siblings argue with my dad, (not very successfully) most of us middle kids learned to follow the rules, keep our heads low and avoid trouble. Our primary goal was to stay out of Dad's crosshairs.

Normally, if us kids were unruly, Mom could usually settle us down by getting everyone to join her in song. When anyone swore, they got their mouth washed out with bar soap. If anyone fought, they got spanked. We never knew the word "time-out," but we were quite familiar with the concept. When a youngster was naughty, Mom would tie the kid to a kitchen chair (using a flour-sack dish towel) to sit quietly for a little while. If we were extra rambunctious, or too old to be spanked, she raised one eyebrow and gave us a silent frown which pretty much meant, "Just wait 'til your father gets home!"

It was not unusual for our relatives' and friends' mothers to ask Mom, "How do you get those kids to behave so nicely?" On more than one occasion, mothers visiting us turned to their children and asked, "Why don't you behave like the Millers?"

Middle kids had way too many big brothers and sisters standing ready to yell at us and/or spank us if we misbehaved. For me as the 13th child, it was like having 14 parents. In a family of our size, everyone develops fight/flight and coping skills at a relatively young age. Fighting was never my thing. Instead, I developed a hyper-vigilant eye for which kid was in what mood, when I needed to try to steer clear of someone, and when I needed to run.

Sister Adrian taught second grade. By the time she met me, she had taught ten of my siblings, and she knew she could lean pretty hard on Miller kids. One day, when I heard her whistle (calling us in from recess), I ran full-tilt around the corner of the school toward the main door. Bobby Bartelt was about six inches shorter than I, and the crown of his head caught my right eye as he rounded the schoolhouse in the opposite direction. I came back to class with a black and blue eye.

As punishment, (girls were not supposed to run!) Sister Adrian assigned me to write out three pages of the dictionary including all the detailed punctuation. I was mad. No fair!

Why should I get punished for running and not him? In our family, if two people were in the event together, both got punished or neither got punished. I whined to my big sisters about how unfair this was. Lucky for me, Kathleen felt sorry for me. She is ten years older than I, and she made quick work of finishing those dictionary pages on my behalf. Under those circumstances, neither of us felt any remorse for cheating on Sister Adrian.

Years later, whenever I caught my two youngest brothers tussling/wrestling/quarreling, they were both automatically assigned to dry dishes. I was oblivious to the fact that one was forty pounds heavier than the other and therefore won most every skirmish, and the younger one was constantly looking for a more sympathetic ear. Mom and Dad had not taught us how to intervene to help the younger ones settle disputes; we just meted out the standard punishment. I'm sorry for my part in the pain that caused.

The nuns and my parents drilled it into us that we needed to live a good life to avoid burning in hell forever and ever, into eternity. In second grade, we prepared for First Communion by memorizing the Ten Commandments and then making our First Confession. At that time, the priest would sit in a tiny three-door confessional booth with two kneeling pews, one on either side of him. He could hear, but not see, the person kneeling down to make their confession.

The day came for me to make my First Confession. I was seven years old. I reviewed the Ten Commandments and could not find any that I had violated. I knew for sure I hadn't killed anybody, and I hadn't stolen anything, and I hadn't lied. The others didn't seem so onerous, and I *needed* to have something to confess so I made myself a list.

I went proudly into the tiny booth, knelt down, waited for the priest to open the solid panel (so he could hear me through the dark screen), and said,

"Bless me Father, for I have sinned. This is my first confession. I did not honor my father and mother two times, I had false gods before me two times, and I committed adultery three or four times."

The priest didn't skip a beat. He must have realized I had no idea what these commandments meant, and he calmly said,

"Say three Our Fathers and Three Hail Mary's, my child, and go in peace."

Whew! I had successfully made it through my first confession. My plan for what to confess worked so well that I used that same list again the next time my parents made me go to confession. That was before Vatican II, when catechism instruction was memorized without being fully understood.

In addition to teaching us to take the Bible literally, my teachers and parents taught us that the Easter Bunny brought candy, and that Santa came down the chimney to deliver Christmas gifts. I memorized my lessons with the same gusto with which I reviewed the Montgomery Ward catalog (the only catalog that came in the mail) to draft my Christmas wish list.

Mom used to say we were lucky to be able to page through such a nice big catalog because when she was a child, a catalog was used in the outhouse in place of toilet paper, and the only other alternative was using corn cobs!

It had come to my attention that some children didn't believe in Santa and the Easter bunny. I was also aware that some people did not believe that Jesus rose from the dead. To me, the notion of believing in the Resurrection and believing in Santa were absolutely synonymous. They both required a leap of faith.

Mom taught us that we had to have *faith* to believe in miracles, and that there are some things we simply cannot understand, and these are called mysteries. We were taught to have faith, even when we did not understand. Mom said only people who had deep faith would go to heaven. As a youngster, I believed whatever Mom believed, so I became convinced that Jesus rose from the dead, and Santa really did live at the North Pole.

As the Christmas season approached, my siblings and I sat on the sofa for hours on end flipping catalog pages to find the one present we REALLY wanted for Christmas. Then we each wrote Santa a letter. We all went down the basement with Dad, watched him read each letter aloud, then throw it in the wood furnace. He said when the smoke rose and reached the north pole, Santa would know what to bring us. We never once got any of those items we had so carefully chosen from the catalog, but it didn't slow us down from trying again the next year.

When I was in seventh grade, Mom and I were in the car on the way to town when she asked, "What do you think Marylu would want for Christmas?"

"Why?" I responded, surprised at such a conversation. "Did you draw her name? [for our family's Christmas gift exchange]?"

"No, this is from Santa."

My jaw dropped. That's how I found out the truth about Santa, and also how I simultaneously lost my faith in terms of taking the Old Testament literally. I still liked going to church, believing in God, and living a good life. It's just that I learned to let go of my fundamentalist' understanding of the bible.

I don't think back on my thirteen-year-old's belief in Santa and the Easter bunny as naïve and gullible; instead, I conclude this could only have happened to a seventh grader in an extremely religious family, and I marvel all over again at the depth of my parents' faith. Mom and Dad's deep and abiding faith carried them through every adversity they ever faced. Honestly, I don't know how anyone could raise a family like ours without a supportive church community, including nuns as teachers and fellow parents who shared each other's values.

To help Catholic parents maintain social contact with other parents, our parish priest instituted "Social Circles." Once a month, Mom and Dad enjoyed going to a church-sponsored

Janet, Marylu, and Kathleen picked fresh strawberries to take to Circle.

card-playing group known simply as "Circle." Their Circle included Milt and Wynn Clemons, Lawrence and Lita Clemons, Cy and Berniece Ostendorf, Mr. and Mrs. Wengronowitz, Mr. and Mrs. Salze, Bob and Ruth Powell and one other couple.

Circle members rotated the job of hosting; each hostess would outdo the last by serving a wonderful meal, after which they played a card tournament (usually a form of gin rummy called 500). The winner took home the grand prize and the loser left with a gag-gift / booby prize. Since nobody except our family had china service for sixteen, people brought their own dishes to each other's homes. Mom always carried silverware, two china plates, and two coffee cups with saucers in her round flannel plate-holder with a drawstring on top.

Mom usually described Circle parties as "lovely." One night they came home in a particularly giddy mood. For my straight-laced German dad to be giddy, something momentous must have happened, so we wanted to hear the joke. The hostess, they explained, was a terrific cook, and had been asked for her dessert recipe the month prior. This month, a not-as-terrific cook who had asked for the recipe said she had tried it and complained it didn't turn out just right. The hostess mused that the recipient must have forgotten the "tablespoon of good judgment" that goes in all her recipes. One cook got embarrassed and annoyed while everyone else had a good belly laugh. My dad told that story dozens of times. I laughed every single time.

My family's supportive community included many, many nuns. A couple of times each summer, we visited our sisters, Sister Perpetua, and Sister Elvira. Ten or fifteen kids put on our Sunday clothes, including hats. We piled on top of each other in the station wagon or van, depending on what year it was. For an hour and a half, we had to sit still on our hour-long ride to the motherhouse of the Franciscan order called Assisi Heights, located in Rochester, MN. We

Ramona, wearing her postulant uniform: white blouse and black skirt. I'm peeking out near her right hand. I have no memory of her before she wore the traditional habit.

Mom serving fried chicken at the motherhouse the year I asked if my eldest sister, shown here in the Franciscan habit, was a boy or a girl.

had not yet heard of seat belts, and sitting on someone's lap was considered part of the fun.

When we arrived, Mom would do a quick inspection. If someone's face was dirty, she'd pull a linen hankie from her purse, dab it with her tongue, and shine that person up. Hats were still required in Catholic churches at that time; if we had forgotten to bring a hat or a chapel veil, Mom would sometimes have to bobby-pin Kleenex on top of our heads!

I was too young to get to know my eldest sister as a postulant, before she wore a Franciscan habit. Nuns were given the opportunity to receive visitors only on rare occasion. Whenever we visited my sister(s) at the motherhouse, we were seated in a huge parlor room. At least

twenty distinct families each sat on formal wingback chairs in individual sections of the parlor separated by marble pillars where the various families could see (and overhear) each other.

The floors were Italian marble, and sound carried well, so all children were instructed to sit still and speak quietly. At age four, I was confused by my eldest sister's new garb, called a habit. Sister Perpetua and the other nuns wore a full length brown robe, a black veil and a white cardboard band across her forehead. I remember whispering to my mom, "Is Sister Perpetua a boy or a girl?"

"She's your *sister*," Mom said, trying to hush me. At the time, I only associated the word *sister* with nuns who wore that type of clothing.

"I KNOW she's my *SISTER!*" I said, almost shouting in frustration. Still thinking the word "sister" just meant that a person wore a certain type of outfit, I demanded, "I want to know if she's a BOY or a GIRL!"

"A girl," she whispered with a smile.

I am in the middle of the family, and, as you can tell from the previous story, I did not remember my eldest siblings living at home. The family life they knew and the family life I knew were half a generation apart. For my youngest siblings, a full generation fit between them and their siblings. As one of my siblings lamented, "The older ones don't think the way we do. Back then it was focused on becoming book smart, stay up all night and get term papers done, it was not focused on what to do for everyday living."

My parents were understandably paranoid about young children misbehaving at the motherhouse. On the way there, when I was about five years old, Dad made one of his famous special deals: if we were *ALL* well-behaved, *All* the way there, and *All* the way back, he would buy us either

a. bedtime snack of sharing a whole gallon of A&W root beer and ice cream, or

b. a five cent baby Dairy Queen cone per person.

We chose the root beer option because we loved fizzy anything, and rarely had the opportunity to enjoy fizz. Dad succeeded in keeping fifteen kids quiet for a full three hours with the promise that we would get to enjoy a gallon of A&W root beer. We sang some songs and then Mom led the Rosary. When we arrived home safe, Dad said, as he usually did after a long drive, "Home again, home again, jiggedy jug." That night, when Dad added Kemp's vanilla ice cream to A&W root beer to make floats, much to our chagrin, the ice cream killed our favorite part, the fizz.

CHAPTER 4:

Everyday Life on the Farm

1955 The Farm
Clockwise starting from the barn: two henhouses, a two-car garage and a machine shed hidden by the trees, our home, a granary, a corn crib, and, nearly hidden behind the barn, a hog- house.

WHEN THEY LIVED in Hartland with only two children, Mom had assisted Dad with farm work; they also had a hired man at that time. After moving to Waseca, Dad had the benefit of help from his father next door and retained hired help less often. As soon as Mom had teenage children, Dad ran the farm while Mom managed the household, with a few exceptions.

Both in Hartland and in Waseca, Mom and the children took care of feeding baby sheep using a 7-up bottle with a nipple on it. It was really fun to feed lambs; they drink milk from a pop bottle faster than us kids could drink orange Kool-Aid, our favorite drink from a cup! Mom also tended any baby piglets that were becoming runts from not getting enough to eat. Mom and the children always kept a large enough flock of chickens for eating and for eggs.

Other than tending lambs, runts, and some chickens, Mom spent nearly all her time raising children while Dad managed what became known as "*the* farm." Our family routinely used the word "the" instead of "our." For example, when our family said, "the farm" we meant the place where we grew up. When we said, "*the* lake" or "*the* cabin," we meant the place where Dad had built a cabin on Reeds Lake. Our farm was always THE farm. Many of our cousins and neighbors who also grew up on nearby farms still know the Miller farm as THE farm.

Our family still holds on to its own "Miller lexicon." Until I moved out of state, I didn't realize it, but when twenty-two kids keep in fairly close touch, there's no way we would have, nor could have, changed our childhood vocabulary. In writing this document, I've retained some of our local vocabulary: "hot dish" (casseroles), kitchen cupboards instead of cabinets, "pick-up" (truck) "gunny sacks" (burlap bags) "went visiting" (popping in on relatives on Sunday afternoons without notice), "sand pile"

1945: Ramona, Al, and Rose Ann in front of their "new" home, forever after known as "the farm."

1944: Ramona and Al, when they first moved from Hartland to Waseca. The farm already had a barn. Dad had built a couple of brooder houses for baby chicks.

(sandbox), "up north" (northern Minnesota), "the cities" (Minneapolis and St. Paul), etc.

We still say "us kids" instead of "my siblings and I." We use the term "got" instead of received and "got to" instead of "were allowed to" and also instead of "needed to." We also used the word "got" to denote past tense. Whereas others would say they "finished their chores;" more commonly we said we "got our chores done."

We use the term "used to be" instead of "had been." Our family uses the term "had to" instead of "were required to." We said "Yup" or "You betcha" for "yes," and "fat chance" for "not likely." We occasionally say "us each" or "us all" as in "She gave us all a cone," instead of saying "She gave each of us a cone."

Instead of saying "very" or "much," we say "way," we say "way better" instead of "much better." We also say places are "way far away." At our house, raiding food was called snitching; we developed expert skill in this particular area.

Our family often uses split verbs in a way that resembles German sentence structure. Most people say, "She put on make-up." We said, "She put make-up on." Others say, "We picked up the kids." We said, "We picked the kids up." My mom "put up" jam instead of "canning jam"

or "processing jam." Potatoes were "put over" [the flame] instead of simply "boiled."

We say "ride bike" instead of ride a bike, and down the basement instead of down *to* the basement. When I lived in New Jersey people used the phrase "down the shore" instead of down TO the shore, and I wondered if there was some linguistic connection.

If Mom purchased food at a grocery store instead of making it from scratch, we called it boughten, as in boughten bread. If we couldn't cook it from scratch, or chose to buy something instead of harvesting it from the farm, we called it store-bought, as in store-bought apples. or store apples for short. Most bakers "baked" sweet rolls whereas my mom "whipped up" sweet rolls. We didn't know anything about being politically correct. We called Brazil nuts "nigger toes," referred to a short boy's haircut as a "heinie" a term that originated in WW1 making fun of the German soldiers' haircuts, and we unfortunately also used the phrase "jewed the seller down" to describe haggling with a vendor.

During my formative years, Dad farmed 180 acres on our home place, and 120 acres on what we called our "other farm" (investment property awaiting a son to take over and start farming). Money was tight; however, our family's financial situation improved as the years went by. Dad made his living farming, but his biggest financial gains actually came from selling land. Grampa Miller borrowed three thousand dollars from his spinster sister, Annie Miller, so that he could afford to buy the Hartland farm in 1940. Knowing that Uncle Francis' farm had cost Grampa $50 an acre, Dad considered $36/acre a bargain. He wrote in his memoir that he was confident he could "whip this farm into shape," and that "We would need a new corn crib, hen house, hog house, machine shed and barn."

Years later, Dad boasted, "I personally built 15 or 20 buildings: even built a Hoghouse, Henhouse, Corn crib and with no electricity. I could build a brooder house in two days, hand sawing." Dad and Mom bought the farm from Grampa two years later, and sold it in 1944 for $90 an acre after having cleared land and built buildings.

Dad purchased the "Fell farm" (the farm where I grew up) for $10,000. In reference to two years thereafter, Dad wrote, *"As we had our farm paid for, we decided to buy some more land, and when Ceil and I had our collective mind made up, we didn't dilly around."* He bought the 122-acre Snake Road farm on June 28th, 1947 for $11,000. Around 1951, he bought 80 acres adjoining our farm from Mrs. Matt Weber for $90 an acre. Dad

did a good job of managing money. He bought and sold four farms during his life, and made money on each of them.

Dad grew primarily soybeans and field corn, although some summers we had planted sweet corn and/or peas for the local canning factory. The big kids bailed a little alfalfa to feed our cow and our horses, some oats for mixing chicken feed, and so that we would have straw to bed

1965: Riding on the hay wagon prepared to help Dad with the farm. Ginny, Linda, Dolores, John, and Art

down farrowing sows, and, for a few years, my father grew wheat as well.

Dad raised about two hundred hogs a year. Dad scheduled farrowing for early spring so the hogs would be ready for market by fall. No kids were allowed in the area when any animals were delivering their babies. Dad kept careful watch. If there were runts in the litter, he sometimes placed baby pigs in a box in front of the propane heater in our family room, hoping they could stay warm enough to survive on their own.

Because our family needed the income from selling pork to pay bills, we butchered only one hog each fall. In the weeks that followed, we splurged by serving two pounds of side-pork (thick-cut uncured bacon) for Sunday breakfast until we ran out. We couldn't wait to have "real" pork chops; my mouth waters remembering the intensity of the flavor of fatty organic pork chops served with mashed potatoes and mushroom gravy, heavy on the salt. Yum!

In the sixties, our family raised around 3,000 chickens each year, and sold eggs for twenty-five cents a dozen. Dad tells the story that, *"After we quit raising a large flock, we bought 120 cockerels for eating. Bob was still home at that time and in the winter he done all the chores (that included feeding 30 sows). One Sunday morning he came into the parlor, and said, "Dad, the chickens are all dead and there is an animal after them!" I figured it was a cougar, so I grabbed the shotgun and a couple of shells and Ceil came along. We walked to the east door of the hen house, and I motioned for everyone to be quiet. When Bob opened the door, a mink ran into the feed room. I fired and killed the mink, and to this day you can still see the hole in the feed room wall! The mink had killed 118 and sucked the blood at their neck. There were just two left!"*

Although we got up early to do farm work, it was rare that any of us kids were awakened by noise before sunrise. As soon as the first person opened their eyes, others would wake up as quickly as possible. Each kid would quickly yell out a number in sequence - because that's the order in which each person got to use the bathroom:

"I go first!"

"Me second."

"Me third," and so on, because everybody had to go, really badly.

Dad awakened whoever was not already up. He bellered each child's name from the bottom of the staircase: Jan-ETTTT', Lin-DAAAA', Hel-ENNNN', and waited until he heard each one holler back, "I'm up." God forbid someone not answer... Dad would start up the stairs to physically roust the lazy one. That happened seldom, because we immediately JUMPED out of bed in panic at the sound of one of Dad's boots hitting the first stair. Dad's Prussian heritage contributed to his no-nonsense style (not unlike a drill sergeant doing roll call). Us kids had no intention of messing with the boss, especially when he was grumpy. But more importantly, no one wanted to be the last one in line to use the bathroom!

When I was growing up, more than a dozen people shared the upstairs bathroom. You'd better get in, get your business done, brush your teeth and get the H out of there, because at least ten people who hadn't peed yet stood in line. While waiting impatiently for siblings who were known to dally, the rest of us banged on the bathroom door.

Dad instituted a strict time limit for bathroom usage; the next person in line turned over the handy three-minute hourglass egg-timer. No one dared to spend time putting on make-up ("too artificial" according to Mom) or curling their hair in the bathroom; Dad would surely have assigned them more work to make sure it never happened again. He used the same egg-timer system to limit long-distance phone calls.

1945: Dad with Ramona, Al, Rose Ann, and Kathleen

On not infrequent occasions, the line to our septic system would get clogged. Who knew if a toy went down the toilet or simply too much toilet paper, and the problem usually happened with the upstairs bathroom. That meant we all had to share the master bathroom downstairs. What a challenge! When I was in my thirties, my brothers finally admitted they'd become adept at peeing off the upstairs balcony into the garden below, even in cold Minnesota winters. Boys had a definite advantage!

We were always in a hurry in the morning, not only because we needed to pee but also because we had to get our chicken chores finished before breakfast.

Because we had so many chickens, Mom served chicken once or twice a week, and she served eggs every possible way: boiled, fried, over-easy, scrambled, toad in the hole, deviled, egg salad, potato salad, soufflé, sponge cake, angel food cake, etc. etc. From time to time, we accumulated too many cracked eggs, so Dad paid us a penny apiece to eat them. This filled us up on pure protein and helped us earn money while getting rid of worthless cracked eggs. Meanwhile, he saved on grocery bills; it was a win/win/win. One summer day while my parents were on vacation, John ate 28 cracked eggs; I was so envious! At that time, twenty-eight cents was more than five weeks' allowance!

When I was quite young, we raised lambs, but we never butchered them; instead, we sold them and/or their wool for income. We bought a leg of lamb to serve for Holy Thursday, our one meal of lamb per year. For a few years, we raised nice 'n plump capons (neutered roosters that grow larger, more tender, and more flavorful). To feed our family, we needed only two capons instead of four chickens. That meant only half as many of our favorite pieces (drumsticks and wishbones), so the drumstick lovers amongst us lost enthusiasm for eating capons.

By the late fall when we ran out of chicken, including capons, and pork that we raised for food, the hunters in the family would have shot enough fowl and wild game to fill a freezer. In all my years as Mom's helper, I only remember completely running out of meat just once. Mom sent me to the freezer in the basement to bring up meat for supper, and I came up empty-handed. Mom turned to Dad and said, "Alvin, we don't have any meat. Can you go find us some?"

Dad went out to the barn and brought back a couple squabs (pigeons too young to fly). Pigeons always hung around our barn, and it didn't hurt the flock to be culled once in a while. Catching birds that can't fly is like shooting fish in a barrel, so Dad came back with enough meat for a meal in less than ten minutes: "Here you are."

We boiled water in a tea kettle, scalded the squabs by pouring boiling water over them into a wide-rimmed metal bucket, dunked them to loosen the feathers, plucked them, dressed them, singed the hairs by holding them over a capful of rubbing alcohol, and then baked them in the oven for supper. We ate those squab less than an hour and a half after Dad had received Mom's plea. Squab meat tastes like dark meat from a chicken, but the birds are much smaller, and therefore more tender and juicy. Delicious!

One evening Dad brought home a snapping turtle for supper. He educated us that there were seven cuts of meat in a turtle. Guess what? Turtle also tastes like chicken. It seemed there was never enough meat or wild fowl to completely satiate our huge family, so we habitually picked every last morsel off the bones. Years later, one of my brothers-in-law made the observation that he had never, ever seen such clean carcasses. To this day, I have to remind myself that chewing gristle right down to the bone is not polite (except at our house!)

By 1955, our farm had all the necessary buildings, most of which Dad had built, or, at least, helped to build. Except for the occasional expansions of our house, the farm buildings looked pretty much the same from the time I was born until I left for college.

When land prices went up in the early seventies, many farmers leveraged their assets. They borrowed enough money to double and triple their acreage, and bought huge tractors, ploughs, cultivators, combines, etc. so they could farm a thousand acres. Because Dad did not like having debt, he continued working the land on our relatively small farm with equally small machinery. That decision saved him from the financial difficulties encountered by so many family farms starting in the seventies. The only

**1955 showing our altar, book case, and hat rack in the background
Back row: Robert, Marylu, Diane, Kathleen, John, Pat
Seated: Ramona holding Virginia, Janet, Rose Ann, Linda, Al holding
Helen**

structures Dad added after I left for college included a grain storage bin and two pole barns.

Dad was always eager to improve his farming techniques; he used whatever information the county Extension Service provided to increase the crop yield and the health of the chickens and hogs. Dad aspired to be a self-sufficient farmer. He knew more about plants and animals that anyone else I know, and he fixed a lot of his own machinery. Dad continued his self-education throughout his life by reading Books of Knowledge, Encyclopedia Britannica, National Geographic, Newsweek, the Kiplinger Report, the local newspaper, and, later when the children were gone from home, adventure books from the county library.

Our family's world view was pretty small; because we didn't watch TV we remained relatively insulated from news of Kent State and the controversy surrounding the Viet Nam war. In contrast to the adventure books that I and many of my siblings loved to read, everyday life on the farm had a definite routine to it. We each had "regular" chores, both indoor and outdoor chores. Dad was expert at delegating. He assigned chicken chores and other chores on an annual basis at the start of a new school year. One teenager needed to feed the hogs ground corn and oats. He never wrote down whose job it was to scoop manure from the barn, the hog house and the chicken coops; it was simply understood that he and the eldest boys would take care of that.

For both boys and girls, our most time-consuming chores involved feeding chickens, gathering eggs, washing and packing them into cartons. Dad was quite particular about who "managed" each chicken coop. One person gathered eggs from each of the east and west henhouses, a second person took care of chickens in the barn's downstairs, and a third cared for the chickens in the barn's second floor. The barn's third floor contained the hayloft.

"What in tarnation are you doing to those chickens?" my dad would ask. He pretended he didn't already know... that some of us waved our hands to scare the chickens off the nests to reduce the likelihood that our hands would get pecked while gathering eggs.

We got away with blaming it on each other, but it was pretty clear that the hens in some of the buildings didn't mind at all when a person came in, while other buildings' chickens would immediately take flight or run for cover the instant someone set foot in that coop. In

other words, the chickens themselves accused the guilty party of scaring them!

Dad was a strict disciplinarian, and he made sure children behaved. He did not often show emotion and he enforced the notion that "the rules are the rules." This is how Dad kept things organized and efficient while minimizing friction. Long before I can remember, he had already made dozens of rules, such as:

- Don't go out deep in the lake

- No little kids at the good table (to qualify, we had to prove we hadn't spilled milk for a long, long time)

- No sharp knives on the table (whoever was serving sliced the meat)

- One scoop of ice cream per person

- Call home before you leave town (in case Mom needs anything from the grocery store)

- When the boat comes ashore, run down to the dock and help unload

- Read "the slip" as soon as you get home (paper hanging above the phone in our kitchen)

- Do all your chores before supper

- Unplug the iron when you're finished using it

- Take your pile [of folded laundry] off the dining room table on your way upstairs

- Check the tires before you drive

- "Gas up" vehicles if the gauge is below a quarter tank

- Don't touch the thermostat for the furnace,

- And, and and

We all hated cleaning out the slimy chicken waterer using corn cobs, so Dad routinely checked up on us to make sure everything stayed tidy. When he caught us shirking our dirty jobs, he'd say, "What in tarnation were you thinking?" If a building full of chickens developed a case of lice or mites, Dad quickly got involved to contain the outbreak. It was nearly impossible to quarantine us kids when we got infested with lice, (Mom had to wash all our hair in gasoline) but it was possible to isolate the source of the problem and to prevent the outbreak from spreading from one chicken coop to the next.

Anyone who broke a rule or didn't behave was subject to an unlimited amount of extra work. Dad's favorite admonishment was "Go paint the white fence."

When I once said to him, "But I just painted it yesterday," he responded,

"Go paint it again!"

If it wasn't the white fence, it was the barn, the henhouse, or whatever else needed a new coat of paint, or even if it didn't! We used oil-based paints for exterior jobs. When we finished painting, we filled an empty two-pound coffee can half-full of gasoline to wash the paint brushes, and used another quart or so to clean the paint off ourselves. It took half the time to paint the fence, and the other half to clean up. Painting the fence was Dad's best way of keeping us busy for a few hours, and our farm buildings and fences stayed in great shape for many years.

There was no question that Dad was the boss in our household; fathers were the family's boss for most my cousins and friends as well. For indoor chores, Dad rotated us through various daily tasks (Mom wrote "the list" before I can remember, but then it became Dad's duty). Every week, Dad updated the list assigning one girl to wash dishes, two to dry dishes, and a fourth to clear the table, sweep the floor, and put away the high chair, rotating those assignments by the day of the week. There were not enough boys in our family to do farm work and I definitely would not have wanted to exchange jobs with my brothers. Thankfully for me, some of my sisters actually liked working outdoors with Dad and so I wasn't needed to cultivate, plough, bail hay, nor clean barns, etc.

Some regular indoor chores were assigned for at least a week. Down the left side of the list Dad wrote the daily cleaning assignments: downstairs bathroom, upstairs bathroom, living room, baby room. Whether for daily, weekly, monthly or annual chores, once Dad wrote the name of the person who was responsible on the list, and taped it inside the kitchen cupboard next to the cereal, that was the gospel.

The good news is that Dad's organizational skills made sure all the work got done. The bad news is that he could be way too bossy, especially when he was over-tired. At a very young age, all of us learned to be responsible and carry our share of the workload out of fear of getting "a good swift kick in the seat of the pants." I got one of those once; that was sufficient motivation for an entire decade of exemplary behavior!

Before I went to first grade, one of my regular chores was to scrub the sink in the master bathroom. With so many small children using that bathroom, the sink needed to be cleaned at least once a day. In second grade, my job was to haul out glass bottles and tin cans.

Even though we never knew the word *re-cycling*, we did what we could. We stacked glass, tin cans and plastic bottles under the laundry room sink. Right after supper, it was my job to haul them to a fifty-gallon barrel in our machine shed. Once a month or so, Dad would empty the barrels at the local dump/landfill. While there, he would retrieve such things as mismatched play dishes and parts from broken bicycles. He washed them and fixed them up so that us kids could have "new" toys without having to fork over any of his hard-earned cash.

My parents believed discipline encouraged a sense of responsibility. It came to my Dad'sattention one night that I had failed to haul out the tin cans. He rousted me out of bed at 10pm to complete my chores. I had to get dressed and walk about 100 scary steps in cold, creepy, darkness to the tin can barrel. I never again forgot to haul out the tin cans.

Whoever owned a dog, cat, gerbil, turtle, goldfish, rabbit, and/or horse took care of their own pet. Children as young as four years old had chores on the list. Before I went to first grade, my brother Art and I were assigned to feed and water the baby chicks in the number two (of four) brooder houses. Each brooder house looked like a little igloo with a number above the front door. Inside, it had corncobs on the floor, a propane burner/hood to keep the chicks warm, and a corrugated cardboard "fence" to keep the baby chicks fenced in, closer to the warmth. Morning and night, we needed to clean and re-fill the chicken waterer and haul feed to them.

We pumped water by hand from the outdoor pump with the long green iron handle. I could not lift a gallon and a half of water, so my younger brother Art took one side of the handle while I took the other. Together we could carry it a short distance to our assigned brooder house.

Similarly, with chicken feed, neither Art nor I could lift a full pail of feed. Instead, I would open the wooden hut we called the "feed bin" and prop the cover up with a stake. I crawled in and handed Art a small bucket of a mixture of ground corn, oats, and "vitamins." Art set it in the little red wagon, then we both pulled the wagon and filled up the metal "feeders" in the brooder house. Once we were old enough to lift more water and feed, we were promoted to a more difficult job.

In seventh and eighth grade, I had the chore of washing twenty pails (wire baskets) of eggs per day. Each pail contained about eight dozen eggs. Uncle George had helped Dad rig up an electronic bubbler in the bottom of a ten-gallon

We gathered as many as 20 rubber-covered wire pails of eggs per day, ate some and sold the rest.

bucket. I set one pail at a time into warm water with special soap that made the eggs light enough to almost float. Washing eggs was like washing dishes, necessary but monotonous.

Every morning while we were at school, Dad assigned egg-*packing* chores by putting a scrap of paper with a name on it into each bucket. Whoever misbehaved got an extra pail. Along the west wall of the basement stood two egg-packing stations: a rickety wooden chair on which to set a pail of eggs, and a crate on which to set a cardboard "case." We became expert at packing eggs. We grabbed three eggs in each hand, six at a time, thirty to a flat (a layer), twenty dozen to a case. For dirty eggs, we scratched them clean using sandpaper-covered rubber blocks, hopefully without cracking the egg.

For odd jobs, and/or punishment (what Dad called extra jobs), he had a separate system. He wrote new notes on the slip, a half sheet of scrap paper on a clip board where Dad assigned ad hoc tasks that needed to be done immediately. We were obligated to finish each one and cross it off before supper.

I hated the severity of my dad's punishments, but I never worked up the guts to talk back to my dad as some of my siblings tried to do (wholly unsuccessfully, I might add.) Our family rarely expressed negative emotions, however, one of my sisters was prone to slamming doors when she was angry. When I was a high school junior, I applied to become a foreign exchange program because I desperately wanted to travel.

The wife of the minister came out to the farm to interview me and my parents. "What does Helen do when she's mad?" she asked my father. He didn't hesitate, and replied, "She slams doors." What? I had never slammed a door in my life... but now was not the time to argue with him, definitely not in front of the minister's wife. I was furious with my father, and blamed him (silently of course) that I didn't get selected to go overseas that year, and I was certain it was

because my dad couldn't keep us kids straight. I talked this over with my mom who knew the minister's wife from their work together on charity events. I'll never know if that helped me get selected the following year, or indeed, if Dad's comment had anything to do with the decision.

When Mom wanted to delegate work, she never ever wrote us notes; she watched who had time and skill to help her, and verbally doled out tasks accordingly. Both Dad's taskmaster management style as well as Mom's verbal interactive communication style worked effectively.

Dad led his own personal crusade against what he called "the four c's": communists, cockleburs, creeping charlie, and crabgrass. Pulling weeds is a whole lot cheaper and better for crops than spraying weed killer. The less weeds that are in the grain, the higher the price. Our family needed every penny we could earn. To increase profits, Dad made sure school-age children spent summers weeding the fields. We called that "walkin' beans."

Dad worked right alongside of us kids as we pulled cockleburs and other weeds out of soybean and seed corn fields. Once the soybeans were too high for pulling weeds, we used hoes, mostly to eradicate thistles. Day after day, we worked from seven-thirty or eight o'clock until three-thirty or four PM, with an hour off to get home and back for lunch.

We took along a gallon thermos jug of water, and no snacks. If Dad saw we were getting too tired, he would occasionally stop at the end of a row. When everyone caught up to him, he pulled an ever-present pack of Juicy Fruit gum from his pants pocket and divided each stick into three or four pieces. That small treat would keep us kids going at least another hour.

After weeks on end of weeding all the fields on the home place, we started in on our other farm. We worked until Dad could proudly declare that our farm had both the *straightest* rows of beans and the *cleanest* fields in the county. Only then were we were allowed to do farm work for hire. Our next-door neighbor paid twenty-five cents or fifty cents an hour, depending on the type of work. Compared to working at home for free, that was big money!

Whenever we weeded bean fields, most of us did not really mind the intense heat of the sun and had no real objection to the work per se. Especially for teenage girls, we liked the chance to improve our tan. Unlike some of my siblings, I absolutely hated thistles scratching my legs, mud squishing between my toes and the pain from remnants of last year's corn stalks poking my bare feet. Looking back, I resented spending so many of my summer vacation days walkin' beans and hoeing thistles instead of having the opportunity to learn to swim, or to play tennis or golf, or seeing more movies, but at the time there was simply no option. That's just the way it was.

I'll never know how summer vacations would have been spent if we had had a smaller family. Was it the size of our family or the fact that we had very little money that made the biggest difference, or are those two things inseparable? We didn't go to places like Disneyland, nor did we attend concerts or professional sporting events. We didn't go anywhere on spring break; in fact, we never even heard of that term. We could not afford to go on exotic vacations, or even to the movies, and neither of my parents had an interest in swimming, playing golf or tennis... Who knows? Maybe if we had had a small family we would have needed to spend twice as much time walkin' beans to get all the weeds pulled.

When I was in first grade, the "Watkins man" came to sell Mom some vanilla. This time he brought a whole new line of merchandise: rubberized shoes. Mom bought each of us a pair of sandals that were made of stiff rubber not unlike CROCs. Mine were orange, and they

Reeds Lake, 1966: Ginny, Bob, Helen, Lor, Rosie, Linda, Diane, Pauline,

were, definitely, the cutest shoes I'd ever had. Better yet, it made working in the field far more comfortable.

Starting when I was in about fifth grade, the Waseca County Library sent a "Book Mobile" to our house once a week during the summer. The library's customized RV filled with books would drive to farms to encourage reading during the summer months. Dad gave us an extra hour's break from pulling weeds. We eagerly reviewed which books were available that week, and we each checked out a couple books. I remember hiding when I wanted to finish reading a book. That's because if Dad saw someone reading when there was work to be done, that person might get assigned another "ten-minute job," one that often took a full hour to complete.

I usually just went upstairs to my bedroom, hoping my siblings who remained downstairs would be recruited for any odd jobs. When necessary, I rode my bike out to "the back forty," (forty acres of land about a half mile from the house.) With so many other siblings available to help Dad, it was extremely unlikely that anyone would make the effort to come get me, even though they knew where I was.

After weeding beans, hoeing thistles, bailing hay, or harvesting phalaris grass seed, we were hot and sweaty, and couldn't wait to go swimming. My parents never took us to a public beach to take lessons nor to go swimming. They were afraid they would not be able to keep track of all of us, and rightfully so. Especially during the hottest days of summer, as soon as we got home from weeding the fields, we changed into our swimsuits, packed our towels and clothes, and piled into the van to head for the lake.

Other than our putting up with cows standing in the water at the east end of the shoreline, we pretty much had Reeds Lake to ourselves. Typically, we swam for half an hour to an hour before Dad would call, "Last dip!" Anybody who didn't want to ride home dripping wet had to run to the "bath house" and quickly get changed. The bath house was a small shed with two partitions, one for girls and one for boys, with nails in the studs on which to hang clothes. Once the others took their last dip, we all piled in the car to go home, finish up our chores and have supper.

In the fall, Dad worked eighteen and twenty hour days harvesting field corn and soybeans, and ploughing the stalks under. Until the seventies, we did not have a grain drying bin, so he sold corn, beans, and grain for "market price" as of that day. Dad filled up his very old two-ton truck and drove load after load to the local grain elevator. Often, one kid was allowed to

1956: Ramona and Al de-tasseling seed corn

ride along for fun. I have fond memories of those trips as a youngster before I went to school.

Depending on how happy he was with that load's market price, he bought five cents worth of salted peanuts from a red bubble gum machine for his helper-of-the-day to enjoy while the harvest got unloaded. Hoping to increase my motivation to help pull weeds the following season, Dad tried to educate me on how prices varied based on how clean the crop tested, but I didn't care. Sorry, Dad. I only rode along because I wanted the chance to eat peanuts.

If the market price was better than expected, Dad and his helper sometimes stopped at the grocery store on the way home to pick up a T-bone steak for him and Mom to share for the following day's lunch, or stopped off at Rindelaub's

The seven little kids plus Bob and Linda, bailing straw

Bakery where he bought a Bismark. Dad loved the raspberry jam oozing out of a frosted donut, and sneaking a roll for his helper without buying some for the rest of the family was their little secret.

The older I got, the less I liked field work. Whereas some of my siblings prided themselves on how high they could stack hay on a wagon before they unloaded it into the hay mow, some of us simply weren't cut out for many types of farm work. Some of us could never lift a bale of hay without pain. Some were not tall enough to pull the tops from rows of seed corn in the days when others "de-tasseled" corn by hand without the benefit of a machine to ride on.

Even though we all grew up on a farm, a few of us actually know relatively little about plants, animals, and farming. As we got older, some of us (including me) barely tolerated the smell of pigs and chickens, and had no real desire to step foot in a barn, no interest in pets, and a total aversion to mice and bats in the house.

1962: Hauling tile
Beside the truck: Ginny and Art In the truck: Lor, Helen

In the sixties, our family had quite a problem with mice in the basement. We also had trouble with bats coming through the chimney access door in the little bedroom. Mom had told us to be very careful because bats could get tangled in girls' long hair and make a total mess. Whenever someone yelled, "BAT!" everyone went into a tizzy, either burying their heads in pillows, or running around armed with fishing nets, badminton rackets or whatever they could find to nab said bat. Damien came up with an ingenious solution: he hung a pail of water on the eves. As the bats tried to exit, they dropped into the bucket before they could spread their wings. Problem solved!

Instead of working with plants and animals, I gravitated toward cooking, sewing, and babysitting. I negotiated with Dad to escape outdoor farm word by helping Mom indoors. Several of my siblings did the reverse because they either loved farming or hated being indoors.

The B had a wooden toolbox which doubled as a passenger seat right next to the big rear wheel. In this 1967 photo, Bob drove while Lor and Art help tile.

To get out of farm work, I'd agree to cook anything, bake anything, or sew anything, and even keep taking piano lessons! I learned to convince Dad he didn't need my help outdoors by suggesting I could sew a new dress for Mom. His eyes always lit up to see his sweetheart in a new outfit, and I got to do something I enjoyed!

I was fortunate to have two brothers close enough in age to me to work the farm. Typical of 1950's families, my brothers worked outdoors and neither cooked nor baked. They became expert tasters, sampling and enjoying Mom's cooking. Dad usually chose the boys first, expecting girls to help Mom. However, if no boys were available, he asked the girls to help out, and sometimes forgot that we had not been trained to do the job at hand. With so many kids to teach, Dad quite frequently forgot who knew what. Did he think we were supposed to absorb knowledge through the ether? When he was in a hurry and needed help, Dad didn't have a spare minute to train us in.

Unfortunately, there were times when Dad desperately needed help, and I was the only kid around. On one such occasion when I still too young to go to school, Dad had spent the morning digging a trough and laying tile for better drainage. He was finished but he still had both a tractor and a truck out in the field; he needed someone to drive the tractor back home in time for lunch. He intended to follow behind in the pick-up truck.

My siblings were at school; I was the eldest kid available, so he volunteered me. I must have been five years old. I was excited to be given the chance to drive the little Farmall "B" tractor for the first time. The 1940's style B tractor was half-way between the size of a riding lawn mower and the size of an old-fashioned tractor. Dad lifted me up on to the driver's seat of the B and turned it on. He shifted it into gear, set the throttle to low speed, and told me, "To stop, just push this silver button and it will shut off the tractor." That was the extent of my tractor driving lesson.

My four-year-old brother, Art, rode shotgun. The B had a wooden toolbox next to the wheel which doubled as a passenger seat. Dad set Art on the toolbox facing backwards and Art hung on to the tractor wheel fender with his right hand. The B was already moving when Dad jumped in the seafoam green pick-up.

As I drove at a snail's pace down the lane toward home, Art happily watched Dad as he followed us. As we neared our yard, we started up the gentle incline next to the old red barn. All of a sudden, Art fell off. The B tractor was still moving forward. Dad slammed on the truck brakes, hopped out, and raced to pick up Art so he wouldn't roll under the tractor wheel.

I pushed the B tractor's silver button, jumped down, and ran as fast as I could to get into the house. I wasn't sure whether Art had gotten hurt, and I was scared I was going to get spanked. Turns out Art did not get hurt, and I did not get spanked. That was the one and only time I ever drove the B.

Fast forward to one fall day when I was around twelve; Dad had just heard the clanking sound of hogs lifting their metal feeder covers. Normally Bob fed the pigs. Dad had assigned him to give the pigs ten pails of feed per day. When Dad heard the clanking of metal on metal, he knew something was very wrong. He asked Bob,

1941: Dad photographed Mom holding Ramona on their new Farmall H tractor, proud to have replaced their team of horses.

"Did you feed the pigs?"

"Yup," answered Bob. Dad went out to the hog yard to investigate. He could see the feeders were completely empty.

"Did you give the pigs ten pails of feed?" he asked Bob, this time with a little more specificity.

"Only five buckets," came Bob's reply, to which Dad exclaimed,

"For crying out loud!"

Bob was fully capable of feeding pigs, and happy to do so, but incapable of realizing each of the five buckets in the granary could be used twice in order to haul ten pails of feed to the hog yard. Oh, no! The pigs were starving. Dad had no way of knowing how long it had been since the pigs had been properly fed. He needed to grind some corn *immediately* to feed those pigs.

Dad looked around for a helper to drive the Farmall "H" tractor. I was eleven or twelve years old, the biggest kid available at that moment, so, again, I got drafted. I climbed up on the H. It was my second time driving a tractor, the first being my disaster on the B. My thirty second lesson on driving the H took place on flat ground. Dad started the H and told me, "If you need to stop, push this pedal." Because it was easier for me to reach than the brake, Dad showed me the clutch.

Moving slowly on flat ground, pushing in the clutch accomplished the same purpose as hitting the brake would have, and it was a lot easier for me to accomplish. I still didn't know anything about changing gears, had no idea what the purpose of a clutch was as compared to a brake.

I proudly drove the H about the length of a football field, from the corn crib to the hog yard north of our yard, trailering a corn-grinding machine behind me. Dad followed me in the pickup, fully loaded with corn. As we drove up the small hill near the hog feeders, he motioned me to stop. I hung on to the steering wheel and pushed as hard as I could on the clutch. The H stopped with a jerk, then started to roll, slowly, backing down the slope. The corn-grinder jack-knifed behind me. I could feel the tractor and grinder starting to tip. I had no idea what to do.

Dad slammed his truck into reverse, backed up, out of my way, jumped out and sprinted toward the H to take control so the tractor and grinder wouldn't roll.

"Dag nab it!" was the last thing I heard from him as I jumped down from the tractor. I was so relieved he caught it in time. Lucky for me, we both walked away without a scratch, and, just as good, or even better, for me, Dad never again assigned me to drive tractor. It simply wasn't safe.

There were other times when Dad didn't have the required knowledge, and precious little time for himself to be trained in, as happened when Mom was away overnight and left Dad in charge of us kids.

One day when Mom was on retreat, Dad was babysitting. Looking for a pair of socks for one of the youngsters to wear to school, he picked up the cardboard box labeled "sock box." He wasn't too familiar with babysitting, and had no idea what Mom did with odd socks. He found out the hard way by counting out forty-seven socks that had no mates!

Each kid had only a couple pairs of underwear and a few pairs of socks. New underwear and socks were both coveted and protected. We were supposed to write our names on the toes of our socks in magic marker, and pin mated socks together before they went in to the laundry hamper. Even so, finding a clean pair of underwear or a pair of socks that matched was a constant challenge. Forget about finding everyday mittens that matched; that would be wishful thinking. We darned mittens and socks until they were completely threadbare. Thank goodness Grama Kahnke knitted pair after pair of mittens for us; we used garter-belt type snaps to hook new pairs to our coat sleeves.

With so many children to protect, Dad emphasized safety on a regular basis. If he found a safety pin on the floor, everybody got punished. If someone left the iron sitting on the ironing board where a baby could knock it over, everybody got lectured. Dad put a belt around the empty freezer to avoid the possibility that someone would suffocate in it while playing hide and seek. He worried about little kids hiding in the dryer; it was declared off limits.

Dad built a fire-escape ladder from our second-floor landing in case the stairway caught fire. We had fire drills at home, just like in school, to practice getting out quickly and safely. Dad's paranoia about us kids getting hurt may be the reason our family suffered so very few accidents. Before we had ever heard of adjustable gates to protect children from falling down staircases, Dad nailed two slats on each side of our second-floor staircase landing, and slid a piece of plywood in between them. Young "creepers" could not get past that makeshift gate, and therefore couldn't fall down stairs. When Dad noticed kids sitting down and going bumpty-bump down the staircase for fun, he carpeted the stairs so it was a safer place for us kids to play.

Every couple days, Dad burned trash in a rusty old barrel near the barn. One winter day, our fluffiest little cat curled up beside the burn barrel's warmth and caught fire. Covered in flames, it raced toward the barn. Dad happened to be nearby, saw it happen, and immediately chased after it with a fire extinguisher, yelling and screaming in hopes Fluffy would not run up to the hay mow and burn down the whole barn. Thankfully, the fire went out before the cat reached the hay mow. After that, Dad surrounded the trash-burning barrel with a chicken-wire fence, and we all got yet another lesson in safety.

When I was young, there was no siren system to alert people to tornadoes. To stay safe, Dad watched his barometer and listened to his battery-operated radio whenever the winds got high, even through the night. If the barometer went too low, or the winds too high, and he suspected a tornado, he yelled up the stair steps, "Hit the basement!" As many as eighteen kids shot out of bed and traipsed down two flights of stairs pretty much instantly.

Dad made sure Mom sat in the very southwest corner (the safest spot) with a baby on her lap; the rest of us huddled close by. If we were smart, we had grabbed a blanket to keep warm. We spent many nights in our basement impatiently waiting for Dad to say, "all clear" before anyone could go back to bed. With so many children to protect, Dad did a fabulous job of staying vigilant, day and night. After our town lost thirteen people to a tornado on April 30th, 1967, sirens were installed to alert people to imminent danger. *"My barometer read 28.25 during the storm, the lowest reading I have ever recorded in 15 years of observation."* That barometer is now part of a permanent exhibit at the Waseca Historical Society Museum.

Cold War dangers meant family planning for a bomb shelter. This pamphlet was part of Dad's safety preparedness.

I grew up in the height of the cold war when parents took the threat of nuclear war very seriously. Mom and Dad even kept enough food to feed us for six months in case we ever needed to use our basement as a bomb shelter. Dad worried about our family's well becoming contaminated by radiation, so he stored gallon jugs of water on top of the brick wall shelf around the entire basement perimeter.

Dad made several rules designed to keep us safe. Linda ignored Dad's "no climbing" rule one afternoon, and ended up injured. Mom and Dad had warned us not to play rough with her because she had had stitches across her tummy following an appendectomy. I must have been four when Linda climbed up the plum tree, fell, and sliced the back of her leg on the huge nail holding up one end of our hammock. Blood streamed out. As she lay on the ground bleeding, I could see white fatty tissue in the deep wound in her calf. I ran to the house screaming, "Linda's guts are falling out! Linda's guts are falling out!" I never saw my mother run so fast in all my life.

My siblings and I violated Dad's safety rules at our own peril, especially when it came to driving. I must tell you one of Dad's favorite safety-related stories, where the joke was on me. Like most teenagers, I wanted my driver's license as soon as possible. Before I could attempt my driver's test, Dad insisted that I know how to fill the car with gas from the 100-gallon barrel housed in our machine shed, and how to change a tire. He tried to get me to check the inside of the vehicle (including the gas gauge) and the outside (including

The green van could hold all of us if we sat on each other's laps.

inspecting all four tires) before I got in. I thought Dad's precautions were bogus, and he knew it.

One winter day when I was a junior in high school, and had already been driving the green van (our largest passenger van, with four seats instead of three) for two years, Dad came across a huge dead cat on the side of the road. He picked it up and set the frozen carcass on the floor between the two bucket seats in the front of our van, knowing full well that I would be driving that vehicle the next day.

Predictably, I got in the van and drove to school without checking the tires for air, without checking the gas gauge, and without noticing a frozen tomcat just inches away from me between the front seats. That afternoon, my girlfriend, Lisa, asked if I would give her a lift home. She climbed up into the front seat, immediately discovered Dad's surprise, and bolted back out

1963: Hunting pheasants with the Korteum cousins John, Marylu, Tim and Billy Korteum; Dad is seated in the pick-up truck

1963: John holding his shotgun and the pheasant he bagged

of the van. My dad got his wish; now I *always* check my vehicle before I start driving!

In the fifties and sixties, while "town kids" were learning to play tennis and golf, and competing in school sporting events, my siblings and I were not allowed to attend extra-curricular events until we were able to drive ourselves, unless we were willing to walk or ride a bike five miles to get home. It took Diane a couple of years to convince my parents to allow her to try out for cheerleading. The fact that she finally won that privilege made it easier for those younger than her to get permission for after-school activities. Art even got permission to play both basketball and track (so long as he ran home after each practice).

In the eighties, when Greg and Damien attended high school, Mom and Dad finally had spare time to chauffeur children to extra-curricular activities, and Greg got to join the school's hockey team. One night, Greg injured his thumb during a school hockey game, and had to be taken to the emergency room. The very next night, Damien had an accident on his three-wheel all-terrain vehicle, and had to be taken to ER.

You know what happened the following day? My parents called an insurance agent. After having 22 babies delivered in a hospital, they raised twenty of those children and launched them into adulthood without health insurance for the children. With only two teenage boys left at home, Dad simply couldn't bear the thought of paying doctors such expensive rates for the relatively minor injuries that Greg and Damien had sustained back-to-back. He signed his teenage sons up for health insurance that very day.

Another risk-aversion issue concerned guns. Dad had several guns for hunting: a Winchester 270 for deer, a Winchester model-12 gauge, an Ithaca single shot model 12 gauge, a Remington automatic 22, a Winchester 2520 from the early 1900's, a Stevens single shot 22, a Benjamin air rifle (pellet gun), a single shot 410, and a single shot 16 gauge.

When Dad was young, his cousin Clare had stood in Dad's bedroom and shot a hole through the window and scared Dad and his brother half to death. "Instant gun training" is how Dad described this incident. With that in mind, Dad insisted all teenagers take gun training, whether or not we had an interest. I must have been in 7th grade when I went listlessly through the motions of learning about guns. I passed my written gun-training test without having touched a gun during that class.

Afterward, Dad took me to a deserted field for my first target practice with a gun. He set up a tin can in the distance, and handed me a rifle. I shouldered the butt of the gun and carefully looked through the sight in the middle of the gun. I could clearly see my target. Without warning Dad, I pulled the trigger. The bullet hit the ground less than ten feet in front of us, and scared the daylights out of both of us. Without realizing it I had pointed the gun downward. Gun training had failed to teach me the most basic of concepts: every rifle has two sights; I needed *both* of them lined up on the target. That was the first, last and only time I handled one of Dad's guns.

Guns were used only for hunting meat for the family, or for shooting birds that ate the eggs of "good" birds. Greg, age 13, remembers "hitting the combination window storm/screen while shooting at starlings (that were eating robin eggs) out the window of the middle bedroom in 1978."

When Dad or my brothers went hunting, they did not use dogs. Dogs didn't generally last long at our house. I don't remember exactly what happened to Ginny's dog, Pepper, but I do remember what happened to our pet German Shepherd that resulted in his untimely demise. One summer day when Marty put bread and milk in a dish to feed the barn cats, the dog came

1968: Damien and Alice with Al's German Shepard, Jo-Jo

1953: John, Al, holding one of our many kittens, and Robert

running, and started eating the cats' food. My brother unwittingly wrapped the full-grown German Sheperd on the nose shouting, "Bad dog!" The dog lunged, and bit Marty in the face; Marty ended up in ER to get stitched up.

Dad was convinced that once a dog bites a child, it can never again be trusted. Dad took out a rifle and shot the dog. With a stiff upper lip, he buried it. We didn't have a pet cemetery, nor were there many tears shed for animals that died on the farm. Dad unceremoniously buried that dog out in the back forty.

The rest of us simply accepted the miracle of life and the mystery of death as a natural part of God's plan. It was Mom's job to smooth things over. With her coaching, we took such things in stride, and just said an extra prayer or sang

an extra song or two or three to move on from minor challenges.

Generally, Mom could settle us down by getting everyone to join her in song. When anyone swore, they got their mouth washed out with bar soap. If anyone fought, they got spanked. "The paddling stick" hung on the wall in the kitchen. It didn't get used often, but when it did, it was bad news. We never knew the word "time-out," but we were quite familiar with the concept. When a youngster got too unruly, Mom would tie the kid to a kitchen chair using a flour-sack dish towel to sit quietly for a little while. If we were extra rambunctious, or too old to be spanked, she raised one eyebrow and gave us a silent frown which pretty much meant, "Just wait 'til your father gets home!"

Dad's typical admonishment was, "You kids, pipe down!" When that didn't do the job, his favorite way of getting boisterous children to settle down was to abruptly say, "Let's play Little Red School House." That meant everyone was required to remain totally still to see who could stay silent the longest. We loved little competitions like this one, so it made it fun for us. Whoever broke the silence was called "a rotten egg."

Music was Mom's favorite way of distracting misbehaving children. Dad had played the trumpet in high school; both Dad and Mom enjoyed music and encouraged all of us to take private music lessons from the nuns. Even though lessons cost extra, (five or six dollars a half hour) developing musical talent was an unquestioned priority. Al, Kathleen, Marylu, Diane, and John played violin. Kathleen, Janet, and Helen played piano. Several played guitar. Art played banjo and had a drum set. Lor learned several instruments including piano, guitar, and recorder.

Finding enough time to practice music was always tricky. Dad used to come in from the field or the barn, wash up, plop in to his "easy chair," and tell whoever was close by to bring him his slippers. He then turned on his reading light, signaling it was time to give him some peace and quiet so he could read the paper before supper.

In order for half a dozen kids to finish practicing their music lessons before Dad sat down to read, us kids learned to block out noise around us. We ignored extraneous sounds and focused on taking advantage of every available minute that we weren't pre-occupied doing farm chores. Each kid would get out their sheet music and start practicing. While one girl set the table for supper, someone would be playing piano, someone else guitar, and a third person practicing violin.

To an outsider, it sounded awful, not unlike a symphony orchestra tuning up. However, each of us heard only our own instrument. That way, multiple budding musicians could successfully practice different songs, on different instruments, at the same time, in the same house, all within thirty feet of each other. After music practice, we ate supper.

When I was growing up, mealtime meant family time. Meals were served on a regimented schedule (dinner at noon and supper at 6PM) and everyone ate together unless they had permission to arrive late from a special event. With the exception of an after-school snack, eating outside of meal times was relatively rare. Every afternoon around four o'clock, Mom chose helpers for that evening's meal: someone to set the table, one teenage girl to serve the food, a pre-teen to feed the baby and a younger person to feed the toddler.

1959: Kathleen, Diane, and Marylu, learning piano and violin, at left.
Timeless: Dad in his reading chair

Our kitchen table (always covered with a flowery vinyl tablecloth) seated fourteen, five to a side and two on each end. When Damien was born, four teenagers had already left home; we still needed to seat seventeen or eighteen people for each and every meal. We had outgrown our kitchen table. To make space, we simply moved the two high chairs away from one end of the table and abutted a small diner table with a gray Formica top, ever after known as "the little table."

Ordinarily, we had assigned seating. The baby's high chair sat next to the refrigerator. Around the two tables we arranged the piano bench on one end, six kitchen chairs, six dining room chairs, two bar-height square-seat stools for the toddlers, two shorter, regular-height round stools for little kids, and unmatched folding chairs for the rest. By the time I can remember, what had once been various complete sets of dishes had become a mismatched assortment. Our spoons, knives and forks came from at least a half a dozen different patterns.

Every single meal required a pitcher of milk, one creamer, one sugar bowl, one honey and one jam jar, two salt and pepper shaker sets, (one glass/one tin), two cafeteria-style napkin holders, and two plates of sliced bread. We also used two butter dishes. When we placed these specific items down the center of the table, we called it "setting the center dishes on."

Shortly before mealtimes, Mom would assign one of the big kids to "call supper." He or she would step out the back door, yell SUPPPP-rrrrr as loud as possible, then come indoors and yell SUPPPP-rrrr down the basement staircase, and again up the second-floor stairs, and immediately turn over the three-minute egg-timer to keep track of who was late (and therefore assigned an extra turn drying dishes). In later years, Dad brought home a conch shell from his and Mom's Caribbean vacation. When the thrill of blowing in the conch shell as a way of calling supper got old, we tried using a bell.

We worked up a hardy appetite doing farm chores, and looked forward to mealtime to take a break. Our family appreciated Mom's home cooking. Even though we were relatively poor, when it came to food, because we lived in a world of incredible abundance, we felt rich. We had top notch homegrown peas, sweet corn, pork and chicken. Mom raised a big garden, and canned a lot of fruit and vegetables while Dad worked the farm. Using produce from our huge garden and several fruit trees, Mom and Dad taught us to pinch pennies on everyday meals so we could live it up on special occasions and share our good fortune with guests (the more the merrier).

When supper was called, everyone was glad to get a break from doing farm chores. At mealtimes, kids came running up to the house, both because they understood the consequences of being late, and also because they knew Mom would have something delicious cooking. Art especially remembers the smells of "food hot outta the oven when yer nose is still cold" from being outdoors.

The smells from meat roasting and dessert baking in the oven always made my mouth water. When no one was looking, I was known to snitch plain butter and quickly lick my spoon clean. I learned this little trick from Dad (except he used a knife to swipe his butter). He would say he was just "checking" the butter; if it had not been covered in the fridge and had acquired the taste of something else, he would have us unwrap a new pound of butter. Then we put the "bad butter" aside, for use on toast. Unlike us kids, Dad didn't worry about getting in big trouble for eating directly from a serving dish, nor for eating before we prayed.

For everyday eating, assigned seating was strategically planned. The two youngest kids who had outgrown high chairs with built-in trays sat to Mom's left at the head of the table. Youngsters and mentally challenged kids got seated between two big kids so they would not need to handle platters. Whoever was "waiting on table" used the pull-out cutting board as their own small table. Mom wrote, *"My husband insisted I myself sit down at meals. Two of the girls would be assigned to wait on tables. Mealtime was the best time to give out rules, and permission to do things."* Before she sat down across from Dad, Mom handed him the main course on one of her two heavy glass meat platters.

Once everyone was seated, we faithfully made the sign of the cross, folded our hands, and said "Grace:" "In the name of the Father, and of the Son, and of the Holy Spirit:

Bless us, Oh, Lord,

and these Thy gifts,

which we are about to receive,

from Thy bounty,

through Christ, our Lord,

Amen."

Then the hubbub of three or four conversations erupted, everyone trying to get a word in edgewise. The first question was always, "What are we having?" then some variation of:

"You won't believe what happened today."

"Dad, can I use the car tonight?" then, "She used it last night. It's my turn."

"My teacher needs you to sign some papers."

"What are we having for dessert?"

"Does anyone know where my pencil case went?"

"Who wants to play football after supper?"

"Mom and Dad, can I go out for cheerleading?"

"Cheerleading? Fat chance!" Or, finally, "No! and that's FINAL!"

Whoever got assigned to wait on table divided the salad, the potatoes, the steamed vegetables, and any other menu items into two serving bowls apiece. They handed the first to Dad, and put a second one at the other end of the table; Dad helped himself and whomever was seated to his right, then passed that serving dish to the left.

We devoured the meat or fish first. Once the entre' was all gone, we ate our vegetables, then filled up on potatoes, bread and butter, and every last crumb of dessert. We were not required to take "a helping" if we didn't like something. Even so, some food didn't quite make it all the way 'round the table.

1959: Fifteen Children
Back row Al, Dad holding Dolores, Mom and Ramona Second row: John, Bob, Pat, Kathleen, and Rose Ann. Third Row Janet, Diane, and Marylu, Front Row: Helen, Virginia, Art, and Linda

Leaving the last bite on the platter was a foreign concept until I was in my late teens. Although everyone was required to politely say, "Please pass the _____," we considered it fair game to take the last morsel from the serving platter or bowl before it reached the one who requested it! Occasionally, Mom needed to move the skinniest girl to Dad's right, where the kid could, as Dad would say, "put some meat on those bones."

No one had to coax any of us to finish our food. After a full day's work, we came to the table hungry. No matter what Mom served, us kids gladly ate it with almost no complaining. Dad, however, maintained his preference for plain old meat 'n potatoes.

Because Marylu's birthday falls on a feast day of the Blessed Virgin, Mom once decorated a doll on her birthday-cake with blue frosting in honor of the Virgin Mary. Dad didn't like the frosting, and wanted to *make sure* no one would ever serve this again, so he issued a simple new household rule: "From now on, NO blue frosting."

As babies, most of my siblings had chunky cheeks. As soon as we learned to walk, we started burning off our baby fat, and kept it off by running around, playing, and doing farm work. We all ate well, but no one got fat working on the farm.

After meals, we threw scraps such bones and eggshells into the "garbage pail," a five-quart plastic ice cream bucket kept under the laundry room sink. We didn't have a garbage disposal, (nor had we ever heard of such a thing). After each meal, Bob had the chore of emptying the small garbage pail in to the five-gallon "slop pail" down the basement. After supper, he "hauled out the garbage," meaning he fed that day's slop to the pigs.

1967 Greg, Damien, Alice, and Angi on the pump, feeding the cats. Art, in front of the granary.

We saved extra milk and toddlers' leftover bread crusts to feed the cats. In second grade, it was my job to fill the "cat dish" after breakfast and supper. We kept an old skillet on the cement slab atop our farm's water well and used it to feed between two and sixteen motley barn cats. We called that slab "the pump."

The pump was the center of our farm yard (surrounded by a circular driveway connecting the granary, the barn, a hog house, four brooder houses, two henhouses, and a machine shed). When anyone stood on the pump and whistled, every cat would come running. If we didn't have enough cats to keep the mice and rat population down, Dad paid us five cents for each mouse we trapped, and twenty-five cents apiece for rats.

After supper, we transformed the kitchen into a study hall so at least half a dozen kids could do their homework. As part of the jobs on the weekly list, one person got assigned to wash dishes, and another to clear the table, put away the baby's high chair, and sweep the kitchen floor. If you planned to be gone after supper, you needed to trade days with someone else. We first folded up the little table and set it off to the side, and put the folding chairs away. Next, we cleared the big table, tucked extra leaves under, and folded down the ends.

One day a young girl who had just met our big family asked my mother how many dishwashers we had. "Fifteen!" Mom replied.

"Wow! What color were they?" she asked.

We used the double porcelain sink in the kitchen exclusively for washing and rinsing dishes. We set the dishes on a rubberized "drain board" to drip, then two people were assigned to dry them with hand-embroidered flour sack dish towels, and put them back in the cupboard. After supper and before we started our homework, we tidied up the house to Dad's satisfaction.

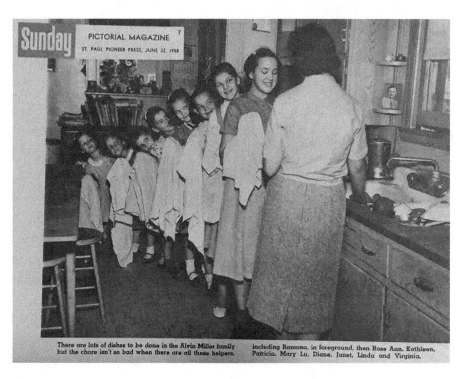

There are lots of dishes to be done in the Alvin Miller family but the chore isn't so bad when there are all these helpers. including Ramona, in foreground, then Rose Ann, Kathleen, Patricia, Mary Lu, Diane, Janet, Linda and Virginia.

Our family had relatively mild standards for cleanliness. We washed sinks and toilets daily, but windows rarely. If us kids put our toys in the toy box, and swept crumbs from the floor, we considered the house clean enough. The only bed that got made every day was Mom and Dad's; it doubled as the baby changing table, so the covers needed to be nice and flat. In the upstairs bedrooms, we changed our sheets on Saturday mornings, but other than that, we rarely spent a spare minute trying to make our bedrooms more presentable.

Dad was the master of making up little contests on the fly to keep kids busy, and to give them an incentive to do more work. When it came to house-cleaning, he sometimes said, "I'm thinking of one thing that needs to be picked up. You've got ten minutes to clean up everything, and whoever picks up THE ONE thing that I'm thinking of wins a prize." Depending on how messy the house was, the winner was awarded half a stick of gum, or a quarter.

When we sat at the kitchen table in the evening to start doing homework, at least half a dozen little kids were playing all around us. When I was in high school, two of my siblings, their spouses, and their combined seven children lived fairly close by. Because it was easy for my elder siblings to leave their children at our house when they needed a babysitter, it was not at all unusual for me to babysit a dozen kids while I was [supposedly] doing my homework. My first niece was born in 1965 and my youngest brother wasn't born until 1966; my youngest siblings and the eldest of my nieces and nephews feel like brothers/sisters to each other, and, to me, they feel like younger siblings.

While the big kids finished up homework, no exhausted little kid needed a curfew to know when it was time to, as Dad would say, "hit the sack." Normally we did not eat between meals unless everyone was served, but before bed, we were sometimes given permission to snack. Dad taught us to add a couple tablespoons of honey to a glass of milk, and called it a "honey malt." If we were still hungry, he let us dish up a bowl of cold cereal. But heaven forbid we didn't eat every last bit of what we served ourselves; he would put leftovers in the fridge with our names on it, and we couldn't eat anything else, even the next day, until we swallowed the last morsel of that soggy cereal.

Before bed, we took a drink of water and called it a day. We used the single stainless steel sink in the laundry room for everything other than dishes: getting a drink of water, hand-washing laundry, bathing infants and toddlers, and washing up after chores. The laundry room sink had both a hot and cold soft-water faucet and a separate lever for dispensing drinking (hard) water, similar to a modern refrigerator door. Outside of mealtimes and tea-party time, we drank only water, never juice nor pop. Our own cold, hard, well water tasted great, no chlorine!

While we were getting ready for bed, Mom was usually putting in the last load of laundry for the day. By the time I can remember, Mom used an electric washing machine to wash multiple loads of laundry six days a week. Each of us had one set of good clothes. We usually had only two sets of school clothes and two sets of everyday clothes, and we typically wore the same outfit for a week. Still, considering diapers and towels, chore clothes and hunting clothes, we needed to do laundry every day.

Whites made up the first load. The soapy water drained from the washer into a huge metal garbage can so it could immediately be re-used for a load of colored clothes. Dish towels, hand towels, bath towels, wash cloths, dish cloths, and rags filled at least one load per day. Diapers usually made up its own load every night. Mom washed jeans and dark clothes last.

We used a clothes dryer only in the winter. The rest of the year, we hung laundry to dry in the fresh air on a clothes line Dad had built. He welded metal pipes into frames that he placed thirty

We kept one plastic cup beside the drinking tap; anybody who wanted a drink of water, even company! used that same cup. When one of us caught a flu bug, you can imagine how fast the rest of us got sick. Mom said it was easier if we all got sick at the same time instead of a few at a time for weeks on end.

feet apart and strung enough wire to hold three loads of laundry. We folded basket after basket of laundry on the dining room table. After supper, each person carried his or her own clothes pile upstairs to put away before calling it a day.

CHAPTER 5:

Leisure and Entertainment

WE WERE HAPPY children; it didn't take much to satisfy us. Much of our family's entertainment centered around playing games with each other, picnicking, and attending celebrations. We never got bored. We played "Simon says," and "Mother may I?" We liked to play hide and seek either indoors or outdoors; we counted to ten or twenty and then said, "Ready or not, here I come!" When we had a lot of people, (more than ten) we played prisoner's base or pom-pom-pull-away. When there weren't so many, we played Statue. I remember saying this nursery rhyme while everyone got into their statuesque positions:

"Star light, star bright, first star I see tonight,

Wish I may, wish I might, have this wish I wish tonight."

There were always plenty of us around so we could find others who wanted to play simple games. All we had to do was stroll through the house and initiate a quick negotiation:

"Hey, wanna play Monopoly?"

"No, I'm busy, maybe later."

"Hey, wanna play Monopoly?"

"That takes too long. Let's play Crocinole instead."

"Hey, wanna play Monopoly?"

"I'll play if you'll play 500 with me tonight."

"Deal."

"Hey, I got a big kid to be the banker tonight. Who else wants to play?"

In the summer, the little kids set up various "play houses" outdoors. Every year, we decorated our slatted-wood corncribs that we used for storing ear corn through the winter in the days before drying bins. Dad parked his three-quarter ton truck between the sides of two corn cribs. The two sides provided the best opportunities for private play houses because we could easily wedge boards across the slatted corncrib walls to make shelving for our tea cups, mud pies and special stuff.

One year, John and Diane built a six-by-six tin shack with old boards covering a four-by-four-foot hole they thought of as their secret hideout deep in the middle of the "tree strip" Mom and Dad had planted on the northwest side of our house as a wind break. Years later, Dad helped Linda build a six-by-six-foot addition.

Before that addition was built, if Linda and I didn't make our play house in the corn crib, we often set up house in the hog yard where the pigs slept. We went out to the pigpen, dusted out the pig "grunt," as we called it, and made the biggest tin hut our house for the day. At night, the pigs regained their home, and the next day we started over. Linda was a tomboy; she always wanted

1964: Rose Ann's over-sized doll had an elegant full length wedding gown and a lacy veil, the envy of all of us girls.

to set up her house in the woods or in the pigpen (instead of the cement floor corncrib which was cleaner and nicer but too near the rest of the family for her taste). It was not uncommon that Mom would come out to the hog yard and tell Linda and me that we *had to* play with Virginia but that meant we couldn't play in the pigpen because that was not Ginny's favorite. Instead, we would use our clip-on roller skates to roller-skate around and around the furnace in the old part of our basement.

Timid, introverted Rose Ann always slept in her own room. I'm not sure why she got her own room; did Mom want the rest of us girls to be more care-free and less burdened with care-giving Rosie? After Dad added floor-to-ceiling built-in cupboards in Rose Ann's room, Mom instantly filled them with off-season clothes, hats, vases, and who knows what else. One year, Santa brought Rose Ann a wedding-dress doll twice as tall as any of the rest of us girls' dolls. We would often go to Rose Ann's room and ask if we could share her doll; she would not let it out of her sight.

I think my mother was quite clever to realize that gifting Rose Ann a nice doll would make the rest of us want to hang out in her tiny room and keep her company. Rosie, as we called her, also had a plastic loom for weaving hot pads, another incentive for us to want to spend time with her.

While one girl was playing with Rose Ann's doll, the rest of us would draw, play school and/or play hangman for hours on end on the four-foot by four-foot chalk board that hung in the hallway right outside Rose Ann's room.

Once in a while, one of us would ask if we could have a tea-party at "our own [play] house." Virginia was an expert at getting Mom to say yes. Mom would get out the costume box so

Alice and Angi, all dressed up, playing house.

we could dress up with fancy clothes, hats and purses, and sometimes, high heels. While we were getting dolled up, she would pack a few crackers or cookies for Virginia to take "home." Virginia would then invite "company" (whoever lived in the other corn crib or pig-pen houses). Interestingly, we were never taught the word "guests," only *company*. Attendees would be treated to real snacks instead of the usual mud-pies decorated with daisies.

In our leisure time on summer evenings, we played outdoors. Dad helped us build an awesome tree house in the pig pasture that provided many a day's worth of entertainment, a fabulous place for young teens to play house. When John was in his early teens, we played touch football almost every night. Our neighbor, Pauly Hurt, was a grown man who had lost one arm in a farm accident; he liked to have fun playing ball with us. John was a good athlete; he would play quarterback on one team, and Pauly on the opposite team. On any given night, at least ten kids wanted to play touch football. Alternatively, since we had two lawns, we had enough space and enough people to play both football and softball at the same time.

We never played baseball, and we played softball way less often than football, in part because Dad made a rule that whoever broke a window had to pay half to have it fixed. When we learned how much it cost to replace a window in the family room door after a bean-bag contest, it made us extra-cautious about playing softball in the front yard lest we break the big picture window.

I never quite got the hang of swinging a bat; I struck out almost every time. In the interest of including all skill levels, the boys changed the rules to give non-athletes like me a better chance: I was supposed to hold my bat straight out. The pitcher from my team would pitch to me; if the ball hit my bat, I could run toward first base.

On Friday nights in the winter, we often watched movies and got to have popcorn for a treat. We had four black and white 8MM silent movies with words that flashed between pictures: Abbott and Costello's No Indian's Please, Andy Pandy, Woody Woodpecker, and Jack in the Beanstalk. Our newest cartoon, Road-Runner, was in color, but it wasn't nearly as funny as our old favorites. We watched all five cartoons whenever Dad got out the projector; of course, every one of us knew all the words by heart, but we still laughed our heads off every time. Then Dad would show us a home movie or two; unlike America's funniest home videos, our home movies were only interesting to children the first time we saw them.

Most of our toys were community property: board games, broken crayons, bats and balls, etc. When Santa brought us a Yahtzee board, it became our most popular form of entertainment for over a year. Individual toys were far less common so if someone got a musical instrument or a favorite doll or an Etch a Sketch, that person really cherished it. Inevitably, something bad happened, and the situation would come to

Mom's attention. "Mom, somebody sat on my new toy and broke it."

"I'm sure they didn't mean it."

"Yeah, but, Mom, it doesn't work anymore."

"There, there, now. Why don't you help Mom bake a pie?"

The next year after Yahtze our new favorite became Shanghai (but Shanghai required all afternoon to play, and we couldn't always commit). Dad was good with numbers, and he liked to help us learn math by playing cards, usually Pfeffer or 500. Five hundred was more flexible than Shanghai; we could play one game or twenty.

On Sunday afternoons, we played 500 for hours and hours and hours on end. Sometimes we had three tables of four playing at the same time so we could rotate winners and losers, tournament style. On the rare occasion that not enough people wanted to play cards with Dad, he could always find at least one person to challenge him to a checkers or Chinese checkers match.

On winter weekends, we built forts in the snow drifts near our house. Dad used the

On Sunday afternoons, we liked to play cards, and we were serious about winning! Here we are in 1967, learning to play Tripoli, a form of rummy. Lor, Art, and Janet

front-loader on the tractor to clear the driveway, and he piled snow as high as a big truck. Around age six, I remember wearing snow pants over my corduroy pants, and hauling a bucket of water to use as mortar to solidify a roof on Art's and my "igloo," the same way we had built a really nice frozen bench to sit on. Building a roof was going well... until Mom found out. Oops. How's a little kid supposed to know that an igloo roof built by a six-year-old is dangerous? Oh well, the fort worked well without a roof.

1975: Art, Pauline, Marcia, Angi, and Alice, playing in the snow Dad had piled high enough to build forts.

"Hey Dad" Its too cold for a picture!!

May 3rd, 1955 late season snowstorm Marylu, Diane, John, Linda, and Janet

The largest pair of snow pants our family owned were designed for pre-school kids. When I outgrew that pair of snow pants, I wore flannel-lined jeans with an elastic waistband. They were not water-proof, and not nearly as warm. When I was in about third grade, I no longer fit into a pair of flannel lined jeans, so corduroy pants were my warmest option. I don't remember complaining to Mom about needing bigger snow pants. Because the girls at school wore dresses and tights, as far as I knew, there was no such thing as warm clothing for girls. You'll have a hard time finding any photos of me playing outdoors in the winter beyond age ten. In order to stay warm, I became an indoor girl.

When I was about five years old, Mom and Dad took us to see the movie "Babes in Toyland." Not having grown up with TV, we could not distinguish between things presented on the screen and reality. The talking, dancing trees scared the heck out some of us. It was so scary that Janet had to take Lor out to the lobby to settle her down. Because movies were considered expensive, the next time we went to the movies, I was already in fifth or sixth grade.

Our whole family absolutely loved "The Sound of Music" and memorized practically every single word. After "Yours, Mine and

1959: Virginia, Art, Dolores, and Helen enjoying the first days of spring. Our next door neighbor's white barn in the background

1970: Greg, Marcia, Alice pulling Damien, in front on John's car

Ours" we also saw "Grimm's Fairy Tales" at the splendid Cinerama wide-screen theater when, in 1968, our family won free movie tickets as a result of winning a contest for the largest family (22 children) in the U.S. The only other movie I remember before I finished high school was "The Castaways." Mom and Dad piled all of us in the van to go to an outdoor movie theater. The kids in the back could neither see nor hear very well, so that was the end of that type of entertainment.

By the time spring comes, Minnesotans have cabin fever pretty badly, and each spring, our family couldn't wait to have our first picnic of the season. As soon as we'd get one of those

gorgeous sunny spring days, we'd gather up all the sticks on the lawn and beg Dad to make a bonfire. Mom would put out four or five packages of hot dogs and buns, make about a gallon of baked beans and splurge on a box of potato chips for us to share. Special for the first bonfire of the season, she'd even let us have five Hershey bars so we could melt them on graham crackers with marshmallows and make *real* s'mores, instead of the chocolate-free s'mores we ate the rest of the season.

Every few weeks in the summer, Mom and Dad would take our whole gang on a picnic. We liked exploring new parks / playgrounds, and eating picnic style.

1959 Sunday Picnic
Lor and Ginny in Sunday dresses, eating fried chicken and baked beans, potato salad and white cake at one of our many picnics.

1956 Springtime in front of the tree strip in our back yard
Ramona holding Helen, Rose Ann, Kathleen, Al middle row: Marylu, John, Bob, Diane, Pat, Front row: Janet, Linda, Virginia

Our picnic basket routinely carried paper plates and napkins, honey for bread and butter sandwiches, ketchup and mustard, salt and pepper, a bread knife, silverware, and everyday cups. We always brought along green onions, butter, homemade bread and a five-gallon thermos jug of what we called "nectar" (Kool-aid) or fresh-squeezed lemonade as well as Mom's famous dill pickles.

<u>Pickles (Dill) for 6-8 quarts</u>

20-25 4" cucumbers

1/8 t. pwd. alum

1 clove garlic, 2 heads dill

1 qt. Cider vinegar

1 c. coarse salt for canning (pickling salt)

3 qt. water

Wash cucumbers. Let cucumbers stand in cold water overnight. Pack into hot, sterilized jars. To each qt. jar of cucumbers add above amounts of alum, garlic, and dill. (Optionally, add a hot red pepper) Combine vinegar, salt, water. Heat to boil. Fill jars. (Optionally, add a grape leaf to each jar.) To seal, cover with a wool blanket until the lids pop, or put jars in kettle of water; bring to boil, take out and cool.

For our picnic supper, we had no particular need for variety and it was easier for the cooks if we served the same simple menu over and over. For family picnics, we almost always served hot dogs and potato salad. In later years, Dad went

Left: 1953 Miller family in front of the school bus owned by my Korteum cousins, (a family of nine who owned the local bus company). Right: 1954 Millers and Korteums traveling via school bus to vacation together for a second year in a row.

to the local meat market and bought "real" wieners; they had natural skin, more meat, and lots more flavor than the light-colored ones.

In the summer of 1952, Mom and Dad took the whole family to a resort in northern Minnesota for their first family vacation. Without reservations, not many places could accommodate such a large group, and they had a heckuva time finding a place to stay. Nevertheless, they had such a fun time that the family took another fishing vacation "up north" the following year.

It became tougher by the year to fit our growing family and the Korteum's growing

family into our cousin's bus to go on vacation; my parents needed to consider another option. Instead of traveling to northern Minnesota to go fishing, Dad and his brother, Leo, put their pennies together and spent $750 for an acre of property on the south shore of Reed's Lake, now called *the* lake by both our family and friends. In 1956, they built a rustic cabin. For the next fifteen years, our family traveled eleven miles from home to "vacation" at *the* cabin. Several years later, uncle Gene and uncle Leo put in cabins next to our property.

Mom recalled: *"One time we were staying at the cabin and the little one next to the baby*

1956: building a cabin on Reeds Lake. Mom in her apron putting food on the picnic table while Bob held his puppy.

typical nectar poured into ice cube trays). We, of course, were beside ourselves with glee.

My parents loved visiting their siblings and having all the kids play together. Us kids longed to spend time with our various cousins, especially our Kahnke cousins who shared our "salt of the earth" lifestyle and liked playing in the barn. We had great fun riding bikes around the yard, circling behind the chicken coop to pick up speed to "fly" over the pump. Our other favorite game was "Kick the Can."

chewed the nipple off the baby's bottle, and we had to go home after another one. It was only ten miles so that wasn't such a hardship, just a nuisance."

At the lake, we sometimes roasted hot dogs and/or burgers on the little brick BBQ grill that Uncle Francis built for us. If the fishermen were lucky, we added catch-of-the-day sunfish and crappies (dredged in flour then fried in butter), to whatever else was being served. In addition to our standard picnic menu, on our annual summer vacation we added popcorn and Oreo cookies to our menu as special occasion treats. Sometimes, Mom bought real Popsicles, fudgesicles, or orange sherbet push-ups (instead of our more

1961: We'd pack our picnic basket, and head for Nerstrand Woods or someplace where we could find berries, flowers, pussy willows, mushrooms, most any kind of nuts, or simply beautiful scenery. Janet, Linda, Mom, and Marylu enjoying orange nectar, watermelon and chocolate cake.

1967: Enjoying time with Aunt Therese' family. Taking advantage of a patch of sun next to the cabin.

1963: Dad built a rickshaw so Bob could wear off some of his extra energy pulling the younger kids around the yard. Shown here: Bob pulling Art while Marty runs alongside.

Which cousins we planned to visit the following week was an ongoing tug-of-war. One Sunday, Dad decided to try something new. "Each of you can pick which family you want to visit this Sunday, and I'll drive to all those places." Of course, some of us wanted to visit multiple cousins in the same day, and begged him to split up the time. "That just goes to show you, you can't please everyone!" he said, and from then on, there was far less arguing about where to go on Sunday.

All our cousins lived on farms. My parents never took us "to town" to play with "city kids." They frowned on "sophisticated" people (college-educated parents or families with more money) who might act "snobby" and look down on us "country kids." If a city kid came to visit

us, our favorite prank was to take him or her "snipe hunting." We waited until it got dark, went out to the tree strip, and told the newcomer to hold a gunny sack and wait there while the rest of us would chase the snipes toward the bag. Then we left him or her there alone and retired to the living room, waiting to see how long it would take the city slicker to come in. A rare streak of cruelty!

After visiting cousins on Sunday afternoons, we came home in time for supper. Once a month or two, we invited cousins to our house for special occasions. I don't remember our family ever getting invited inside anyone else's home for a sit-down meal. There were simply too many of us.

Because nobody had a house big enough to serve meals to twenty or thirty kids, if any of our cousins wanted to share a meal together, hosting a picnic at a park wasn't actually a choice; it was both a necessity as well as the perfect solution. Sometimes we got together at the lake, and other times we explored various parks with playgrounds, or off-the-beaten-path picnic grounds.

When multiple families met at our cabin, or at a public park, everybody brought potluck food. Baked beans and fried chicken were two of the few variations to our standard picnic menu. In the early summer, Mom often fried spring chicken, everybody's favorite! For Sunday picnics, Mom made her fabulous baked beans with ham, using the pressure cooker when she didn't have time to slow-cook them. On the 4th of July

weekend, some farmer would drive a semi-truck up from Texas and Dad would treat us to a watermelon and three or four muskmelons for our picnic supper.

When we didn't have melon, Mom made red Jell-O with real whipped cream and walnuts, just like Grama Miller's, and served it in "the Jell-O bowl," a fancy opaque glass bowl with a red rim. Potato chips were considered a treat. Ripple chips and store-bought chip dip were a REALLY special treat.

Our family's picnics were usually within an hour's drive from home. All summer long, us kids pleaded with Mom and Dad to take us on vacation. A few nights a year, Mom and Dad relented, and loaded up the car with supplies

Mom and Dad liked to celebrate their April 16th Anniversary by going on a picnic and enjoying grilled steaks. When I was in 6th grade, at the peak of the 1960's loud-colors fad, I sewed the dress Mom's wearing on this photo.

1975: Angi, Dad, Damien, and Greg, displaying the day's catch inside our rustic cabin.

for some cherished R and R at the cabin. Often this happened over the 4th of July long weekend. When the whole family slept over at the cabin, we considered that one long weekend our summer vacation, and we thoroughly enjoyed ourselves.

The cabin had a gas stove, a sink and one tiny little cupboard for storing serving dishes. The cabin had no electricity; we kept a kerosene lantern on the kitchen table. In lieu of running water; we brought drinking water with us, washed our dishes with lake water, and used a two-holer outhouse.

Roughly sixteen feet wide and twenty feet long, with four "rooms," the cabin was uninsulated so the studs and the rafters were all visible. It had three partial-wall bedrooms made out of sheets of raw plywood, half-way up and half-way down, like stalls in a lavatory.

In the late fifties, Bob always slept in the far bedroom, (Mom made sure the challenged kids had priority on beds instead of sleeping on the floor), younger girls in the middle room, Mom and Dad in the first room. Rose Ann slept on the couch. The rest of the kids grabbed a quilt or a feather tick and slept on the peg board floor.

In the sixties, Dad bought a tent with mosquito netting at the annual church auction; it had been donated by Herter's, a nationally known sporting goods store headquartered in our home town. After Dad bought that tent, camping on the lawn at the cabin became a favorite for some kids. Years later, Dad added a screened-in porch to the cabin; teenagers could sleep out there in sleeping bags or on quilts. Finally, EVERYBODY could easily fit in the cabin, on the porch, or in a tent. Every summer from then on, we stayed at the lake for at least a few nights.

Each kid took a brown paper grocery sack and stuffed it with a swimsuit, towel, shorts, tops, and sandals. Mom packed enough food

We had never heard of life jackets at that time!
From the left, back to front: Ramona, Eileen? in the hat. Second row: Marianne, Karen,
Kathleen, Jeanie. Third row: Al, Bob, Karyl, Paul, Rose Ann touching the water
Fourth row: Marylu, Joe or Kevin?

and water for one day. One trunk's worth of supplies was never enough. Some of the big kids had to go home twice a day to feed the chickens, gather the eggs, milk the cow, and pick up more water and food. Except for a quick visit home at chore-time, we swam and fished all day long then ate a simple picnic supper. Especially when some of our cousins joined us to go swimming and/or fishing in the afternoon, we could not have been happier.

None of us will ever forget waking up in the middle of the night at the cabin, knowing full well what was involved when we had to go to the outhouse to pee...having to step over six or seven sleeping bags where tuckered out children lay snoring away... hoping we didn't mash anybody's fingers...as we struggled to find the

only flashlight... avoid the poison ivy along the outhouse path... and ignore the stench... while fighting off the mosquitos... then return via the same route, step across the sprawled out snoozers, and let our head hit the pillow again. We went right back to sleep, absolutely thrilled to wake up the next morning, eager to play at the lake for one more day.

For us, the 4th of July weekend epitomized summer vacation. For sure on that holiday, and at least a couple more times per summer, we would have company at the lake. Company usually meant at least one of Mom's three brothers or three sisters, and their five or ten kids.

Of course, everybody wanted to see the fireworks. We'd pile into the van, little ones sitting

1976: Greg and Damien after their successful fishing trips

on the big kids' laps, drive half way to town, park on a hill where we could stay in the car (away from Minnesota's notorious mosquitos) and still get a chance to enjoy the fireworks.

The night our cousin, Collette, stayed over with us at the cabin, she belatedly learned one of my dad's rules. Whenever Dad came in from fishing, his rule was that kids should come (quick) to help unload fish and fishing gear. Poor Collette was standing on the shore when my dad started shouting, "Don't you know you're supposed to help??" Dad didn't realize that the person he saw near the dock was not one of his own. Recently Collette recalled, "Oh, yes, I remember him scolding me; I was almost in tears."

The next morning, we were toasting bread on the cabin's stove by balancing two slices against a square metal grate over a gas burner. We were enjoying Wonder bread (light and fluffy compared to home-baked bread), which our family

Although I had absolutely no idea where we were, Dad made me promise I would not tell anyone where we found this lady slipper because he was afraid they would dig it up. I had to laugh when, years later, I took the snap shot out of his photo album and saw on the back, "Nerstrand."

considered a real treat. Collette was astonished when we opened the second loaf. "You use TWO loaves of bread for breakfast?" she asked.

"More like four" I said, knowing that Wonder bread was such a delight that we would keep eating toast until none remained.

Collette's jaw dropped. It was the first of the thousands of times in my life that someone reacted in total awe to something I had considered "normal." Watching other peoples' reactions is how I learned what they found most unusual about our huge family, and it never ceased to surprise me.

It should shock no one to know that my siblings and I got precious little "alone time" with either of our parents. I didn't really miss not having one on one time with Mom and Dad until I came to know my friends' parents and witnessed the fun they had together. As an adult, it struck me that one of the downsides of such a big family is that children don't always get sufficient validation at the right points in their development, so they sometimes continue to seek validation from others as adults.

I have fond memories of one particular afternoon alone with Dad when I was in second grade; we went in search of Minnesota's state flower, a pink lady slipper. It's the only time I can remember spending an entire afternoon alone with Dad. We drove about an hour from home, walked deep into a woods, found our state flower, and he took a picture that will forever be my favorite childhood photo.

If alone time with our parents was rare, being home alone was even rarer. We virtually never had time completely alone. I was in my forties before I knew what it was like to spend any significant amount of time alone.

Much as I loved picnics, socializing with cousins, and staying overnight at the lake, I longed to travel, like my friend Susan's family. When I was in 7th grade, I begged my parents to take some of us on a "real" vacation so that I would have something exciting to talk about on the first day back to school. I had three vacation goals: 1) to go far away to some place we had never been, 2) to see something famous, and 3) to stay in a "real" hotel.

My parents finally relented and took me, my next older and my next younger sister on a *real* vacation that summer. We drove a few hours north to Hibbing, MN to see something that was world famous. I had never been so far from home, so I was pretty excited.

I felt especially privileged to stay in a hotel for the first time. That night, Mom and Dad slept in a full-size bed and the three of us girls crowded together in the other full-size bed in the cramped Super 8 motel room. No room service; no free breakfast, just a place to rest for the night. We never ever locked our house, both because there was usually someone home and because we lived in a safe neighborhood. Having a chain lock on the hotel door seemed kind of frightening.

The next day the five of us stood on the rim above one of the worlds' largest open-pit iron ore mines. Dad was fascinated by the big machines. Not me. I looked at the huge hole in the ground and only saw lots of trucks hauling what looked like dirt. No big deal. For lunch, we ate sandwiches from our picnic basket. Then the three of us girls sat silently on a smelly sofa for an hour while my mother and dad visited quietly with one of my Mom's old-lady relatives who lived not far from the mine. Afterward, we drove about five hours "straight home."

I had travelled far away from home, saw something world famous, and stayed overnight in a hotel. My three goals were fully accomplished, but... I decided *real* vacations were not all they were cracked up to be; going to the lake was a LOT more fun.

Part of the reason I was so naïve was that I was raised without TV. All of my friends' families had a TV. In fact, to this day, I have never met another Minnesotan my age who grew up without watching TV. Dad had bought a small black and white TV in 1949 as a gift to Mom when she delivered Diane. At that time, Dad liked watching Bonanza and Lawrence Welk for entertainment, and kids liked watching cartoons, Ted Mack, and American Bandstand.

One day when I was about four years old, kids were bickering over which TV channel to watch. My siblings tell me that Dad stood up from his easy chair, unplugged our family's only TV, and took it away without any elaboration. He put it in storage on the floor of our dusty granary. He then talked it over with Mom; together they decided TV was a bad influence on kids. From then on, the TV stayed in permanent storage.

Without a TV to occupy us, there were plenty of times when we were less than angelic children. To avoid disagreements, Mom would sometimes answer a question by saying, "Go ask your father," and Dad would respond separately, "Better go ask your mother." Long before I was born, they had learned how to prevent their children from playing them against each other.

If a child had a disagreement with Dad, rather than arguing, Dad would simply say, "I'll betcha a dollar." No long arguments, one side or the other needed to come up with proof, and voila! that person won a dollar. Never more than a buck, and never less. My dad very much enjoyed telling complete strangers, "Betcha a dollar you can't guess how many children I have." No one ever guessed right, and he didn't expect to be paid. Betcha-a-dollar became a common phrase, even when no money changed hands.

Removing the TV from our household had a more positive influence on me and my siblings than any other single decision my parents made. In our limited leisure time, we developed additional reading, writing and arithmetic skills. My parents noticed that everybody's school grades improved. On winter weekends, we played cards and board games for hours on end: Crazy Eights, Old Maids and Candyland until we graduated into Hearts, Spades, and Monopoly. In addition, we developed creativity by inventing our own toys and games, like when my brother strung

1969:
Back Row: Helen, Diane, Robert, Sister Ramona, Pat, Marylu, Al, John, Janet, Virginia
Middle Row: Pauline, Lor, Kathleen, Linda, Art,
Front Row: Greg, Marcia, Dad, Damien, Mom, Alice, Marty, Rose Ann, Angi

twine onto coffee cans so we could walk around our basement on "stilts."

My parents' decision insulated us from extraneous concerns of the world around us. We were sheltered from the violence of both movies and war; Viet Nam was almost never discussed. My parents used the phrase "hotsy-totsy" to describe people whose values they did not want us to emulate. For example, when I brought home an anti-war book from a friend, my dad promptly burned it with the trash, even though he knew someone else owned that book. Our

understanding of the developing world came from our priest and our teachers at school, both of whom took up collections of pocket change for pagan babies and all the "poor starving children" in India, China, Africa or wherever they were serving as missionaries.

The day before Neil Armstrong landed on the moon, Dad rented a TV just so we could see this historic event. The day JFK died, Dad took all of us to Uncle George and Aunt Marg's to watch Walter Cronkite tell the world that JFK was the first person killed on live TV. I was in third grade. Uncle George wanted to make sure I realized that JFK's death was not like cowboys and Indians (*just* TV).

Because everyone in our Catholic school had knelt on the cold, hard, linoleum floor beside our desks that morning to pray for our President's recovery, and having learned about death when I attended my Zimmerman cousins' wake as a youngster, I understood all too well how real JFK's death was. That our President was Catholic made the assassination all the worse for families like ours.

For me personally, JFK's death marked a pivotal transition. Prior to that, my world pretty much ended at the county line. I didn't really know who was President, or what it meant to be President. Our family lived in relative isolation, oblivious to politics. Dad had once said that his father was a Republican and his mother a Democrat so there was no sense of them voting. I had no idea if my parents voted, or for whom. Once I gained a tiny window in to a bigger world, I started to read more, and began to discover life outside of farming.

Many of my siblings' primary entertainment consisted of hunting, fishing, or their pet(s). Al, Marylu, Janet, and Linda are the horse-lovers in our family. Each of them became quite proficient at riding and at animal caregiving. My interest in horses ended abruptly when our favorite horse, "Blaze," took a sharp corner leaving me in a ditch. Our family owned a pony named Trigger, and a gelding named Silver. For a year or so, we also boarded a gorgeous Arabian stallion named Colonel. His owner hoped that having several different riders would reduce the horse's spunk. After I left home, Dad agreed to buy Angi a horse on the condition that it was big enough for him to ride. He needed to prepare for an antelope hunting trip where he planned to pack in to the campsite. Done deal!

Our next-door neighbors owned a pony and one other horse; the horse-lovers in their family often rode horse with my siblings while my neighbor, Connie, and I watched TV and played board games like "Clue." When I went to Connie's house, her mom always kept nectar in her fridge because she was diabetic. I was treated to something sweet to drink almost every time I went there, and, unlike at home, I could drink as much as I wanted; what a treat! Her mom would often stir up a cake or a batch of cookies and let me lick the beaters because she knew how much I enjoyed that, and how seldom I was given the privilege of licking the beaters at home.

One of our family's favorite forms of entertainment was to attend weddings. The first time I remember going to a wedding was in 1960; I was five years old. My cousin Eileen had several bridesmaids who looked like princesses. They wore blue suede shoes to match their cocktail-length dresses. Simply gorgeous! Wedding receptions offered a terrific opportunity to get dressed up, enjoy yummy food, and have fun with all our cousins.

One of the predicaments of having such a large family is that you never get enough time to talk with each person. At a Miller wedding, holiday gathering, graduation, family reunion, or similar event, dozens of people who had not seen each other in years converge for a few hours. Some of those you haven't seen for years happen to be your very own siblings! You often leave hoping that no one took offense that you didn't get the chance even to say "hi."

When the first of my sisters got married, I was in eighth grade. Pat married Glen Rice at Sacred Heart church. From then on, our family had most of our family photos taken in this space. I was old enough to pick out a wedding gift, and proud to pay for it with my own money. Mom mentioned a few things from the bride's registry, and I have to chuckle when I recall how delighted I was with myself that I could afford to buy the new bride and groom a sixty-nine-cent rubber spatula with my very own money. Realizing how expensive a wedding can be, my dad joked that if any of the rest of us girls wanted to elope, he'd pay for the ladder. However, he no longer thought of it as funny when I eloped at age 27.

The only time in my life that I had a babysitter who was not one of my siblings or grandparents was when I was in third grade. My brother Al, and his new wife, Donna, celebrated their wedding with a reception followed by a ballroom dance, but I was considered too young to attend. My brothers and sisters had been practicing how to polka, waltz, and schottische; those of us who had to stay home were pretty darn unhappy. After that, I had many chances to attend wedding dances, and loved every single one. My sisters and I also had lots of babysitting opportunities, some fun and others not.

Our family got babysitting jobs outside the family from people we did not know well. It seemed like whoever's kids were out of control would rely on Miller girls as babysitters. The wife would call Mom to request a sitter, and Mom would say, "Oh, sure," then assign the eldest available sitter, based on how difficult that family was to babysit.

When I was fifteen, Mom assigned me to babysit seven bed-wetters while their parents went on a snowmobiling vacation. How could all seven kids still wet the bed when the eldest was already in sixth grade? It was twice as hard to babysit those seven little rascals as it was to babysit my nine younger siblings plus several nieces and nephews.

My favorite babysitting job was being on-call for a couple who lived at the end of our section. The mom was an ER nurse with two lovely daughters; she paid me twenty-five cents an hour to be on-call whenever she was on-call, and fifty cents an hour if I was actually needed to care for the children. It worked out well for both of us.

To me at that time, fifty cents an hour was big money. After baths on Saturday evening, Dad got out "the money cup," a dented tin camping cup that held his spare change, and passed out allowance. First graders got five cents, ten cents for second graders, fifteen for third graders, and so on.

We could choose whether to spend part of our allowance to buy a candy bar from a stash that Mom hid for that purpose. She kept a square metal cake pan high up in the cupboard; she called it the "treat box." Saturday night was

the only time we ever ate candy bars, and was also the only night of the week on which Mom did not serve dessert.

Depending on the week, we had our choice of Hershey bars, Almond Joys, Mound bars, Snickers, Mars bars, black licorice, Heath bars, Salted Peanut Rolls, Babe Ruths, m&m's and Nut Goodies. I sometimes spent an hour that afternoon deciding which delectable candy I would choose that week, and hope that by the time it was my turn to pick, that brand was not already taken! On rare occasions, I froze my Mars or Snickers bar to enjoy the next day, but usually we each impatiently polished off our treat within a few minutes.

Dad encouraged us to put our allowance in our savings book/piggy bank. Each of us had our own bank and our own savings passbook. Whenever we took our little banks to the Farmers' National Bank, the teller would open each bank and record the savings in our passbook. Dad replicated the teller's key just by looking at it; having a key at home allowed him to open up our banks in case we needed money for a special event.

Especially on weekends, my dad outdid himself telling stories. He didn't care if we'd already heard it, and often said, "At least one of you won't remember this one." Here's the story most of us have heard at least a dozen times:

"Those days [late 30's] there were chicken thieves, 3 or 4 guys about 30 years old. All the neighbors knew. One night a lady stuck her head out and yelled, "I know who you are!" But that didn't stop them.

One night it snowed, and I saw their tracks in our yard, but didn't know if they actually stole anything. So, the next day I went to the neighboring town of Wells and borrowed a black dog for a couple months so I could hear the barking. I kept my automatic rifle loaded and occasionally rippled bullets into the woods to scare the thieves.

One night I heard the woven wire crinkling, so at midnight I went to the chicken thieves' house and there was a kerosene light burning in the kitchen and "the Mrs." came to the door. "Say," I said, "someone is after my chickens and I need help." She went to the bedroom door and said "John, Mr. Miller says someone is after his chickens and he needs help." I could hear him whisper, "Can't go," and her say, "Gotta go!" But of course, John couldn't go because it was either his Pa or his brothers. Well, that night cooled those thieves down!

By day, these thieves worked alongside me and my brother, Francis. One time, Francis told the thief, "We're going to go to a Knights of Columbus meeting this evening; could you come by and pitch manure in the morning instead?" The thief said "Sure." So Francis and I left the farm together in the car. Down the road a bit, I jumped out and walked back and lay there by the straw pile waiting for the thieves. The thieves came, but they must have seen me in the moonlight (or maybe they had a spy at the meeting who knew I was missing). At any rate, the next day the guy came to work and just grinned ear to ear and said, "How was the meeting?"

Not long after, Francis and I went to a wedding dance in Albert Lea. I was supposed to be running shot gun that night, but my brother Leo's girlfriend, Veronica, couldn't go that night so Leo picked up Ceil (because she lived next door to Veronica) and Leo stayed on the lookout. When I came home, our neighbor Joe Herbs was there and Leo had two guys cornered by the fence and whispered to me, "I only got two shells left." Leo had shot behind them on purpose and the chicken thieves dropped their sacks of chickens, and one thief ran to the slough, but later gave himself up.

I'm glad I wasn't running shotgun that night because I might have dropped those guys on the spot. The sheriff came and arrested the thieves and I went to bed at 1:45AM. The first guy was questioned and he spilled the beans... They had stole hogs, too! Imagine! They had had the audacity to have come over to our house with some freshly ground pork and one of them asked if we wanted some. How DARE he."

There were no locks on our door at that time. At 3AM the sheriff came right in and said "There's another guy!" Dad jumped in the sheriff's car and went to the suspect's farm. There was a kerosene lamp burning. "Hey, anybody home?" said the sheriff. The accomplice simply picked up a deck of cards and got in the sheriff's car. He knew right then he was going to jail.

The thieves were caught in New Richland. One of the them used to milk cows with us. The other one was a big tall guy (6'2"), could carry enough chickens (six pounds each worth 30 cents a pound) to buy an acre of land. One was an usher at church; he got parishioners seated and then stole chickens from them during the service. Later, he admitted stealing from a list of guys several inches long... Two thieves got sent to Stillwater prison and two to St. Cloud prison."

Every time he told that story, he would re-iterate the value of working hard and making money. Whenever Dad earned more money than anticipated, whether on that day's load of grain or that year's sale of land, our family spent extra on something yummy to eat. We typically celebrated special occasions by inviting company and cooking up a feast. On rare occasion, we ate "high off the hog" without inviting guests, like when Dad sold "the other farm" in a single day.

In the early sixties, Dad had bought a farm a few miles away from home on a winding road called the Snake Road. For several years, he rented the entire farm to Archie Draheim. Later, he erected additional buildings in hopes that his eldest son would start farming there. Just like his father and grandfather had done before him, my father wanted to launch each of his sons on a farm of their own. He rented the farm house

In 1967, a cluster of tornados killed 13 people in our town, destroyed all the buildings on our other farm (shown here), and also completely wiped out our Uncle Francis' and Aunt Harriet's home place.

to a family by the name of Hinna, and worked the land himself. Just after he had completed building a corn crib and a machine shed, a cluster of tornados struck that farm and leveled all the buildings and most of the trees in a matter of seconds.

Years later, Dad reminisced: "On the Snake Road I built a corn crib, and machine shed. 'Just got machine shed done when the tornado came. The way I built a corn crib, there was cement, a burr sticking up, then a plank fastened to it. The

tornado took it all the way down to the burrs, a 2 x 6 was still there, and the rest was gone. The hay rack was wrapped around a tree in the grove."

Seeing the extent of the devastation from the tornado, Dad was too dejected to want to re-build those buildings. He had no enthusiasm for starting over on that property. He promptly went to see a realtor who sold the other farm that same day.

Dad came home from Donahue Real Estate super-excited with the relatively high price he had negotiated. He announced to Mom his intent to go grocery shopping and buy something really special so our family could celebrate in high style. He needed someone to help him pick out "celebration kid-food." Lucky for me, I was readily available, so he invited me to go back to town with him. He gave me the chance to choose anything I wanted to buy for supper.

To enjoy this once-in-a-lifetime opportunity, I walked down the aisles of Wolf's grocery store with a whole new perspective, feeling extremely privileged. I started browsing individual items on each of the shelves, especially the ones I was unfamiliar with, and wondering what would be the very best food I could find. Dad was hungry and in a hurry. He wanted me to quit "just shopping" and just tell him off the top of my head what I wanted so he could help find it and rush back home.

I was in 7th grade. For this momentous occasion, I chose the first things that came to my mind. Here's what Dad bought for our party:

- one loaf of Wonder bread,

- one box of breaded shrimp,

- one can of frozen orange juice (not Hi-C!), and

- a package of Hydrox cookies.

My food repertoire was so extremely limited that I felt certain that I'd hit the jackpot bringing such delicacies home for our feast. I couldn't wait to get home and tell my siblings what we were having for supper!

CHAPTER 6:

Living Off the Land

My MOTHER AND father loved both plants and animals. Mom taught each of us how to plant, to weed, water, and pick flowers, and she usually displayed the prettiest ones as a centerpiece for our table. Mom planted flowers all around our yard: gladiolas and tulips by the mailbox, yellow roses near the swing set, marigolds next to the willow tree, crocuses and daffodils along the white fence, petunias, begonias, impatience, clematis, a jack in the pulpit and morning glories next to the house and by the shrine (plus desert cactus so the prickly thorns would stave off cats), philodendron, geraniums and Christmas cactus in the porch, hydrangeas

Left: John and Helen, clematis and climbing roses 1958
Right: Ginny, Linda, and Helen by Mom's irises,1956

1967: Dad's pride and joy, the ever-sprawling yellow rose bush.

Flowers surrounding the shrine in our back yard.

and peonies near the clothes line, ferns and lilies of the valley on the north side of the house; flowers galore virtually anywhere she could find open space to plant.

As soon as the frost was gone, Dad tilled the vegetable garden. Every year, or so it seemed, Dad moved the garden fence. When the family was *growing*, he usurped a few yards of the pig pasture each spring to extend the garden. As the big kids left for college one after the other, Dad realized we needed less vegetables, and started moving the garden fence closer in again, year by year.

1983: Mom weeding her extremely shrunken vegetable and fruit garden after most of the children had left home.

Dad fertilized the vegetable garden with sheep manure from my aunt and uncle's farm. He believed horse and cow manure were too strong for our vegetables. Mom showed us how to use a how to dig a trench just deep enough for a particular kind of seed, then carefully taught one of the children how to gently plant a row of seeds, cover them, water them, and label that row. In this way, she supervised while the whole family helped plant a huge vegetable garden and each child eagerly awaited signs of growth on their special row. We did not use chemicals like weed killer and pesticides, so we fought off way too many mosquitoes while we weeded the garden.

All summer long, we feasted on garden-fresh vegetables of all kinds as they became available. Leaf lettuce and radishes came up first. Then came asparagus, rhubarb, and scallions. As soon as the carrots, tomatoes, cucumbers, and beans were ready, we practically lived on vegetables at lunch time. Mom served garden leaf lettuce with cream and vinegar almost every summer day, and kept a full dish of sliced cucumbers in the fridge with that same watery dressing.

Dill and basil thrived throughout the season. About a third of our garden's square footage was dedicated to growing strawberries. Each teenager had their own row, and made money selling berries for fifty cents a quart. We must have picked twenty-five quarts a day at the height of the season. Toward the end of the summer, everybody helped harvest sweet corn, beets, cabbage, onions, potatoes, and ground cherries. Squash and melons came last in our very prolific garden.

Our grape vines and currant bushes were somewhat intertwined. Neither produced a lot, but both gave us a few meals' worth each season. We had two plum trees, a crabapple tree, a Jonathan-gold apple tree and a tree with hard red apples. We also picked pears from our aunt's tree.

Coleslaw, cabbage with poppy seed dressing, or shredded carrots with raisins and mayo provided variety for our summer meals. We never heard of okra, and never grew fresh spinach, but other than those, we raised all our own veggies. Us kids thought carrots or acorn squash baked with butter and brown sugar constituted a special treat. The only produce I can remember buying from the grocery store included lemons, limes, iceberg lettuce, celery, and, once a year, a crate of peaches.

At the end of the summer, Mom worked morning, noon and night canning or freezing excess garden produce. Mom liked to set cucumbers into ice water and make them into pickles the same day they were picked. Strawberries were even fussier; she strived to get them in the freezer within a few hours. Mom even used dandelions to make wine.

Although Dad deployed a herbicide called 2, 4-D on some of our fields for a short time (until he heard that a farmer died two days after he spilt some on his leg), our produce was otherwise chemical free, so I think it would be fair to say that our garden was organic. We didn't eat organic just because it was healthy; we ate that way because we didn't have enough income to buy processed food and so we lived off the land. Mom was a terrific cook who could make do with whatever nature provided. When food is perfectly vine-ripened, and immediately processed, it doesn't get any better than that!

My father was an expert at foraging. He taught us to forage in nearby woods for any edible plant we could find, including: blueberries, wild raspberries, huckleberries, hazelnuts, walnuts, and mushrooms. We picked gooseberries (even the prickly kind), for making jam and pie. Dad brought home blueberries from his fishing trips up north.

If fruit, vegetables, or nuts were going to waste within ten miles of home, we went after any and all free food. We even looked for honeysuckle blossoms to enjoy the tiny bit of sweet juice in the tips. It's not that we were starving; Mom and Dad were just extremely frugal, highly experienced in penny pinching, and delighted to be able to live off the land.

Dad recognized poisonous mushrooms from edible ones, and he would go mushroom hunting by himself every spring. In early May, he took us along whenever he went looking for morel mushrooms. Because morels are unmistakably distinctive, he didn't worry that a little kid would pick a poisonous one. Morels and various other

We spent whole Sunday afternoons enjoying the smell of spring, the pretty violets and other spring flowers while foraging for morels.

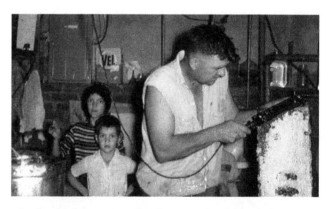

Linda and Art watched as Dad melted the honeycomb edges with a hot knife, centrifuged out the honey by hand-turning a crank on the big barrel containing frames from the beehives, and processed the beeswax in the shiny bucket on the antique wood stove.

wild mushrooms were sizzled in butter and served as a side-dish.

When Dad went hunting or foraging, he often brought back wild roses for Mom, a simple but heart-felt gift. They both loved roses; Dad maintained a sprawling yellow rose bush for the fifty years he lived on the farm, then took a slip and planted it in town when they retired. In later years, his "new" yellow rose bush was nearly ten feet tall!

Every year, we gathered all the black walnuts from a half dozen huge trees on our neighbor's abandoned farm; we spread them on our driveway where cars ran over them until the husks fell off.

One year, we picked gooseberries, hazelnuts and butternuts in the cow pasture in the woods belonging to Dad's friend, Archie Draheim. Anticipating excessive bugs in the deep underbrush, he required everyone to wear long sleeves, long pants and shoes, so we were sweaty before we even started. He figured that if everybody went, we could get the job done faster, with fewer bug bites. We would happily do most anything if we could go swimming afterward. However, it was pretty tough for him to motivate us to go there the following year.

Dad had custom labels printed and we had no trouble selling honey for two dollars a quart or five dollars a gallon.

Dad enjoyed tending beehives in our woods/cow pasture. Our own honey had both a lighter color and a more delicate flavor than the clover honey found in most grocery stores. We sold honey to friends and neighbors. Dad heated honeycombs on the wood stove to make beeswax candles; they smelled just awesome.

Us kids liked honey; in fact, we liked all sweets. By the end of winter, we sometimes used up all the vegetables we had stored during the summer and the meat we had butchered in the fall. If Mom didn't have adequate choices in the freezer, and because money was tight, Mom's go-to meal consisted of white rice with raisins and cinnamon. At the table, we each added our own

1951: Bob, swollen from a bee sting, Pat, Marylu, cousin Phil, Rose Ann

milk and sugar or honey. Eating something that sweet as a main course suited us just fine.

Milk from Bossie filled a three-gallon stainless steel bucket we called "the milk pail." We

1962: Dad milking Bossie one summer morning. In the evening, John or Bob milked the cow.

never pasteurized it; we just put it through a strainer to filter out cow hair and dirt. Right after our cow delivered a calf, she gave too much milk. When that happened, Mom made more hot chocolate, custard, tapioca, rice pudding or rice with cinnamon and raisins. Because Mom could serve these soft foods to babies as well as to adults, excessive milk lightened her workload.

If we still had too much fresh milk, we poured it into a green tank called a "separator," added water, waited an hour for the cream to float, saved the cream and tossed the milk, or fed the milk to the pigs.

We never had too much cream. We served whipped cream in cream puffs or on pie. We substituted "straight cream" for milk on our

1959 Al, holding the 18 mallards Dad brought down with three shots.

1964: Joyce Brown (practically one of the family), and Marylu, holding the catch of the day

1970: Damien, Marty, one valuable mink caught in a trap, and Greg

cereal. With snow, and a lot of elbow grease, we turned any excess cream into hand-churned ice cream. Enjoying all that cream as children, it's no surprise that most of us had "Gerber baby" chunky cheeks!

It's a blessing that Dad liked hunting. Bringing home wild game/fowl was not just sport, it was essential in order to feed such a big family without going broke. Dad hunted with a gun or with a bow and arrows, depending on the season and the prey. Often Dad would ask us kids who wanted to go along hunting. We would drive to a woods, then he would instruct us on how far apart to walk, and whether to stay silent or to make noise. His goal was for us to create a line and nudge the target animal toward where

1985: Bob holding dead chickens and Mom holding a dead mink that killed 118 of our120 chickens in the west henhouse in one night. Dad nailed that mink with his first shot.

AT LEFT: 1959: Linda and Art, target practicing
AT RIGHT: 1966: Dolores and Art with their bows and arrows

Dad would be standing. We hunted mostly deer and foxes in this manner.

Dad maintained an ever-growing collection of Indian arrowheads he had found throughout the county, often combining hunting and arrowhead collecting at the same time. He taught anyone who wanted to learn to shoot, and had a target set up on the front lawn for bow and arrow practice. He also taught several children and cousins how to trap mink, muskrat, and foxes.

Because Dad was such an avid outdoorsman and an expert marksman, Mom often shaped the evening meal around whatever wild meat Dad brought home. Frog legs right out of our slough were sautéed in butter, and were prepared in addition to a main course. Small game got stretched to serve the family; she rolled rabbit or squirrel in flour with salt and pepper, fried it in butter, and then cooked it on top of the stove. For duck, goose, pheasant, pigeon, and squab

1967: Marty, Alice, and Angela, holding pheasants in front of our back door/porch.

1961 dead deer inspection by Art, Janet, Ginny, Helen and Linda

she supplemented the meager amount of meat drippings with butter or bacon grease, Kitchen Bouquet browning sauce, and/or mushrooms. Having lots of gravy made up for the small amount of meat being served.

Mom served venison about twice a month. Because both Mom and Dad were deer hunters, our meat freezer was stocked with venison every fall. Venison and, in later years, elk, were the only two types of wild meat routinely stored in our freezer. Otherwise, we typically ate the rewards of the hunt within a day or two. While some hunters like bagging trophy-size bucks for sport, our family shot mostly does, because the meat is less wild tasting.

If Dad butchered an elk or a deer himself, he marked most of the meat packages as either chops or hamburger. If Dad had done a particularly good job of making sure there was no hair/hide on the meat, he marked that package "A-1."

At our house, A-1 meat meant it was eligible for serving to company. If, instead, Dad took deer or elk to the butcher to process, he came home with chops and burger, and also yummy venison sausage. Everyone in our family liked sausage.

Mom normally did a terrific job cooking wild game. Fried deer chops, and venison roast served with potatoes, onions and carrots taste best when served piping hot before the tallow cools and gets waxy. When one of us girls tried to cook wild meat, it sometimes got "culinarily massacred." Thankfully, that was a rare occasion.

When I was in my early twenties, Art lived with me. One day, he played a little joke on me and roasted a wild critter drenched in marmalade. When I arrived home from work to find dinner already on the table, I complimented him on his creativity. Half way through the meal, when he told me we were eating raccoon, I about gagged. I didn't *dare* risk asking whether the raccoon was road kill; I didn't want to know. (Still don't.)

Sometimes on weekends, Dad took an overnight hunting trip. When Dad went hunting or fishing, it was Mom's opportunity to serve "kid food" for us and prepare a separate meal for the hunters. Mom packed a half dozen sandwiches in Dad's wooden lunch box. We bought sandwich meats for fall hunting trips (ordinarily considered too expensive). Dad liked summer sausage and cheddar cheese; Mom preferred Braunschweiger with no cheese. No chips, in case hunters needed to stay quiet. Although Dad wasn't partial to cookies, he always appreciated something sweet; for hunting he liked to take along raisin-filled cookies or oatmeal cookies with raisins, and of course, his stainless-steel thermos filled with coffee, cream and sugar.

Whenever Dad was gone, Mom got a chance to have the foods she liked best (vegetables in a white sauce, nutmeg instead of cinnamon in apple pie, Roquefort cheese, cottage cheese and peaches, Mulligan-style stews and most any

Hamburger Pie: a favorite "kid-pleaser"

kind of salad, especially three-bean salad) and us kids got to have foods Dad didn't like:

- "hamburger pie" (mashed potatoes over green beans over sloppy joe meat/sauce,

- chow mein,

- tuna/hard-boiled egg broiled on toast,

- tuna hot dish,

- what our family called "regular hot dish" (macaroni with hamburger and home-grown tomato sauce),

- anything with mayonnaise

- anything with macaroni or spaghetti noodles

1971: Mom holding a walleye she caught up north on one of my parents' many fishing vacations.

- summer salad with seashell macaroni, mayo, diced ham, celery, cheese, and raw tomato,

- and chocolate cake.

When Dad went hunting, my favorite treats were hamburger pie or macaroni with milk, salt and pepper, with or without cheese. Typical of his German upbringing, Dad did not like foods mixed together. He particularly disliked it if we stirred our cake and ice cream together. While he was away, I have fond memories of stirring dense, moist, Devil's Food chocolate cake to-gether with whipped cream; it was as intense as eating fudge.

I could include more of my parents' gazillion hunting stories and photos, but I'll leave it to the hunters in the family to author our parents' sub-stantial legacy on that score!

Arguably, our family loved catching fish and eating fish even more than we liked hunting. When Dad wanted to spend some time alone, he took off to go fishing. When Dad wanted to enjoy vacation time with Mom, or with his pals, he went fishing. When Dad wanted to have fun with a bunch of us kids, he took us fishing.

Dad honed his fishing skill by reading and practicing. He had a subscription to both

1961: Dad showing off the buck he shot with his bow and arrow. Note our clothes line filled with diapers, and our bike rack next to the white fence.

Dad with his good buddy, Erv Sanders, walleye fishing up north in 1975

Outdoor Life and Sports Afield, and enjoyed telling us stories of other people's fishing success. Herter's showroom was in our home town, and each year they sent out a huge catalog. Long before Cabela's hunting and fishing stores came into existence, Dad spent hours reviewing Herter's catalog and perusing their showroom to check out the latest and greatest tackle. Occasionally he carved his own fishing lures, but usually he bought them.

Dad made good use of his little fishing boat with its ten-horsepower motor; when we arrived at Reeds Lake, Dad went directly to his fishing boat to attempt to bring back sunfish and or crappies (or possibly a northern pike) for supper.

He usually took a few enthusiastic young fishermen with him. The rest of us used the remaining cane poles and bobbers to fish off the dock, using worms from our garden as bait. We fished sunfish and crappies off the dock at least once a week all summer long.

Every other year or so, Dad went up north to seine smelt; he came home with several five-gallon buckets filled with loads of this itsy-bitsy fish. Mom fried them in butter until they were super-crispy so we could eat the whole thing, bones and all. Yum!

In the winter, Dad towed his ice house (which he called his "dark house") out on the frozen lake

1960: Diane accompanied Dad spearing when the Crane Creek watershed flooded.

1966: Time for cleaning fish on Dad's fish cleaning station on Reeds Lake: Dolores, Helen, Virginia, Marty

to go spearing. His dark house contained a tiny little wood stove, a stool, a minnow bucket and a tackle box. He used a special long-handled "ice chisel" to chop a twenty by twenty-inch hole through at least a foot of ice, strained the ice chips out so he could see better, then waited anxiously inside the dark house, holding his spear over the hole waiting for a good-size walleye or northern pike to come through. Because the fish house had only enough room for two people, it was a

In 1965, I had the privilege of watching Dad spear a big northern

rare treat for any of us to join Dad to watch him spearing.

A few times a year, Dad and his pals drove up to northern Minnesota (or into Canada) to fish Walleye and Northern pike. He almost always brought back a cooler of fish and a boatload of fun stories. He put enough fish in the freezer to last a month or two 'til his next trip. He often took men and boys up north but insisted that the wilderness was "no place for girls." I vehemently disagreed! I

1959: Linda and Marylu with the catch of the day, probably walleyes.

1966: Pan fish, including sunnies, crappies, and trout, became the main course at least once a week in the summer if Dad wasn't too terribly busy. Art, Lor and Angi

felt jealous. Why should boys (and not girls) get vacation trips?

It took me until 1979 to convince Dad to take girls on a fishing trip. Dad and my eldest brother, Al, took me, three of my sisters and two of my nieces fishing for a few days. We drove fourteen hours to the English River in Canada, and camped on an island to stay safe from bears. The day of our arrival, we caught our limit of fish in less than one hour in the late afternoon. The next

1970: Dad and his cousin, Lawrence Clemons, holding a northern. In the background, you can see the granary, the double corn crib, a tip of the hog house, and the barn.

morning, Dad awakened us at dawn (*his* idea of the best part of any fishing day). Having learned that we could so easily catch our limit of fish in the afternoon, we saw no reason whatsoever to get up at the crack of dawn while on vacation. Our primary vacation goal was to get a tan, and only secondarily, to catch fish.

Stumped as to how to convince us, Dad spent that morning fishing without girls. By the time he came back a few hours later, us girls were busy shampooing our hair in the same pristine lake in which he'd been fishing. Seeing bubbles, Dad nearly had heart failure. Concerned about how many fish the soap had killed, he vowed never again to take girls up north.

That afternoon, he tried hard to get us to use the "right" lure from his tackle box based on the weather, the depth of the water, the time of day, the type of fish, etc. We paid no attention whatsoever to his expert fishing advice. We chose flashy lures from his tackle box as if we were selecting jewelry, and still caught fish like they were going out of style. My niece Becca was about eight years old, and she caught a walleye so big that Dad thought she had snagged her lure on a log! We continued to have success regardless of which bait we used and what time of day we fished. Much to his chagrin, Dad had to admit we caught more fish than ever before. On the way home from that trip, us girls bought T-shirts that read: "Anything boys can do, girls can do better."

One of the dilemmas of a big family is keeping things relatively fair with limited

Dad shot this photo of me in Canada on the girls' fishing trip, holding the two biggest fish I had ever caught. Later he wrote on it, "Should we be looking at the fish?! 1979

resources. The children are hyper-vigilant to noticing who got more of Mom and Dad's attention, who got more clothes, shoes, toys, food, especially dessert, or more this, that, or the other thing. They keep track of who got certain privileges at what age, and they sometimes pre-maturely insist they are ready for the next step in the process of "adulting."

Introverts in the family would crave their own bedroom and alone time to enjoy their hobbies. Extroverts would want to join teams spend time with friends. Some of the children would register differences in Mom and Dad's treatment of them as simply unfair, others would take it more personal. As immature children, we would sometimes generalize and complain we "always" get the short end of the stick.

Dad took so many fishing trips with Mom, with my brothers, with my brothers-in-law, with his pals, and/or with his brothers that writing about Dad's fishing trips would fill an entire book. As with hunting, I'll leave it to the

fishermen in the family to tell those tales. Mom and Dad are shown here in 1967 with northerns caught in Reeds Lake.

After swimming, fishing, and going bare-foot all summer, when it came time to go back to school, inevitably our feet had spread out and we had outgrown last year's school shoes. Whenever possible, we picked out a pair of everyday shoes from our huge cardboard "shoe box" of hand-me-down shoes.

The week before school started, Mom lined us up to see who needed Sunday shoes, and who needed school shoes. Mom wrote down who needed which shoes, and took a few kids at a time to the second-hand store to try on shoes. Anybody still needing shoes after that shopping trip went with Mom to one of two local shoe stores. There was usually only one salesman on

duty to serve about ten of us. He measured us, one at a time, and brought out shoes as fast as he could go. We tried them on for fit, not style. We were not allowed to be fussy. If the shoe fit, and was sturdy, Mom bought it.

Mom usually purchased all the Sunday shoes, school shoes, and boots we needed in one thirty or sixty-minute shopping spree. I remember one particular year when that meant she needed to buy fifteen pairs of shoes, and we drove a half hour to Mankato, MN to shop. Many years later, I happened to meet the shoe salesman who had waited on her that day. It was his first day on the job. He went home that night ecstatic with his first day's commission for those fifteen pairs of shoes.

I don't remember any of my siblings ever going clothes shopping with Mom anywhere but the second-hand store. In a pinch, Mom ordered something from the Montgomery Ward's catalog. The younger half of our family almost never shopped for clothing at all; we used hand-me-downs and sewed our own clothes.

Mom taught us to sew in a similar fashion as she had taught us to cook. She was expecting company one afternoon and saw that a few of our dolls had no clothes. "Put some clothes on the dolls," she told me.

"I can't find any."

"Then get out that box of scrap fabric over there in the corner, and make some."

"How do I do that?"

"Just take a piece of fabric and wrap it around."

"OK."

"Now cut a hole for each arm."

"Then what?"

"Take a needle and thread, and sew it together so it stays on. Here, I'll help you."

I quickly learned to sew before I learned to read. I started my sewing lessons on doll clothes, followed not long after by learning to make stuffed toys. Sewing became my first, and my favorite, hobby. As soon as I could, I graduated from doll dresses to sewing clothes. Once I could read, Mom taught me how to study a pattern and follow it. My sisters and I were inspired to sew pretty dresses after watching Kathleen get elected Homecoming Queen when I was in second grade.

Kathleen wore a hot-pink satin gown with a tight waist and a gathered skirt. Her bouffant up-do showed off her sparkly tiara. I attended the parade where she sat next to Mr. Handsome himself on the roof of a flashy new convertible. Not long after that, when she played the lead role in the school's class play, she even kissed that same Mr. Handsome on stage!

At that time, the only Disney princess I'd ever heard of was Cinderella, and I was certain my sister was *way* prettier. I beamed with pride as my girlfriends oo'd and ah'd as they watched the king and queen, and snickered when she kissed that boy. After watching Queen Kathleen in her hot pink princess outfit, I asked Mom to cut off my waist-length braids so I could curl and tease my hair. My sisters and I wanted to wear beautiful dresses and grow up to be as pretty as our *royal* sister.

Although Mom did a lot of mending, she lacked time to do much sewing. The last time I remember Mom making dresses for us was when I was in first grade. That summer Mom sewed eight sleeveless gray V-neck jumpers for us girls, and bought each of us girls a new type of blouse (called a knit turtleneck) to wear under them. Getting brand new clothing was almost a foreign concept. We were super excited with our new jumpers, and our very first turtleneck tops.

Mom embroidered under the V-neck on each jumper to match the new turtlenecks, using kelly green on mine. When I was in second grade, I outgrew my favorite jumper, and grew into the blue jumper. In third grade, when I was too big for the blue-trimmed jumper, the one with the red V fit just right. You'll never guess what happened in fourth, fifth, sixth, seventh and eighth grades... more gray jumpers!

At our house, if you wanted to wear something pretty, you had better get busy sewing! I hand-made any clothes Mom would let me try. My teenage sisters asked for bold-print "tent dresses," a new style that became trendy in the sixties. Mom usually requested "house dresses," any dress that buttons up the front so she could nurse a baby. One day, Mom told me she wanted a "maternity dress." I had never heard the word maternity; I just assumed a maternity dress was

1962: Homecoming Queen Kathleen

a new style, something like a tent dress. I went to the fabric store and asked the clerk to help me find a pattern for a maternity dress for Mom.

"Is she pregnant?" asked the clerk.

"What does that mean?" I asked.

"Is your mother expecting a baby?"

"Not that I know of."

"Is the maternity dress for your mother?"

"Yes."

At that point, the clerk must have understood that I had absolutely no idea that Mom was pregnant. She simply helped me find a pattern and fabric for my new project, no doubt snickering to herself. I cheerfully made a maternity dress for Mom without ever realizing we were about to welcome another sibling.

Not long after that, my eldest brother's wife came to visit. I commented to Mom that my sister-in-law was getting fat, so maybe I should make her a maternity dress, too, still thinking that *maternity* was a new style. My mother informed me that she wasn't fat, she was "expecting..." And that is when and how I learned that babies did not get dropped off by the stork.

Because I liked to sew, Mom help me re-cover her mother's quilts which were hand-made from scraps of men's wool suits and coats. These quilts were toasty warm, and extremely worn. I used scrap fabric of every color and texture to create new tops for some of those old quilts. We fastened the quilt tops to a rustic quilting frame made of two-by-fours, and tied the quilts with yarn.

In subsequent years, Mom taught most of us girls tougher skills like how to embroider hankies and how to make French knots, how to knit and how to pearl, and how to crochet a scarf, giving us the opportunity to see if we liked any of these options. While my sisters chose various crafts, I always returned to sewing.

Mom happily taught all of us whatever she had learned. Each of us built on that foundation. One of the many wonderful things about having such a big family is that at least one sibling mastered a certain skill or developed a passion for almost any topic and shared some of that knowledge with the rest of us. We learned a lot from each other, still do, and always will.

We usually wore hand-me-downs, or something from the second-hand store. We knew three generations' worth of most of the other parishioners (at least by their last names) and they knew us, so we were sometimes gifted clothing from people in our community. Mom also sorted through Catholic Charities donations and brought some home from there. The rest of our clothes were hand-made. In my teenage years, I got excused from chicken chores and cleaning barns by sewing day and night.

I had just finished making new dresses for two of the teenage girls when both dresses turn up with a four-inch tear. I was furious, and blamed it on my sister, assuming she did this out of jealousy. It couldn't be proved so nobody got punished, and I mended both by making them into V neck dresses. In my fifties when I

By the time I was in eighth grade, I sewed a lot of our clothes, including all but two of the dresses that are visible on this family photo taken on Fathers' Day in 1968 at my eldest brother's farm.

witnessed my special need's brother trying to fit into my clothes because he was fascinated by cross-dressing, the mystery of the torn dresses was finally solved. I had been dead wrong.

Somewhere in those early years, I quit leaning on Mom as a sewing teacher and started teaching myself. We were required to wear skirts to school, and dirndl skirts were popular. My parents had friends whose only daughter was heavy-set. The mother kept buying her daughter dirndl skirts that the daughter either didn't like or quickly outgrew, and barely-worn dirndl skirts often ended up in our scrap-fabric box. All I had to do was cut off the waist band to get about three yards of like-new fabric, enough to use for a dress, a skirt or anything I wanted!

For my high school graduation, I found a full-length dress at J.C. Penney's that cost eighteen dollars, and I really wanted to buy it. Mom said it was too expensive for her to buy, but she agreed to pay half, and that made me feel very special. It was my very first store-bought dress that I got to pick out for myself.

CHAPTER 7:

For the Love of Food

IN THE FIFTIES and early sixties, my parents served simple, interesting, cheap, healthy food that was quick to make: homegrown vine-ripened fruits and vegetables, farm-raised meat, local fish and wild game. Mom once told me she cooked to feed us and she baked to brighten everyone's spirits. It worked! Her specialties included:

1. Crusty fresh bread,

2. Perfectly sticky caramel nut rolls,

3. Poppy-seed Kolackies,

4. Flaky pie crusts,

5. Apple pie with just the right amount of juiciness in the fruit,

6. The world's best fried spring chicken,

7. Intensely flavored, no-lump gravy,

8. The fluffiest angel food cake,

9. Wonderfully moist turkey with crusty, flavorful plum dressing,

10. Yummy dense chocolate cake from scratch,

11. Lightly seasoned potato salad, and

12. Spooky Pops (brittle caramel with Jack-o-Lantern faces)

Mom became an expert at creating camaraderie within our family by turning relatively simple meals into social occasions. Likewise, she created community by using good food as the centerpiece of social occasions. Relatives, friends, and perfect strangers who originally came to our home to enjoy Mom's cooking and baking found themselves staying for friendship. Once our family established a relationship, those same people came back to our house *first* for friendship, and *secondly* to enjoy good food.

What made Mom's meals so special that we still long to eat at her table?

- simple recipes
    - anything and everything could be made by a ten-year-old
    - non-complex food left us satisfied but not bloated
- interesting meals
    - the joy of anticipating favorite tried and true family meal menus
    - variety together with the ritual of traditional menus made up for an absence of restaurant dining
- serving great meals while penny-pinching by
    - baking cakes and pies, etc. from scratch,
    - avoiding ready-made food
    - serving steak or lobster only for special occasions, otherwise

For our mother, (always wearing a dress and an apron) preparing food was never a chore; instead, it gave her an opportunity to enjoy and share the benefits of some of her favorite hobbies (gardening, hunting and fishing). She radiated sheer joy whenever she was cooking and baking. It would not be a stretch to say that Mom's apron strings bound our family together.

- serving home-grown meat, or buying the cheap cuts of meats.
    - healthy, mostly organic, food

- vine-ripened fruit and vegetables from her garden
- canning and freezing homegrown food for the winter
  - her ability to prepare meals super-fast
    - salad, meat, vegetables, and dessert miraculously appear all at the same time
    - while she simultaneously juggled half a dozen youngsters under the age of seven

Honestly, I don't remember ever seeing Mom use a recipe. I'm #13 in the line-up, so by the time I can remember, she had memorized her favorite recipes and cooked most everything by heart. Us kids would get particularly hungry for something (usually to satisfy an insatiable sweet tooth), and ask Mom how to make it. She first referred us to the kitchen

recipe drawer where she kept a Waseca County Cookbook, a Better Homes and Garden cookbook, index cards, newspaper clippings, and scratch paper snippets collected from friends. By the time I was interested in cooking, all the paper in that drawer was, like the "Velveteen Rabbit," severely tattered from having been so well-loved.

Mom's first love was children; she gladly taught most anything to whoever wanted to learn. I don't remember her instructing us on how to care for a baby; I think that lesson got absorbed through osmosis. Mom kept babies safe from inclement weather and took everything else in stride. She usually put the babies on a schedule. At our house, babies slept through lots of noise. Mom pasteurized baby milk for the first several months of bottle feeding. After that, raw cow's milk like the rest of us drank. For sure we all came in contact with germs. Mom didn't find it unusual when a baby developed diaper rash or a cold or a fever; it was all normal, old hat so to speak.

She spent most of her time in the kitchen which was bookended by the laundry and the baby room. In between cooking, taking care of babies, and doing laundry, Mom taught us how to read, how to write perfect Palmer script, how to change a diaper, bandage a wound, comfort a sick child, play violin, dance an Irish jig, and perfect our cooking and baking skills. Mom shared her passion for growing flowers and vegetables, riding horse, knitting, crocheting, and embroidering, etc., etc., etc., according to each child's natural inclination, all the while adapting each lesson to accommodate widely varying abilities.

To teach us girls how to bake, Mom had us get out a blank index card, and gave one instruction at a time so we could both follow the instruction and also write down the recipe that she knew by heart, thereby creating a new "recipe card."

"Turn the oven on ___ degrees," she'd say.

"OK, what next?" I responded.

"Did you write that down?"

"Not yet, but I will."

"Fine, now get out the mixing bowl and a rubber scraper.

"Then what?"

"Check and see if we have any chocolate chips."

"I already did. We have a whole package."

"Good. Start by putting in a half a cup of butter and a half a cup of lard," she'd say, as she continued to nurse the baby, sort laundry, or scrub the floor... Before or after we added ingredients for baking something delicious that we loved, we wrote each one down, and ended up with the ability to bake that recipe by ourselves the next time.

[I wrote Mom's bread recipe on an index card before baking my first batch. Based on the handwriting, I was probably in third grade.]

I have tons of memories working with Mom in the kitchen, including when she showed me how to knead bread, and how to pinch the crust on pie dough. My favorite memories are of making rolls, pies, cakes, cookies and "bars"

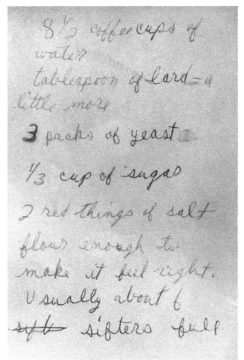

Mom used the loaf pan above starting in the forties, and the one on the right starting in the fifties, (if you look closely, you will see a "22" stamped into that pan.) This pan is part of the museum exhibit in Waseca.

(square-cut cookies) for the hundreds of people who came to celebrate every possible occasion.

Mom taught me and my sisters to cook and to bake, and coached us on the joy of entertaining. We often baked eight or ten batches of cookies or bars in preparation for a family get-together. Each of us gained a reputation for baking something we particularly liked, for example, Ginny was an expert at baking seven-layer bars. Linda specialized in Danish pastry.

If I had to pick Mom's most-used everyday recipe, hands down it would be her bread recipe. Every other day, our family made bread in a bowl we called "the bread pan." When I was young, our bread pan had a base that kept it stable. It was probably tin or some pre-WWII metal alloy that eventually wore out from overuse; Mom replaced it with a two-gallon stainless steel bowl.

Mom's bread recipe called for about nine cups of water and three packets of dry yeast, resulting in ten loaves of bread. We used Dad's big coffee cup as a measuring cup, and it holds about a cup and a third. No need for such precision on this recipe!

Mom said, "Start with yeast and sugar in warm water. Let it set a few minutes, then add a long handled big serving spoon of lard."

"Ok"

"Add two red scoops of salt."

"Ok"

"Mix in flour until you can pick up the dough."

"Ok"

"Put a dish towel over it and set it on top of the warm oven for a few minutes."

"How many minutes should I set the timer for?"

"Ten."

"Let me show you how to knead it."

"Ok"

Greg and Dad carving a whole hog on a piece of plywood for one of our annual graduation parties. See the "new" bread pan in the lower left hand corner.

"Don't add too much flour when you are kneading it. When the strands no longer break when you stretch it while kneading it, it's ready to put back in the bowl. Let it rise until it is bigger than the bowl."

"It doubled in size."

"Good, punch it down and let it rise again."

"Ok"

"Grease nine pans with lard. Be sure to tuck the ends under on each loaf."

Whenever we could talk Mom into frying some of the bread dough in pure lard, she made enough dough for ten loaves. She rolled chunks of piping-hot fried bread in sugar and served it with jelly as an after-school snack. Mom warned us that if we ate too much fresh bread while it's still hot, the dough would goo up like bubble gum in our stomachs, and make us very sick. This thought slowed us down a tad, but it certainly didn't stop us from wanting to eat fried bread until it was completely gone.

When the bread loaves turned golden brown, we took them out, immediately buttered the tops, ran a table knife around the edge of each pan, dumped the loaves on the big bread board (a three-feet by three-feet sheet of plywood) and cooled them.

Until she left for college, Patty baked most of the bread, then Janet took over the bread baking. In later years, the bread-baking job skipped over me and landed with Lor, and later, Alice, both of whom always made excellent bread, and still do.

In addition to our frozen food, Dad had lined the new part with floor-to-ceiling canning shelves which Mom filled to the brim. Every year, Mom canned hundreds of quarts of apples, plums, peaches or pears in a light syrup, and filled the canning shelves with 750-800 quarts of pickles, tomatoes, sauce, jam and jellies. Keeping track of what us kids liked to eat, and making sure that she canned enough of it, was Mom's idea of fun.

As I transcribed Mom's well-worn, batter-spattered recipe cards, I attempted to give credit based on the author's handwriting, and copy them *as is*; including youthful spelling,

Top: We loved cherries; thankfully, that year we could afford to buy a whole crate for canning.
Left: Because dill pickles were a family favorite, every year Mom would can about a hundred quarts. I preferred baby dills, but she could can faster using big cucumbers. Mom liked bread and butter pickles; she soaked them in three-gallon batches in a crock jar. She also canned watermelon pickles, beet pickles and some sweet pickles, but these weren't as popular.

like *Cholate* instead of *Chocolate*, *resipe* for recipe. These mistakes endear me all the more to whomever wrote a particular card. I, and many of my siblings, used to beg Mom to make our favorite cookies, candy, bars, cakes, pies, and other desserts. Over half the recipes in Mom's collection have sugar as their primary ingredient. Knowing children documented most of them, that makes perfect sense.

At our house eating in haste was called "*scarfing it down.*" After I left home, I was introduced to a before-meals prayer that fit our household perfectly: "Father, Son, and Holy Ghost, whoever eats the fastest gets the most. Amen." When we got to college and had access to unlimited cafeteria food, most of us put on our "Freshman 15" (extra pounds), but very few of us have problems with obesity. We grew up eating healthy, and returned to those patterns when we started cooking for ourselves.

One day when I was about a year old, Mom held a baby in her arms while she cooked sweet corn in a twenty-three-quart pressure canner to save time. She started to open the lid without realizing it was pressurized. Suddenly, the steam "blew." She quickly shielded the baby, but Mom's chest got badly scalded. From then on, Mom rarely used that canner, and she preferred to can only after all the babies, and most of her kids, were asleep.

How many jars of jam and jelly Mom put up through the years might well compete for inclusion in the Guinness book of world records, or in some Sure-jel hall of fame. Whatever strawberries we hadn't sold for fifty cents a quart became jam or jelly. She also took advantage of apples for apple butter and used grapes, strawberry-rhubarb, raspberries, black raspberries and currants for jams and jellies. After us kids were sleeping, she used every odd-shaped little jar she could find, poured in the jam or jelly, ladled melted paraffin on the top to seal each one (cheaper than buying new lids or sealing rings), and then stored them on canning shelves in the so-called new part.

FEB • 62

In 1962, the living room transitioned to our dining/ sewing/ baby room. This picture says it all! Clockwise around the dining table starting from the far left stands the china cupboard, the sewing machine, a lamp on top of a small dresser filled with diapers as well as sewing stuff, Mom's Christmas cactus in front of the picture window, the piano in the upper right corner, and the baby crib with a tiger pajama bag.

For use in cooking what we called Spanish Rice, hamburger pie, hot-dish (aka goulash) and homemade tomato soup, Mom canned a couple hundred quarts of tomato sauce per year, crushing batch after batch through the Foley food mill to strain out peelings and seeds.

Mom and Dad bought their first freezer in the fifties, and by the time I can remember, they had three freezers. The chest freezer held wild game from Dad's hunting excursions, and pork from our farm. The tall, upright, freezer stored about a hundred quarts of garden vegetables, plus a hundred quarts of factory raised peas and sweet corn, and the older freezer stored home-grown strawberries and raspberries, ice cream, cookies, and everything else.

When I was young, Mom froze blanched veggies in two-quart red and white milk cartons. Mom didn't write anything on those cartons. If I was asked to run down to the freezer and bring up a vegetable for supper, I would grab a milk carton from the veggie freezer. It was anybody's guess whether the carton contained beans, peas, or corn, but it didn't really matter which it was. By the early seventies, finally, we could afford to buy freezer bags and brand new white cardboard canning cartons with labels for identifying contents. Mom's frozen vegetables tasted a hundred times better than the canned

vegetables served at school. No wonder so many of my schoolmates hated vegetables.

Sometimes our family's hunters shot two deer or an elk in early December and we ran out of freezer space. Since Minnesota winters are so cold, Dad was able to use the outdoor temperature to his advantage by storing meat outdoors in our winter freezer, just as he had always done before they acquired an electric freezer.

EF Johnson manufactured two-way radios in our small town, and we owned one of the earliest models. Dad used it to keep in touch with Mom when he was out in the field. One day he radioed her to "Go out to the corncrib and get a steak." Not knowing our family had a makeshift winter freezer, our neighbors listening in on that two-way radio conversation thought we were either speaking in code, or just, as we used to say, *plum nuts*.

Finding places to store things was a constant challenge. For example, we stocked up on toilet paper fifty to a hundred rolls at a time. We could fit about six rolls of t.p. in the cubby hole under the end of the bath tub. We stored another five rolls in a toilet paper holder in the downstairs bath. We crammed the rest of it in the top shelf of linen closet upstairs, or tucked some in the back of Rose Ann's clothes closet.

We bought one hundred pounds of sugar at a time and dumped it into a big, tiltable "sugar bin" under the kitchen counter. Our kitchen cupboards included a pull-out bin about 30 inches tall and 24 inches wide just for sugar. Having that large of a sugar bin seemed *totally normal* to us.

Because we needed a second bin to store fifty pounds of flour at time, Dad lined an ordinary ten-inch-deep kitchen drawer with tin. Our family still called this old-fashioned drawer "the flour bin." In those days, flour did not last long at our house nor did it keep well. We generally inspected it for tiny bugs before we used it. *"Fifty pounds of flour would last us for two weeks as I would bake ten loaves of bread every two days."* Underneath the flour bin sat "the bread drawer." Our bread drawer held about eight loaves of homemade bread.

Above and beyond our garden's produce, Dad bought food in bulk when it made financial sense to do so, and of course we needed a place to store it. Dad drove the pick-up to a farm in Hollandale, MN (an hour away) to buy root vegetables to last us through the coldest winter months. Just before the first hard frost, Dad bought Idaho Russet potatoes a thousand pounds at a time, ten 100-pound burlap gunny sacks for three dollars each. He also bought

a hundred pounds of carrots and a hundred pounds of onions, all of which needed cool, dark and dry storage so they would last a few months. We layered the carrots and onions with newspaper into a crock jar three feet in diameter, and three feet high, stored it in the basement alongside of the gunny sacks of potatoes, and covered all of them in blankets.

Dad built shelving along one wall of the new part of the basement to store as many as a thousand quarts of home-canned goods. He installed four-foot-high vintage bookcases there as a pantry, storing cans of soup, jars of mayonnaise, ketchup, mustard, and salad dressing, a few of the items we bought in cases from the warehouse. Other store-bought staples were stacked on the floor next to the canned goods.

The basement stored root vegetables as well as canned and frozen food, but was too damp to store paper goods and dry food. It was a constant challenge to know where to find enough square inches of unused space to store them. We stored one three-feet by three-feet case of Wheaties, and another of Cheerios, on the landing of the staircase leading to our second floor.

Another example is paper plates; we bought paper plates five hundred at a time, and stuffed them into the broom closet, which of course housed a dust mop, a wet mop and a bucket, but also stored the bread pan, empty plastic and paper bags, and Mom's stash of rainy day activity stuff. Every nook and cranny got filled!

Mom hung a green and white cloth sack in the broom closet for storing extra plastic bags used to wrap homemade bread. She called it her "rainy day bag." That's where she hid new coloring books, crayons, colored pencils, Cracker Jacks, and other surprises in case she was having a tough time keeping us occupied indoors whenever it rained all day.

We had to get creative to find new places to tuck things, but once we found a place, we kept that item in the same spot. For example, our family used two diner-style stainless steel napkin holders at every meal. Because she had to drive a half hour to Mankato to buy them, Mom bought tall-fold napkins 10,000 at a time, and for all the years I can remember, they were squeezed into the little closet in our front entryway, right underneath our Sunday coats which were all on wire hangers, jammed together in a relatively tiny space.

Because Mom canned, and cooked every possible thing from scratch, and because Dad hunted and fished so much, most of our grocery shopping involved bulk purchases of staples. In

When I was a toddler, Dad brought home this load of groceries in the old pick-up truck, shocked at how few groceries he got for $150.

the mid-sixties, our family tried catalog grocery shopping a few times. We mailed in our order; a semi-trailer would pull up to our back door without an appointment to unload case after case of groceries. Catalog shopping worked out only so-so. Invariably, the supplier would be out of something important, and Dad ended up driving forty-five minutes to the "Faribault Warehouse" anyway. Dad always used cash, never credit cards. Because Dad was the only one who knew what he could afford, he was the one who placed the order for bulk food from "the grocery truck."

At the warehouse, we stocked up on cases of soups, a carton of Wheaties (a dozen or more family-sized boxes), a carton of Cheerios, a quarter of beef, cases of fruit cocktail, of sliced peaches and/or pears (after sky-rocketing sugar prices made canning fruit less affordable), a carton of Hershey's, Babe Ruths, and other candy bars that came 24 to a box, and sometimes a case of baby food. We never bought single serving packages at the warehouse. We also never bought snacks like chips or cookies in bulk; they would have been inhaled within a week!

Here's a page out of the grocery catalog ordering two 50-pound bags of flour and one 25-pound bag of brown sugar.

rendered into lard. Because Wolf's employees knew "the Miller kids," they didn't ask for payment when we shopped; the clerk simply wrote down the amount, and Wolf's got paid when Dad wrote out checks at the end of the month.

In between warehouse trips, Mom shopped at the local grocery store, Wolf's. There was always a teenager available to babysit, so Mom almost never took kids along grocery shopping. Even when we did get the chance to go with her, children did not get to choose which foods to buy. In fact, I don't remember ever even asking for grocery store items. We were well trained to save money by buying only the things we neither grew nor bought by the case: hot cereal, rice, oil, hot dogs, chips, celery, olives, condiments, and specific types of candy bars.

Mom preferred Wolf's because the butcher donated any excess fat tidbits, which Mom

We seldom bought vegetables because we grew our own or harvested locally grown veggies. Whenever the local Birds Eye factory harvested a field of peas or sweet corn, we'd drive there at sundown on picking day (or the morning after) to gather whatever fell off the truck. We had such fun shucking fresh peas: one handful to eat, then one handful to freeze, YUMMY! Sometimes Birds Eye let us pick up freshly-picked corn on the cob from the pile outdoors at the factory; when that happened, we got busy canning in a hurry!

As a farm family, we ate good food, and plenty of it. We ate our own farm-raised pork and chicken. A couple of times, Dad bartered with a neighbor (half a side of beef for pork). Otherwise, we bought the cheapest cuts: hamburger for meatloaf, or a two-pound chuck roast from the local grocery store. Once in a while we had Polish sausage on sauerkraut. Because we lived in Minnesota, the land of lakes, and knew how to fish, we wouldn't even *think* of buying fresh or frozen fish. Why spend hard-earned pennies on anything we didn't *need* to buy?

Occasionally we churned our own butter, but we preferred to use up the cream and buy butter. When the health craze started in the 60's, we tried adding the red dye to oleo; yuck! After that, we tried margarine to save money; nobody at our house could stand the taste; shortly thereafter, we returned to butter. Ours was the only household I know of where it was acceptable to eat butter with a knife or a spoon, or devour half a stick on a couple pieces of toast...

For most of my childhood we had a cow that provided about two and a half gallons of milk twice per day and our family had no trouble using up that amount. When Bossie dried up, the "dairy man" came to the farm twice a week. Each time, he delivered [only] five gallons of milk, ten pounds of butter, five quarts of vanilla ice cream (more if we were expecting company) and two cartons of half & half. That also seemed so very normal to us.

Every morning, Mom got up at the crack of dawn, made coffee, nursed the baby, spoon-fed Pablum (pre-cooked, dried rice flake mush) to the next older child, and set the table for breakfast, all before Dad awakened us. A few years ago, I asked Rose Ann if she could remember what Mom served for breakfast.

"Cereal, toast," she said with no hesitation whatsoever.

"Anything else?" I asked.

"Nope."

I'd have to agree with her recollection. In winter, or whenever our sole cow didn't give enough milk, Mom cooked hot cereal. For a treat, she added raisins or prunes to oatmeal. We also liked Malt-o-meal with brown sugar and butter. Cocoa Wheats were an infrequent luxury (chocolate was not considered as healthy). The rest of the year, Mom put out Wheaties (Dad's favorite), Cheerios, Corn Flakes, and either Rice Krispies or Shredded Wheat. Kix and Raisin Bran were special treats; sugarcoated cereals were considered unhealthy as well as out of our price range.

On school days, us kids were always in a big hurry. Before school, we had to feed three

Twelve of us boarded a 72-passenger school bus every morning. If one person wasn't ready, my siblings walked out one at a time, slowly. If Maynard, the driver, could see a kid coming down the driveway, he was required to wait. If we had to, we could stretch out Maynard's stop at our house by an extra six, eight, or maybe even ten minutes!

thousand chickens, a couple hundred pigs, lots of rabbits, several cats, two horses, one cow and assorted other pets. Then we raced to wash up, change into our school clothes, and sit down for breakfast. My friend asked me one day how Mom kept track of who had eaten. Simple. Every person had to be seated at the breakfast table before anyone was allowed to eat. That rule kept sleepy heads on their toes lest they face the wrath of the hungry ones.

We ate breakfast without much socializing, except to answer Mom's questions on whether we remembered homework and sheet music for our lessons, whether we had our hats and mittens, etc., etc. While we were eating, Mom braided three or four girls' long hair, one after the other. She didn't like hair in girls' eyes, and she could make perfectly tight French braids really, really quickly. The rest of the girls either wore short hair, pigtails or ponytails. For picture day at school we talked her into rolling our hair with strips of an old sheet. "Rag curls" made perfect ringlets.

After feeding chickens and pigs, we had no time for frying eggs on school days, so after one bowl of cereal each, we filled up on toast. We reserved the smaller of our two electric ovens exclusively for broiling toast, eight slices at a time. John did the best job; he almost never burned the toast. Whoever slept in the northwest bedroom waited by the little window to alert the rest of us when the orange school bus crested our neighbor's hill. Typically, one person kept making toast right up to the bus's arrival.

During the summer, we ate a full farmer's breakfast: cereal, eggs, and toast, so that we'd have enough energy for pulling weeds, bailing hay, or whatever else. We had a neighbor who had even less money than we did. Pretty much every day for two summers, three boys and a girl showed up at our house for breakfast and/or lunch. They liked their eggs scrambled, and covered with ketchup. Ketchup on eggs was a brand-new concept to us. Mom was not a fan of ketchup for breakfast, and didn't want her children to follow their lead, so one day she tried avoiding the subject by making pancakes. Guess

1963: Family photo including David Ostendorf (who lived with us at that time), and our neighbor's four children who often joined us for meals.

Fourteen of fifteen Miller kids in front of our home in 1958 after Ramona left for college. We shared six one-speed bikes and two trikes. I am riding the rocking horse, third from the left.

what? They liked ketchup on pancakes, too! In fact, they liked ketchup on cheese sandwiches, and they even liked ketchup on plain pickle sandwiches. Persistent as Mom was, the day after the pancake fiasco, she served Johnnycake for breakfast with butter and homemade syrup. Alas, she finally found something they liked without ketchup.

Mom never minded when we brought friends home to eat; what difference would it make to have one or two extra hungry children? Mike Charlebois had begun staying with our family for several weeks at a time during the summer when he and I were both in fifth or sixth grade. His parents lived in the suburbs and wanted Mike to experience life on a farm. Mike's German-born mother pressed all his clothes, including his T-shirts and blue jeans. I was assigned to press his clothes the first month he lived with us. After that, he had to learn to do it himself. We were not about to start pressing everybody's jeans and T-shirts!

Mike moved in with us full time when we were in ninth grade. One day, a bunch of Mike's and my mutual friends showed up at our house at supper time. Mom made a new request: "If you're going to bring ten or more people home at mealtime, please let me know ahead of time so we have enough food." That made sense to both Mike and me; we just hadn't thought about it!

Later that night, Mike was telling jokes to our guests in the living room after everyone else was in bed. Dad came out of the bedroom wearing the grayest pair of tidy whities those guests had ever seen, and shrieked, "If you kids don't pipe down immediately, I'm going to throw the circuit breaker and you'll have no electricity," then turned around and went back to bed. He had absolutely no idea that the audience was not his own kids, before or after his outburst. Mike's and my friends couldn't stop laughing!

During the night, if the baby needed a bottle or a dry cloth diaper and clean rubber pants, Dad got up and did night duty so that Mom could sleep a little more. Mom and Dad probably averaged less than five or six hours of sleep per night. Over thirty-some years, they had a limited amount of sleep; even that was frequently interrupted by children's needs.

Mom nursed each baby until the baby's appetite exceeded her milk supply, challenging the notion that a woman can't get pregnant while nursing. After that, the baby got fed cow's milk. Since there were no microwaves in those days, she simmered it on the electric stove until a skin formed on the top, then tested the temperature by squirting a little milk on her wrist. Waiting for an electric stove to heat up, it took several minutes to prepare a baby's bottle. She consistently used two specific little aluminum pans. When one was dirty, she used the other. Diane now has these two pans as her favorite childhood souvenir. Separately, Mom kept a kettle of steaming water on the back burner for sterilizing glass baby bottles and rubber nipples.

As each baby got old enough to eat Pablum, Mom delegated spoon-feeding to one of us preteen kids. Except when Marty was little, Mom seldom used baby food from jars although she kept some in the diaper bag for emergencies. When the baby was big enough, Mom used a fork to mash whatever veggies or fruit she was serving the rest of us in order to make baby food. At that time, I had never heard of a blender or food processor.

Using a flour-sack dishtowel, we tied the baby in to the well-worn wooden high chair, flipped the food tray down (avoiding the baby's head), and fed the baby before everyone else sat down for a meal.
My nephew, Aaron

From the time Marty quit nursing until he was at least two, Mom opted to buy baby food by the case. Because Marty was born three months' premature and also physically and developmentally challenged, Mom really had her hands full. At that time, three children each sat in their own high chair, and needed to be spoon fed before each family meal. Mom sent one of us down the basement to bring up two jars of junior baby food for Marty and Pauline, and pureed applesauce in a tiny jar for Alice.

Using store-bought baby food freed up at least a half hour of Mom's time per meal so she could visit her mother in the local nursing home which we called a "rest home." In the sixties, Grama Kahnke had had a heart attack followed by a stroke; for years, she lived in a semi-coma. Mom visited her mother at lunch time because meal-time offered the best chance of catching Grama on the rare occasions when she was conscious.

At first, Mom started using store-bought baby food just so she would have time to lead the Rosary at Grama's nursing home. After Grama Kahnke passed, Mom kept leading the Rosary for the nursing home residents and their visitors. Leading the Rosary in honor of her comatose mother marked the beginning of Mom's thirty-three years volunteering there (as if she wasn't busy enough!) My mother spent her whole life dedicated to those she loved, tirelessly offering her time and talents. From Mom, my siblings and I learned to appreciate acts of service.

Mom used very few processed ingredients, and cooked most meals from scratch. At home, we called our noon meal *dinner*, and our evening meal *supper*, but at Catholic school, for twenty-five cents a day, we called the noon meal hot *lunch*. On rare occasion, when the school cafeteria was closed for the day, Mom packed peanut butter and jelly sandwiches using homemade bread. All the other kids at school ate Wonder bread sandwiches. Thinking that my friends would realize we were too poor to buy "good" bread and therefore had to bake our own from scratch, I felt embarrassed. I hid my homemade bread from having my classmates, and, because of this, sometimes didn't eat lunch at all!

For the little kids who didn't yet go to school, and for those siblings not capable of attending school, Mom usually served leftovers, soup and/or salad for lunch. I asked Rose Ann what she remembered Mom serving for lunch while the rest of us were at school. She immediately responded, "Potato Salad."

"Anything else?" I asked.

"Nope."

If we couldn't think of anything else, potatoes and eggs became a default breakfast, lunch or dinner menu. Between owning a chicken farm and having an Irish Mom who ALWAYS served potatoes, no wonder Rosie thought that. Or perhaps she remembered it so well because she was our *numero uno* potato peeler. Imagine anyone peeling a couple dozen potatoes for supper, day after day, week after week, for over twenty years. Not to mention Rosie's other job of peeling at least half a dozen boiled eggs a day, and dicing celery. Peeling, slicing and dicing were some of the few jobs that Rose Ann was capable of doing, and she genuinely liked being helpful.

After we prayed, Dad couldn't wait to enjoy his "big white cup" filled with weak coffee, sugar, and lots of cream. He drank his first cup of coffee with his meal, and washed his meal down with a second cup as soon as he was finished eating. Sometimes he requested a third cup, and he would get very specific: "Fill this half-full," or "Fill this up two-thirds of the way."

Inevitably, one of us would over-fill or under-fill his special white cup, and he'd get upset. It's a well-worn family joke that Dad put up with millions of other things, yet he would virtually come *unglued* about once a week because his third cup of coffee got measured imprecisely.

In summer, Mom served tomatoes, cucumbers, scallions, and leaf lettuce for every noon meal. To balance the acidity, she kept cottage cheese on hand, and served it with chives. Besides a three-ounce package of Roquefort for Mom, cottage cheese and Velveeta were the only cheeses we ate because they were the most economical.

In the fall, we looked forward to what Mom called "end of the garden soup." It always started with a tomato base, carrots and onions. She added green beans, potatoes, or whatever garden produce was still plentiful just before the first frost.

During the winter, Mom added something hot to the noon menu. Chicken anything was a staple; chicken soup could be varied to include homemade noodles or dumplings, or it could be served with chicken-fat-rice (a pressure-cooked fatty stew hen to which she added rice, carrots, onions, and celery). The whole thing dripped with grease, and we loved it. Homemade tomato soup with lots of cream in it was also a favorite treat. Once in a while, Mom liked to make potato soup or cream of onion soup.

No one I knew as a kid ever drank tea, but all summer long we performed a daily ritual called "tea-party time" between three and four PM, rain or shine. At tea-party time, somebody older than three was assigned to make nectar. This may have been the first recipe each and every one of us learned.

"Fill the big pitcher with drinking water from the hard water tap," Mom advised.

"Dump in two packets of nectar (Kool-Aid), two heaping cups of sugar out of the sugar bin," she continued, and

"Remember to put in a tray of ice."

The *big pitcher* was made out of aluminum, and looked like a mini-cream-can with a spout; I have never seen another one like it. These days, that big pitcher contributes to our family's legacy atop a permanent exhibit at the Waseca Historical Society.

Serving nectar was Mom's way of keeping children from dehydrating. "Fussbudgets" were frowned on at our house; no one dare complain about the flavor: orange, cherry, or grape. Most of us drank out of opaque twelve-ounce plastic cups. Whoever was lucky got the chance to use one of our four or five brightly-colored, brushed aluminum cups, much preferred because they were bigger, and, when it came to nectar, bigger was definitely better. We served our tea-party on the picnic table on our front lawn; if it was raining, we simply moved in to the garage. I can't remember a single time in all those years when there was any nectar leftover.

Before or after tea-party time, we lugged a thermos of water, lemonade or coffee out to whichever field Dad was planting, fertilizing, cultivating, spraying, or harvesting. Dad's stamina was matched only by his work ethic; he always worked tirelessly from dawn 'til dusk. Tea-party time for kids coincided with a short break for him to re-hydrate.

At tea-party time, we usually ate a snack. Once a week or so, one of us girls would bake cookies. We could eat cookies faster than anyone could bake them. There was no use having a cookie jar; if Mom wanted to save any cookies, they needed to stay in the basement freezer. Frosted graham crackers (or graham crackers with butter and honey) were welcome substitutes when we didn't have real cookies. Otherwise, saltines constituted our stand-by snack.

My sisters and I helped bake cookies before we learned to read while the boys spent their days outdoors helping Dad. Before Mom taught us how to use the kitchen, we practiced by making mud-pies on our play-oven next to the "sand pile." We didn't have a sand box, just a big pile of sand that Dad either scooped up along the roadside near the Mississippi bluffs, or, once in a great while, purchased from a gravel pit operation. We decorated our sand creations with individual daisy petals. We pulled one petal at a time away from the yellow center, convinced of the power of the saying, "He loves me; he loves me not."

When it comes to cookies, Mom's specialty was her mother's favorite, raisin-filled cookies. She rolled sugar-cookie type dough, used crinkle cookie-cutters for round tops and bottoms, and filled each with raisin pie filling. The only person I know who still bakes them is Diane. Like most kids, my siblings and I liked chocolate chip cookies and mint surprise cookies best. Because of the expense of chocolate, our family baked these only for parties.

Whenever a cookie recipe called for shortening, we were taught to use half butter and half lard. Mom rendered lard from pigs we raised and/or from the grocery store donations; she kept a crock jar of it next to the stove both for cooking and baking. Unlike my mother, Grama

Miller used only lard for her chocolate cookies, and only butter for yellow cookies.

During the school year, even though we didn't call it tea-party time, we still had a snack. Instead of nectar we drank milk or hot chocolate. We jumped off the bus, set our books on the book shelf, checked the slip for what chores Dad had assigned, then changed into everyday clothes. We gulped down some milk and ate one peanut butter and honey sandwich apiece, sandwiches that Mom had prepared. If we were still hungry, we made our own PB&J's, or toast with butter and jam, then hurried out to do our regular farm chores. After the outdoor work was completed, we did our indoor chores, including feeding the goldfish we kept in a small aquarium.

It amazed me what tidbits of wisdom Mom stored in her recipe box. Before supper was goldfish feeding time, for which Mom's recipe card file contained the following instructions:

- Feed often, a little. Should be eaten in ten minutes.

- Too much sunlight causes algae.

- Cryptocoryne is a good plant. Elodea they like to eat.

- Arrange sand uneven deep in back and shallow in front.

- Let water from faucet set 'til it is same temp as that in tank before changing.

- Siphon water out of tank.

Another treasure found in Mom's recipe box was a typewritten card.

"Recipe for having a happy life is having a Mom like YOU."

Signed, Rose Ann

Our collective metabolism rocked. Even if we had scarfed down five pieces of toast after school, we ate a full supper an hour and a half later. We never heard of the term "balanced meals." It was simply understood that supper consisted of meat and potatoes, a simple tossed green salad, a steamed vegetable, and a dessert.

As soon as we got home from school, Mom routinely assigned five girls to prepare that evening's meal: the youngest helper was assigned to set the table. One teenage cook browned two pounds of meat and roasted it. Our most common entrée was homegrown chicken, a homegrown seared pork roast, or a beef roast. Whenever Dad brought home rabbit, squirrel, ducks, pheasants, geese, or fish, we served it as soon as possible.

Mom assigned a third helper to steam two one-quart packages of frozen peas, beans or corn in the waterless vegetable pan and top them with butter and salt. That person also baked, boiled, or mashed a couple dozen potatoes. Potatoes were a year-round filler-upper; Mom cooked them every possible way to maintain children's interest. My favorite was whipped potatoes with thick, greasy gravy like Grama Miller used to make. Dad's favorite was riced potatoes (boiled potatoes squeezed one at a time through a coarse metal sieve). Because it's hard to keep riced potatoes hot, and equally difficult to time the rest of the meal around them, we didn't serve riced potatoes very often. True to our German and Irish heritage, most of us kids would happily have enjoyed potatoes and gravy for every single meal of our childhood.

A fourth, middle-size, helper got the job of prepping a garden salad. During the winter, salad consisted of iceberg lettuce, a sliced cucumber and a tomato or two. To make eating salad easier for children, we always dressed and tossed salad before serving it. For a while, Dad liked Catalina dressing, then he switched to Western dressing. Once Mom discovered dry packets of Ranch to mix with buttermilk, that became a life-long favorite. Mom also enjoyed bleu cheese dressing, and kept her own little bottle in the fridge. The rest of us thought "bleu cheese anything" stunk up the house.

Unless Mom had already baked something sweet for supper, a teenager got tasked with baking dessert. We ate cake every couple days, apple crisp a couple times a week in season, strawberry shortcake every other day in season, and lots of pie and ice cream, most frequently on Sunday. Cookies were not considered dessert. However, every few weeks we served brownies or blonde brownies, or red Jell-o with whipped cream and nuts for dessert.

If time ran short, Mom cooked up some silky-smooth custard or pudding or served what we called "sauce" (sliced apples or peaches in syrup), for dessert. She kept an open jar of sauce in the fridge to mash up for baby food. In 1971, when the local Birds Eye factory sold various flavors of overstocked pudding and Cool Whip for nine cents a quart, our family ate pudding and/or Cool Whip about three times a week.

Because our kitchen had only about three feet between the appliances and the table, very specific routines developed to maximize efficiency in such a tight space. Rosie always peeled potatoes on the far side of the kitchen table where

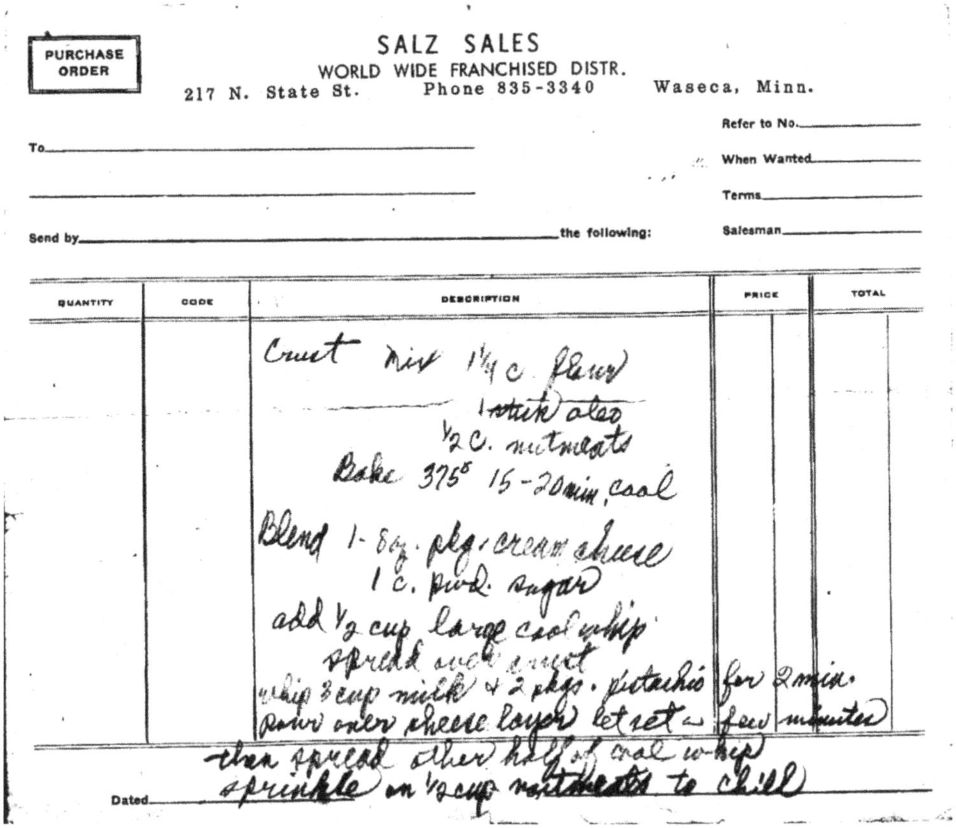

PURCHASE ORDER

SALZ SALES
WORLD WIDE FRANCHISED DISTR.
217 N. State St.   Phone 835-3340   Waseca, Minn.

To_____
_____
Send by_____ the following:

Refer to No._____
When Wanted_____
Terms_____
Salesman_____

QUANTITY	CODE	DESCRIPTION	PRICE	TOTAL

*Crust mix 1¼ c. flour
with also
½ c. nutmeats
Bake 375° 15-20 min, cool
Blend 1-8oz. pkg. cream cheese
1 c. pwd. sugar
add ½ cup large cool whip
spread over crust
whip 3 cup milk + 2 pkgs. pistachio for 2 min.
pour over cheese layer, let set a few minutes
then spread other half of cool whip
sprinkle on ½ cup nutmeats (to chill)*

Dated_____

The local ladies made up Cool Whip recipes to offer some variety, and shared them with each other on scrap paper as shown here.

she faced the back door and monitored the ins and outs. Even the stove burners had assigned tasks: potatoes got boiled using the front burner on the left side, while frozen vegetables steamed on the back burner on the right side. The little burner on the back left was reserved for keeping coffee hot and the little burner on the right front reserved for warming baby's milk. We kept the right-hand kitchen counter free to sear meat in a waterless electric skillet using lard and flour which were stored within easy reach.

When I was in my teens, a traveling salesman volunteered to cook dinner for any family who would invite him, and said he'd bring all the food. Free food? Of course! My parents accepted the invitation with great enthusiasm. That night, the salesman cooked dinner for 16,

We ate baked, fried, grilled or stewed chicken at least once or twice a week. It was cheap, and it was easy to go out to the henhouse and butcher the following day's dinner. We almost never had leftovers when it came to meat of any kind, especially fried chicken.

showing Mom how to perfectly cook frozen vegetables without using a steamer, and without adding any water, using Miracle Maid waterless cookware.

He seared meat then roasted it in the same pan. It was the first non-stick pan we'd ever seen. Instead of being coated like a Teflon pan, it was a heavy, non-stick electric fry pan with a high top, great for roasting. This amazing invention for waterless cooking was called "the L'ectra Maid." Mom and Dad spent a small fortune ($300) on

a full set of waterless cookware because it was healthy, and because it had a lifetime warranty, but boy, did they get their money's worth!

We used the twenty-by-fifteen-inch electric skillet at practically every meal; for breakfast on non-school days, we fried bacon and eggs in it then stored it under our kitchen sink. For supper, we often roasted a cheap cut of beef in it, then added a dozen potatoes, onions, and dozen carrots forty-five minutes before mealtime.

After that, our family never used anything but waterless cookware. Frozen veggies were cooked perfectly such that they still retained their flavor and a bit of their crunchiness. We wore out a couple of sauce pan lids, and they were replaced at no charge until, unfortunately, the company went out of business. I was shocked to learn not every big family in America owned waterless cookware, especially the L'ectra Maid that both seared and roasted.

Our family used very specific containers and utensils for certain foods, but not the way you might expect. Mom kept a brushed aluminum canister set behind the rubber-mat "drain board" near the kitchen sink: the canister marked flour contained powdered sugar, the one marked sugar held brown sugar, the coffee canister needed to contain coffee (so as not to confuse guests), and our tea canister contained rice. It never even occurred to us to re-label those containers!

As mentioned earlier, we kept large amounts of flour and sugar in bins under the kitchen counter. Dessert got mixed by hand or with the little handheld mixer on the kitchen table instead of taking up counter space with the big Hamilton electric mixer. The assigned baker had to make sure to get out sugar and flour before it was time to set the table. That's because the girl assigned to set the table had to pull out the built-in cutting board (directly above the sugar) to slice two loaves of bread for a meal, depriving the baker of access to the sugar and flour bins.

By the time I learned to cook, Mom had over fifteen years of practice orchestrating daughters preparing meals. Most nights, we worked around each other perfectly. As the five cooks carried out their assigned jobs, each knew what job the other girls had, and could anticipate their needs and their movements without even thinking about it. Relatively speaking, our meal preparation was well-organized, none of the problems typically associated with too many cooks in the kitchen... we worked independently, but stayed in synch, as if we were part of a kitchen dance where cooking together had been choreographed. The skill of working independently while coordinating with others to meet a deadline became a huge asset in our adult lives.

Dad insisted on something sweet with every meal. For special breakfasts, Mom baked banana bread, pumpkin bread or zucchini bread. For celebrations, Mom baked the best sweet rolls I have ever eaten; my favorite type was apricot Kolackies (sweet rolls with jam in the center). Yum!

Until I was in grade school, our family had a four-burner stove where the back burner was a deep fryer. My mother kept it half-full of pure lard. Twice a year or so, Mom deep-fried old-fashioned cake donuts, usually timed to be sampled right when we got home from school. She often used it to fry bread, and to fry chicken. As much as we loved potatoes, I don't remember her ever frying homemade French fries; instead, she crinkle-cut potatoes, spread them on a cookie sheet, and baked them. They were never crispy, but they were healthy!

Especially for Sunday dinners, Mom made fabulous pie; everybody loved it. During the winter, Mom made a lot of peach, cherry, lemon meringue or blueberry pie; in season, she baked apple, plum, pumpkin, rhubarb cream or gooseberry pie.

Because Mom could make a pie faster than she could teach us to bake one, I didn't learn how to make pie crust from scratch until I was a teenager. Mom got up at dawn to roll out pie dough so that the kitchen table space needed for rolling dough didn't interfere with room for serving breakfast. Mom baked three pies at a time, each sliced into eight pieces for serving. Our oven held four pie pans at a time, so whoever woke up the earliest got to use any leftover pie dough to make "pie crust" or "cinnamon rolls."

Whenever Mom bought cheap over-ripe bananas, the little kids sat out on the pump and used a hammer to crack black walnuts so she could make banana nut bread.
Damien, Marty, Marcia and Greg, 1969

Pie crust meant sprinkling sugar and cinnamon on pie dough scraps in a pie pan, and tucking them in the oven while the pies were still baking. To my mother, a pie pan meant an aluminum pan while a pie plate meant a glass Pyrex pan. She used both, depending on the type of pie.

To make *cinnamon rolls,* we added a few raisins to the unbaked cinnamon pie crust, rolled up the dough, and cut it with string so each cinnamon roll was still round. We'd be lucky if we had enough leftover pie dough for six cinnamon rolls, and there'd be about ten kids who wanted one. To have half a chance at getting one, you had to be

I have fond memories of using the red and green handled donut hole cutters as cymbals when I was a toddler. I couldn't wait until I was finally old enough that Mom let me cut out donut holes.

Mom's brother Herb (shown here in 1957 along with his daughter Mary and Ramona) could have eaten a whole pie whenever he came to our house.

waiting in the kitchen when they came out of the oven. Whoever "won" quickly scarfed down their cinnamon roll or pie crust scraps (sometimes with jelly), while they were still piping hot.

Learning to cook something new or bake something new involved creativity. Occasionally we asked Mom to replicate school hot lunch entrées, for example, spaghetti and meatballs. My Irish and German mom hadn't eaten spaghetti as a kid, so, like she did with many dishes, she made up her own recipe. She put chopped onions, salt and pepper in with burger, rolled enough one and a half inch balls so every kid could have at least one, and browned them. Then she boiled spaghetti noodles, added home-grown stewed tomatoes or a can of plain tomato soup, and topped it off with the meatballs. We

didn't know that her version of spaghetti and meatballs bore precious little resemblance to what Italians serve; we craved Mom's version. The word pasta had not yet entered our vocabulary. We were only familiar with regular macaroni, what we called seashell macaroni, and spaghetti, or as we often said, "bussghetti." Later, when I married a Sicilian, I learned a lot about manicotti and other types of pasta, so it's hard to imagine how much I once craved Campbell's tomato soup and meatballs over noodles!

CHAPTER 8:

Annual Celebration Menus

I LOVED HELPING Mom entertain: first, dreaming about how much fun we would have, secondly, preparing just the right menu, thirdly, making memories by serving large quantities of high-quality, delicious food to an appreciative audience, and, finally, after our company had left, savoring stories and re-living those memories.

Special occasion dining at our house was always a celebration amongst friends. Whenever our family wanted to celebrate anything, we first decided what to serve. For annual holidays and Holy Days, our traditional menu for each specific occasion had been decided long before I was born. For ad hoc special occasions, we spent multiple days discussing what would be most enjoyable and most festive. Only after getting the menu in mind did Mom decide whom

to invite, and whether to serve a buffet or a sit-down meal.

1962: When Al came home from the army for Christmas, he gifted each of us girls a fancy apron.
Kathleen, Rose Ann, Pat, Marylu, Diane, Janet, Linda, Virginia, Helen, Dolores

My mother knew her family and guests appreciated all the fussing that preceded such company meals. She made special occasions festive, and endeared herself to all who joined us for them. Like many depression-era parents, Mom and Dad honored guests by getting dressed up, having us kids dress up, decorating the house, and sharing all the best food they had to offer. In return, guests honored Mom by "pigging out!"

For special occasions, Mom wore her Sunday dress, nylons, high heels (even when she was pregnant), and old-fashioned clip-on or screw-back earrings that always hurt her ears. She made sure she kept her apron on until the moment it was time to sit down at the table.

Mom had a couple dozen aprons including: her Christmas apron with poinsettias, the hand-crocheted pastel-colored Easter apron, the chiffon one with the roses on it that Al had sent home as a Christmas gift when he was stationed at Fort Knox army base, the pink and white gingham check one with white rick-rack and cross-stitches, one with an appliqued apple and green strings, a blue smock Kathleen had sent from Germany, and a white bib apron used for baking to prevent flour from dusting her clothes. By the time Mom put on her good clothes and her good apron, the food already smelled fabulous

Us kids were usually responsible for decorating. We gathered wild flowers in the woods, or asked Mom if we could pick some from her garden. Helen, Ginny, Jan, Lor, and Art picking violets, 1964

and kids started hovering around the kitchen, excited to enjoy another feast.

When we had company, we used our good dishes and dressed the good table (veneered white birch dining room table) with a freshly pressed white damask tablecloth and matching napkins.

After we broke most of and orange and green set of china, we used beautiful pink rose-patterned china; Mom and Dad had won a full set by requesting a song, (Let Me Call You Sweetheart),

1958: Virginia, Helen, Art and Dolores, picking flowers in our back yard

stainless steel flatware, we set the good table with our good silverware, which we pronounced "siv'el ware." That meant first unwrapping knives from their teal flannel cloth, [the cardboard holder in Mom's mahogany silverware chest had long since suffered too much wear and tear] and polishing the silver.

When I was in third grade, my folks received a silver service (coffee pot, cream and sugar set) for their 25th anniversary. Once in a blue moon, we'd polish these and use them for company. We didn't use the decorative pot very often because the coffee cooled off too quickly.

that the "Play or Pay" TV show orchestra was not able to play.

Over time, my siblings and I chipped much of the rose china. Mom longed for the day when she would no longer have to entertain using chipped and/or mismatched dishes. When Dad retired and they moved to town, Lucille *Rose* bought a third set of china, also with lovely pink roses.

Instead of using our unmatched assortment of

Our family's good dishes were china with the orange, pink, blue and green pixelated flowers with gold accents. Hmmm. That makes me wonder about the origin of the use of the word "China" to describe valuable dishware

Our everyday relish tray included two of the following: carrots, celery, radishes, green onions, sliced tomatoes in season, and homemade pickles, usually dill. For parties, Mom typically added more of these options plus an eight-ounce jar of green olives stuffed with pimentos; in one meal, us kids could eat as many olives as she would buy. On special occasions, we sliced the carrot sticks with the ripple cutter to make them decorative, and stuffed celery sticks with cream cheese. We thought ourselves quite fortunate to have such fancy treats!

Mom never served hot appetizers. Even the term "hors d'oeuvres" was not part of our vocabulary. Sometime in the seventies, we began eating less home-canned food and started adding Colby or cheddar cheese

Every celebration meal started with a relish tray and home-made bread or rolls.

with saltines or Chicken-in-a-Biscuits to our standard relish tray for special occasions, and that's when we were introduced to the term *hors d'oeuvres.*

Mom made two side dishes that some people would consider appetizers. Other than a relish tray, these are the only cold appetizers I remember: corn relish (cold sweet corn, red and green pepper and a little vinegar) and headcheese. Compared to how much I detested headcheese, corn relish was good stuff. I swear no one but a calloused farmer or a butcher would eat headcheese if they saw how it got cooked. Mom put a hog's head, teeth and all, into a pot and boiled it until the meat fell off the skull, then chopped meat, fat, and gristle into little chunks, added seasonings, and chilled the result in a glass loaf pan. The bone marrow and lard

congealed until it looked like a tasty French country pate' but, for me, after having seen that grotesque head of a pig dropped into a kettle of water, I couldn't *bear* the notion of even tasting headcheese.

For company, we never penny-pinched, and we never skimped on calories. Just like everyday, special occasion dinners for company included meat and potatoes, vegetable and salad, except there was more of it. We usually made enough food for company dinner so that we could serve leftovers for supper for our family. In addition, Mom baked cloverleaf buns (three little dough balls in each muffin pan hole served in our aluminum bun warmer) and wonderful desserts. We reserved desserts like Mound Bars or Rice Krispy bars with chocolate on top for this type of special occasion. For an elegant event, she also bought a can of mixed nuts and tiny pastel mints to fill one-ounce paper "nut cups" and set one next to each water glass. On such occasions, we even wrote up place cards; assigned seating ensured that each little kid had a big kid nearby to help out.

**1958: Grapefruit from Arizona, courtesy of Alice Haley
Clockwise from bottom right: John, Marylu, Al, Linda, Helen, Kathleen, Dolores in the high chair, Virginia, Pat, Art, Dad, Janet, Robert, Rose Ann, Diane**

Mom served milk, water, coffee and, on rare occasion, green tea; we almost never offered cocktails to guests. We never put alcohol in punch. However, for graduations and New Year's Eve, Mom bought ginger ale to "spike" the punch. The only time we drank pop *straight up* was when we were sick and had a fever higher than 102... then Mom offered small sips of 7-up or ginger ale.

If root beer was rare at our house, real beer was only slightly more common. Dad bought the world's cheapest beer. He occasionally split one with Mom at tea-party time. Dad said Mom would produce more milk to nurse the baby if she drank half a beer; Mom quietly agreed.

Other than beer, Dad's idea of alcohol was to buy a bottle of Mogen David for Easter and to keep a fifth of whiskey and a pint of brandy in his gun cabinet. If booze and guns seems a weird combination, the similarity is that they are both off-limits to children. Mom and Dad never drank hard liquor at home, but they took whiskey to wedding dances at the local American Legion Hall, and that small bottle would typically last a year or two.

Our company would occasionally bring something wonderful to eat. When Mom's Aunt Rosie Lynch came over before Christmas, she always brought a grocery sack filled with oranges, apples and nuts. When Aunt Therese came over, she sometimes brought us pears. When I was about four, my eldest sister's Arizona friend spent a holiday at our house. She brought the biggest oranges I had ever seen (or so I thought), and I was super-excited. Turns out they were yummy pink grapefruit, and each kid got to eat an entire half of a grapefruit – what a delightful extravagance!

Just after the movie "Sound of Music" came out, our family started a new tradition; instead of saying grace before special occasion meals, we sang a prayer to the tune of Edelweiss. Many of my sisters and brothers have great voices, and several siblings play a musical instrument, so at least two people usually accompanied us on guitar and/or piano as we loved to sing:

Bless our friends, bless our food,

Come, oh Lord, and sit with us.

May our talk glow with peace,

Come with your love and surround us.

Friendship and peace, may they bloom and grow,

Bloom and grow forever,

Bless our friends, bless our food,

Bless our dear ones forever!

Our good table seated ten. After 1962, when the new family room extended the space, we

Before we built the new family room, whenever we had company, the big kids sat at the good table. The rest of us squeezed together around the oak kitchen table.
1961: the little kids and some Clemons cousins at our kitchen table; note Marylu feeding two toddlers in the high chairs.

strung the twelve-person kitchen table and dining table together for special occasions. To seat plus or minus forty for holidays, we added as many card tables as needed. We had plenty of folding chairs, but if we ran out of table space, we either assigned more big girls to wait on table, or asked the little kids to sit on the stair steps to eat. After each meal, we took down all the extra tables and chairs and put them away until the next meal, even if that was only a few hours later.

Birthdays in a family of twenty-two are almost a weekly event; birthday celebrations gave our family plenty of opportunities for special occasion meals. Each child's birthday was the only day that person was given the opportunity to provide input into menu planning; Mom gave the birthday kid his or her choice of food to serve, like chicken vs. pork, or peas vs. corn. Even that small amount of discretion felt pretty darn special!

Mom gave birthday kids their choice of both the flavor of cake and frosting, and also their preference for decorated cupcakes, layer cake with filling, or a rectangular cake. I always chose layer cake in order to have sweet filling between the layers AND frosting on top. My siblings agree, filling *makes* a cake, especially Mom's pineapple or lemon filling. Once in a blue

When the birthday kid chose layer cake, Mom put the birthday cake on her crystal, pedestal-style cake stand shown here for six-year-old grandson, Nicholas. If she had time, she used a toothpick dipped in food coloring to write something on the frosting.

moon, we were allowed to choose a non-vanilla ice cream as a birthday treat. We each got one small, red-handled ice-cream scoop-full served with our birthday cake.

First thing in the morning on our birthday, Mom would give us one present, most often something to wear. Birthday boys and girls got excused from doing dishes and other chores; that was a huge gift! However, the best part of having a birthday was being allowed to have

Mom delicately turned a fluffy angel food cake on to her round cake-saver board, covered it with the well-loved black and white tin cake-saver top, then snapped on the wire handles to transport it safely.

was an expert at maximizing the gooey part and still being able to turn it upside down without cracking it. We couldn't serve that kind for birthdays because it has no frosting and besides, it doesn't go as well with ice cream.

What was so great about Mom's cakes was that if they were supposed to be light, they'd be super-light. Mom could fold egg whites into batter better than anyone. When fresh strawberries or raspberries were in season, she baked an Angel Food cake a couple times a week. If

friends sleep over as a special, birthday-only, privilege.

The first time I was allowed to attend a friend's birthday party, (in about third grade) I watched in awe as my friend's mom cut a cake into 12 large pieces instead of 20 "regular-size" pieces. She then served each person *two* big scoops of ice cream, after which we *even* got to have second helpings of dessert! What a treat!

Mom made terrific heavy cakes such as spice cake, applesauce cake and ginger cake. Dad loved pineapple upside-down cake, and Mom

Big-white-cup originally meant Dad's coffee cup; however, Mom used that specific cup for baking (instead of a measuring cup). When referred to in recipes, big white cup meant about a cup and a third.
Given Dad's desire for precision on the volume of his third cup of coffee, I wish we could have used a measuring cup for his coffee, and let us cooks reserve his big white cup for baking!!

she had to use up more eggs, she made a yellow sponge cake, which is something like a pound cake.

If we got really lucky, Mom would call her sister, Marg, and ask Aunt Marg if she had time to bake the birthday cake. Aunt Marg was Mom's closest sibling in age, and, I daresay, her best friend. When Mom's sister, Marg, married Dad's cousin, George, the newlyweds moved to the farm behind ours and became the best neighbors anyone could ever want. Amongst other hobbies, Marg liked to decorate cakes, and she knew how to make dainty roses out of decorator frosting. Inevitably, us kids would bicker over who got to eat the decorations.

Outside of birthday cakes, Mom baked Grama Kahnke's cream cake recipe the most often because this is the recipe Mom used for what we called Strawberry Short Cake. I hand wrote an index card and used the following recipe for the very first birthday cake I baked, *by myself.* Based on the handwriting, I was likely in second or third grade.

Cream Cake: Grama K[ahnke]'s Cream Cake

2 eggs

cream

1 c. sugar

1 t. vanilla

1 2/3 c. flour + salt

2 t. b.p.

Put eggs in a [Dad's] big white coffee cup. Fill with cream. Beat. Add sugar, vanilla flour + b.p. + salt. Bake at 350 degrees.

Dad usually requested white cake and vanilla ice cream. He particularly liked pineapple filling underneath sticky white seven-minute frosting, or angel food served with strawberries. On Dad's 60th birthday, our family enjoyed a little get-together at home. On Dad's 70th, Mom invited company to help celebrate. For Dad's 80th, Al and his wife Donna hosted family, friends and

Marty, celebrating his second birthday with a layer cake covered with Dad's favorite: sticky white frosting

relatives on April 26th, 1997. They roasted a hog, filled a couple banquet tables with side dishes, celebrated with music, planned a program including a slide show, and ended with a bonfire. Dad had T-shirts made highlighting his favorite hobbies. Dad very proudly invited the local TV stations to show off his twenty-two healthy, happy, grown children. On the ten o'clock news, KSTP TV aired a quick interview of each of those who attended.

The older Dad got, the more he enjoyed bragging about his big family, which oftentimes embarrassed the crap out of us kids. Whether he was on vacation or at an ice cream social, Dad got a big kick out of walking up to strangers and taunting them, "I'll bet you a dollar you'll never guess how many kids I have." He would proceed to pull out a tiny well-worn family photo from his wallet, and tell a few of his favorite stories.

Before Dad's 90th birthday, he felt relatively healthy, considering that he was still recovering from an emergency hip replacement. He requested we place an ad in the local newspaper inviting "anyone who wanted to come" to his 90th birthday party. He insisted that so many friends would attend that we needed to roast *three* whole pigs in celebration. Knowing Dad lived in Northfield (an hour from Waseca) with Marylu, I couldn't imagine many of his aging

Back Row: Marty, Angi, Greg, Damien, Janet, Bob, John, Lu
Middle Row: Rosie, Linda, Marcia, Ramona, Pat, Alice, Kathleen, Al
Front Row: Art, Helen, Mom, Dad
Missed the party: Diane, Ginny, Lor, and Pauline

friends driving an hour for a birthday party. I put a small ad in the paper, hired a caterer to roast just one hog, and another caterer to bake enough birthday cake to serve one hundred fifty people, including nearly 100 of our immediate family.

To facilitate out-of-state traveling, we planned Dad's birthday party for the Sunday directly after his 90th birthday. On the morning of his 90th birthday, Dad impatiently asked several times, "Did the mailman come yet?" "Did I get any birthday cards?" "I want to see that ad for my birthday party."

As soon as the mailman arrived, Dad looked at his birthday party invitation in the local paper and thoroughly enjoyed his birthday cards. Less than an hour later, he passed away peacefully. That Sunday at his funeral reception in Waseca, several hundred people, including everyone who had planned to attend his birthday party, celebrated his life with a whole hog roast. It was as if Dad had planned the timing of his funeral (or could it be that Mom helped plan one last birthday party from somewhere up above?) ☺

Just like birthday parties, Miller graduations offered a routine opportunity to celebrate a special occasion. Every year since I can remember, at least one family member graduated from high school or college, or got an advanced degree. As each of us graduated from high school (and sixteen of us graduated from college; the others lacked the aptitude), Mom beamed with pride. Family tradition dictated hosting a graduation reception not only for our aunts and uncles, almost none of whom had gone to high school, but also our cousins, our nieces and nephews, and our neighbors, most of whom had also not attended college.

Our annual Graduation Party buffet menu offered:

- open-face pimento or pineapple-spread sandwiches on thinly sliced squares of boughten rye bread,

- tuna and/or chicken salad crust-less Wonder bread sandwiches cut into strips,

- a decorated sheet cake from Rindelaub's bakery,

- mixed nuts and pastel-colored mints,

- homemade cookies/bars: for sure chocolate chip cookies, thumbprints, mint surprise cookies, brownies, blonde brownies, and seven-layer bars,

- our standard relish tray, and

- store-bought midget dill pickles.

Mom's crystal punch bowl got used exclusively for graduation parties. First, she arranged maraschino cherries in pineapple slices on the bottom of a Jell-O mold, covered them with grapefruit juice, and froze it to use as an ice ring. Then she spiked canned Hawaiian punch with ginger ale and 7-up. Us kids loved graduation punch because the fizz made it special.

In 1977, because four Millers graduated, we decided to move this extra-large graduation party outdoors. In addition to our family's two picnic tables and three card tables, we borrowed

First Annual Hog Roast, 1977
Here we are, all 22, with Mom and Dad, on our front lawn at the farm. Mom with her apron on, and camera ready; Dad is kneeling, on the left.

banquet tables and wooden folding chairs from the church. Dad suggested we all wear name tags showing our birth order number so the relatives could tell us apart. That was the first family event for which we wore nametags. Initially, we resisted the idea; after that, we considered it normal to wear nametags on special occasions. It wasn't very long before we realized our young nieces and nephews also needed us to wear nametags to keep us straight.

Instead of our regular graduation menu, we substituted a whole hog and fifteen dozen potato buns, added baked beans, potato salad, cookies, bars, and a keg of beer. Guests looked forward to the feast: juicy wood-fired pulled pork, hot off the grill, with lots of sides and desserts, then stayed for our mini-hootenanny; both the feast and the fabulous talent show were a huge success.

Our relatives and friends loved it so much that we quit serving reception sandwiches and

1977: Mom played violin for the Graduation party talent show, while Linda turned the pages.

roast" had become a June tradition, whether or not *anyone* graduated.

For three weeks in advance of any graduation party, my sisters and I baked and froze at least two dozen batches of chocolate kiss cookies, thumbprints, mint surprise cookies, chocolate chip cookies, Rice Krispy bars, blonde brownies, brownies with walnuts, and lemon squares. Of course, there was never any snitching... Ha, ha!

My sisters and I snuck plenty of bars before the remainder went to the freezer in preparation for a celebration. My sister Ginny had to make her seven-layer bars *right before* any party; otherwise they'd completely vanish from the freezer beforehand!

cake, and started a new pattern of serving a whole hog every year for graduation parties. The crowd got bigger each year, always hoping that we'd roast another hog (or do another program) as awesome as that first one. Regardless of how many people graduated in subsequent years, we never had any trouble polishing off a 200+ pound whole hog in one afternoon. After a few years, "the Miller hog

Nephews Reggie and Lucas, hammin' it up, hootenanny style

Mom often warned us that if we ate too many sweets, that we'd get sick to our stomach. I couldn't imagine getting sick from eating too much dessert. The year that Patty graduated high school, I had just turned old enough to get the job of arranging sheet cake onto trays, and storing any leftover cake on the wood stove in the basement. While in the basement (away from prying eyes), I slammed down 14 pieces of cake that day, (yum!) and, better yet, never got sick. However, I must admit, I haven't touched sheet cake since.

Ordinarily, if Mom wanted to save cake or pie for someone who had missed supper because they had gone babysitting, she'd set it on top of the refrigerator (where little kids couldn't reach). If it was saved for someone in particular, and somebody else ate it, the mad kid would demand the guilty party be punished. After Patty's

Brother-in-law Wayne Smith, Al and cousin, Steve Wesley carving a whole hog. Mom's six-quart roaster looks tiny in this photo.

high school graduation party, we were short on refrigerator space, so Mom asked me to store a baking sheet full of tuna salad sandwiches down the basement. She would have expected me to set leftover sandwiches on the cast iron range to stay cool, but the leftover sheet cake filled that space.

Unaware of the potential for salmonella, I set the tuna sandwiches on the only available clean flat surface, the top of the upright freezer, not realizing it was warm. The next evening, Mom sent me to fetch those sandwiches. We heated them under the broiler, and served them as open-face sandwiches.

I had inadvertently created the ideal conditions for food poisoning. Everyone except Dad got sicker than a dog for 24 hours. Twenty people getting diarrhea and retching our guts out wasn't pretty. We had two bathrooms, and needed twenty. Dad brought out every bucket he could find, and then just laid down newspaper all the way from our beds to the bathroom. Sorry to say, Mom and the youngest child ended up in the emergency room. Thankfully, we all survived.

Dad stayed healthy that night only because he hates mayo; no wonder he no longer wanted mayonnaise served in anything. That night

Grama Edith Stangler Miller's siblings lived within an hour of us. Each of them had several children, so by my generation, the extended Stangler family included hundreds of people, and we all got together for an annual family picnic.
Back row: Marie Stangler Grubish, Albert, Henry
Front row: Bertha Stangler Curran, Frank, and Grama Miller

ranks as the worst sleepless night of my childhood. Getting sick was especially memorable because us kids were *poster-child* healthy, and for the most part, still are.

We did, however, have teeth issues. Unfortunately, most of us were born with our parents' relatively bad teeth. To make matters worse, we ate tons of sugar and had less than stellar brushing habits. Mom and Dad took us to the dentist when our teeth hurt. They couldn't afford Novocaine, so we had to endure the pain. Ouch! Even if we had had good brushing discipline, many of us would not have avoided spending a small fortune on dental work.

For our family, illness was a particular kind of special occasion, and indeed, came with its own menu. Whenever one of us got sick to our stomach, that person was allowed to sleep downstairs in the living room, eat soda crackers and drink pop. If the sick child could keep that down, he or she might get served Jell-O. Generally speaking, us kids liked these perks so much that we didn't mind having a flu bug.

As a family, we had near zero familiarity dealing with illness. We didn't "waste money" on wellness visits or health check-ups. In fact, the only times any of us kids ever saw a doctor outside of in-school vaccinations were for a pre-first-grade physical and a pre-college physical. Once I accompanied my next older sister while the doctor stitched up a cut on her forehead. Oh, yeah, and the time all of us went to the hospital together to get the oral polio vaccine.

We had our fair share of stuffy noses and change of season colds. Mom would have us drink hot lemonade or chicken broth. When Dad got a cold, she made him a hot toddy. We loved getting special attention from Mom. Having learned bedside manner from Grama Kahnke, who had spent many years taking care of sick people in their homes, Mom made a terrific nurse.

In the late fifties, several of us contracted measles back to back. When I developed the German measles, my temperature rose to 107. Mom calmly said that if it went up to 108 she would have to take me to the hospital. I didn't feel worried or scared, just hot. I was happy for the ice packs she brought, and her calm voice and comforting smile. Mom let me sleep downstairs on the new couch in the new family room and drink an unlimited amount of ginger ale and 7-up. What a treat! When I got better, I remember ice-skating on the frozen pond, quite sure I was nearly as good as the Olympian ice-dancer I had watched on TV at my friend's house.

By contrast, when I lived with my stoic, no-nonsense Grama Miller as a teenager, she didn't fuss over me at all when I got sick; she just brought out blackberry brandy and told me to drink it until I felt better. I hated brandy, and immediately "got better."

Family reunions offered an annual special occasion. Rain or shine, the Stangler family picnic started at noon on the first Sunday in June at Clear Lake Park. Someone would set up about a half dozen picnic tables end-to-end for all the food. Each family brought their own plates, cups and silverware (we didn't start using paper plates until the mid-sixties and plastic silverware much later than that). All the cooks tried to out-do each other with yummy food. We could always count on heavy-set Aunt Marie to bring huge caramel popcorn balls. Mm mm good!

Mom brought a large quantity of at least two of her picnic specialties: chicken, baked beans, potato salad, and pie. She fried five or six spring chickens that had a crispy crust but still dripped with juice, melt-in-your-mouth tender. Whenever she fried that many, she stood a much better chance of limiting quibbling over who got drumsticks.

For potato salad, Mom's trick was to under-cook the potatoes, then chill them so the potatoes could absorb the seasoned liquids, and correct both moisture and seasonings once again just before serving. Typically, Mom also brought baked beans slow-cooked with a ham bone (the bone marrow creates just the right stickiness), and bacon strips on top to keep the

Thirty-seven of Grampa Vincent's and Grama Mary Kahnke's fifty grandchildren (plus their parents) attended the 1958 family reunion at Grama's house.

beans moist. If she had apples in the freezer left-over from the prior season, she baked cinnamon apple pie. Otherwise, she served fluffy angel food cake with strawberries.

Stangler family picnics involved well over a hundred people; we had to play in the park until everyone arrived and it was time to eat. We could choose from dozens and dozens of foods: hot dishes, salads galore, and lots of desserts, too. I, for one, didn't waste any time exploring options. I went straight for our very distinctive

oval cast aluminum roaster to make sure I got a drumstick or a thigh, and so did several of my siblings. Mom's six-quart roaster was always the first thing emptied.

At one of the Stangler picnics, my sister told me to check out a rice hot dish that had tator tots on top. I went back and, thankfully, there was still some left. It had hamburger mixed with rice and cream of mushroom soup, topped with crispy tator tots. I skimmed the rest of the tator tots off the top without taking any rice. Yummy!

If Mom had caught me doing this, she surely would have wagged her finger and said, "Shame on you!"

Being shamed by Mom was effective punishment. I for one feared being shamed as if it were a curse. If the situation called for more than a raised eyebrow, a wag of the finger, or a few minutes of sitting by yourself on a chair in the kitchen, she'd turn the trouble-maker over to Dad to assign us an extra job when we got home.

After lunch, one of our relatives organized contests: gunny sack races, wheelbarrow races, etc. One particular year, because the prize was a Nut Goodie bar, I was motivated! I knew I couldn't run fast enough to win a race. However, I could pop a balloon by sitting on it faster than any of my cousins, because, unlike my cousins, I didn't care if I fell on the grass and got my dress dirty. I wanted that Nut Goodie bar, and I got it!

"Another time we were at the park for a big Farm Bureau picnic. A group of us men were sitting at a picnic table, and they were just starting a sack race. I mentioned that I thought a Miller kid would win. When asked why, I said to take a look, seven kids and all were Millers!"

Before Grama Kahnke moved to the nursing home, our cousins on my mom's side met at her

Linda, Ginny, and Janet with a soon-to-be jack-o-lantern, circa 1957
Laundry drying on the clothesline, and a puppy I was too young to remember.

house once a summer. Just like the Stangler family reunion, Mom would load up fried chicken, potato salad and pie for the potluck picnic. On Grama Kahnke's kitchen counter, red and white striped peppermint candy filled a glass canister. I'd never seen these marshmallow-looking hard candies, and I couldn't wait to have some. Mom said us kids weren't allowed to ask for candy or food when we went visiting. Lor figured out how to beat the system. "Mom says we can't ask for candy," she said to Grama Kahnke as we came through the door, and, of course, Grama

1962: Halloween Piñata
Diane, John, Marylu, Linda, Pat, Dolores, Virginia, Robert, Helen behind Art
From youngest to eldest, each child uses a bat trying to bust the piñata, while the others anxiously await candy spilling out.

immediately took the lid off the canister and let us each take one.

I don't remember going to anyone else's parties for Memorial Day, 4th of July nor Labor Day. Instead, we celebrated those holidays as a family. We never attended other families' High School graduation parties because we were always hosting one ourselves.

For Halloween, we carved two jack-o-lanterns, one for the front door and one for the back door. We had to be a bit careful with burning candles in them because afterward, we cut them up to make pumpkin bread, pumpkin cake, and pumpkin pie filling to be used on Thanksgiving.

Bob's favorite day of the year is Halloween because he likes costume parties. On Halloween, we pulled out our costume box to find whatever could be turned into a costume. Hoping we could find a plastic mask, or make costumes out of old clothes, and assorted high-heels and purses, we sorted "rags" until we found something suitable. We never went trick-or-treating at other people's houses. Instead, we each put on a costume, then, one or two at a time, we walked out the back door, knocked at our own front door, and asked, "Trick or treat?"

For treats, whoever was in charge gave us homemade popcorn balls and corn candy. Mom also made Spooky Pops (brittle caramel, shaped like pancakes, and decorated with chocolate chips to resemble jack-o-lantern faces). Frankly, most of us preferred eating Spooky Pops to trick-or-treating in town with our friends.

Spooky Pops

[Ramona's handwriting]

2 cup sugar

1/3 c. dark syrup

½ c. water

1/8 teas salt

Cook to 250 degrees until it makes a firm ball in cold water. Add 6 tbsp butter, cool until brittle in cold water. Put one tbsp at a time

1958: we had only a couple dozen people for Thanksgiving, and one turkey sufficed. As our extended family grew to our typical crowd of closer to forty, Mom added more main courses. Clockwise from the upper left: Bob, Art in the high chair, Kathleen, Mom, Marylu, Pat, Ramona's pal, Ramona, Linda, Janet, Al, Diane, John, Virginia. Dad probably took this photo.

on buttered cookie sheet. [Create jack o' lantern faces with chocolate chips to get "spooky" pops.]

After trick-or-treating on Halloween, we played "Bob the Apple." Half a dozen store-bought red Delicious apples floated in a couple gallons of water in our bread pan; we dunked our faces in until we succeeded in pulling out our special treat without using our hands. The prize? A store-bought apple with no worms!

When Kathleen traveled to Mexico after her high school graduation, she brought back the custom of making a piñata. The big girls mixed flour and water to create glue, and used it to paste strips of newspaper around a balloon to create a piñata. They filled it with wax-paper-wrapped homemade fudge and homemade caramels. They hung it on a string and everyone took turns hitting it with a kid's baseball bat, (littlest to biggest), until the piñata broke. Then we quickly scrambled to grab the most candy.

Dad craved brown sugar/maple fudge; us kids preferred chocolate fudge. My sisters and I tested every fudge recipe we could find, trying to make it fast yet keep it from crystallizing. Mom tried to teach us but we never got it right. Fudge was too tricky; our inability to replicate Mom's technique, not the recipe itself, caused us problems.

1953: Thankful for eleven happy and healthy children
Back row: Rose Ann, Kathleen, Ramona holding Linda, Al
Middle row: Robert, Diane, Marylu, Pat
Front row: Janet, John

As soon as Halloween was behind us, we started preparing for Thanksgiving. For farmers, Thanksgiving is a truly special occasion, because it marks the first chance to relax after completing all the fieldwork. We genuinely thanked the Lord for a bountiful harvest, after which Mom served a huge traditional feast: as big a turkey as fit in the big oven, ten or twelve pounds of mashed potatoes, a quart or two of gravy, turkey stuffing plus a stainless steel mixing bowl full of dressing on the side, a cake pan's worth of sweet potatoes covered with marshmallows, two pounds of fresh cranberries boiled with a bit of sugar, a few quarts of vegetables, often green beans with French onions on top, four

dozen homemade cloverleaf dinner rolls, and, of course, a relish tray. For dessert Mom baked pies, served with homemade whipped cream and/or ice cream.

Every year, I make an effort to share this message (that my IBM boss had passed out in the late 70's), with all Thanksgiving guests:

If you woke up this morning with more health than illness, you are more blessed than the million who won't survive the week.

If you have never experienced the danger of battle, the loneliness of imprisonment, the agony of torture or the pangs of starvation, you are ahead of 20 million people around the world.

If you attend a church meeting without fear of harassment, arrest, torture, or death, you are more blessed than almost three billion people in the world.

If you have food in your refrigerator, clothes on your back, a roof over your head and a place to sleep, you are richer than 75% of this world.

If you have money in the bank, in your wallet, and spare change in a dish someplace, you are among the top 8% of the world's wealthy.

If your parents are still married and alive, you are very rare, especially in the U. S.

If you hold up your head with a smile on your face and are truly thankful, you are blessed because the majority can, but most do not.

If you can hold someone's hand, hug them or even touch them on the shoulder, you are blessed because you can offer God's healing touch.

If you can read this message, you are more blessed than over two billion people in the world that cannot read anything at all.

You are so blessed in ways you may never even know.

In order to serve Thanksgiving dinner between noon and one, Mom started cooking the day before. Otherwise, she would have run out of cook-top space and oven availability. She mixed refrigerator-roll-dough the night before so that on Thanksgiving she just kneaded it and shaped three-clover leaf buns, and baked them in muffin tins. Before dawn on Thanksgiving, she made pie crust from scratch and baked one mincemeat pie and three pumpkin pies.

Meanwhile, Mom filled the bread pan with sage and sausage plum dressing and stuffed the turkey. She roasted an 18 or 20-pound turkey, as big as would fit in the "big roaster," a blue and white speckled oval enamelware pan. Mom cooked turkey in the big oven with the cover on until it was nearly done, then took the cover off to let the skin crisp up. While the turkey baked, she'd prepare a second meat entrée, whether that meant stuffing a goose, a pheasant, a wild duck or preparing a ham with pineapple and cloves.

The second main course belonged in the little oven along with sweet potatoes in square Corning Ware pans. Cranberries were boiled before the potatoes were put over, then set in a serving dish in the fridge to cool. Mom had learned to cook on a wood stove, where she put food over a flame so she used the term put over whenever she was talking about boiling something on the cooktop. As soon as she finished making cranberries for our Thanksgiving feast, she'd wake up a few helpers to clean up the dirty dishes so far, feed the babies, and peel potatoes so she could keep on cooking.

Mom had a specific routine so all the food was ready at the same time. She boiled Idaho russet potatoes on "the big burner." The little burner simmered giblets or boiled a second kettle of potatoes until it was time to make gravy.

Mom and Dad both preferred wild duck with plum dressing over turkey and stuffing. Duck became a family favorite supplemental entrée; John roasted this one for Mom and Dad after they retired.

Vegetables steamed in the three-quart and one-quart saucepans. While the potatoes were being mashed, the big burner was re-used for making gravy. If we ran out of burners and ovens, we cooked ham in the electric skillet or in a crockpot, and used canned cranberry jelly (no cooking required) and/or canned sweet potatoes (warm and serve). Potluck food from guests was welcomed but clearly not expected.

On the way to church on Thanksgiving morning, we sang "Over the River and Through the Woods," reminding us of Mom's childhood horse and sleigh ride to Grama's house. By the time I can remember, we always served Thanksgiving and other special occasion meals at home instead of traveling to our Grama's celebration.

The first time my then-husband attended a Miller Thanksgiving, we brought along twenty pounds of crab claws from my customer's restaurant supply business. My husband's jaw dropped to see our family devour an entire crate of crab claws as an appetizer, without the least bit of concern as to whether it would curb anyone's appetite. It didn't.

Thanksgiving morning in 1973, a WCCO radio announcer interviewed Mom about how spiraling inflation affected families of different sizes. The news reporter and his cameraman came to film our family's Thanksgiving dinner. As the TV cameras rolled, the journalist asked Mom to compare how many people attended Thanksgiving, and how much it cost to host this year's feast versus a few years prior.

Mom candidly told them that she *never* counted how many actually attended, nor did she have any clue how much it cost, because most of the food came from her garden. That stunned the reporter; he didn't know what else to ask! He turned the camera to Dad and asked the head of the household to please carve the turkey. On camera, Dad looked over at me and said, "Do you have any idea how to carve a turkey? Mom usually does this. I don't know where to start."

After that, the frazzled reporter asked us girls some [ridiculous] question about doing dishes in the absence of a dishwasher. At that point, my little sister picked up a spoon of baked beans and flung it at the [unwelcome] camera, and Oops! hit it right in the lens after which my mother quietly admonished, "Mind your manners." The rest of us kids wish we had had the nerve to do that! Needless to say, our family didn't get much exposure when that Inflation Segment aired.

The Christmas season included a series of special occasions. More than half the pleasure rested in our joy-filled high hopes while we prepared for each. First, we cut pine boughs and made an Advent wreath with purple candles for the three weeks of anticipation, and one pink one for a week of celebration. Next, we practiced Christmas music on the piano, guitar, violin, or recorder. We also played Christmas music on

"the stereo," a console radio/phonograph Mom and Dad bought in 1961 to enhance our new family room.

Every year on Ramona's birthday, Dec. 21st, Dad cut down an evergreen from the tree strip; the Christmas tree's fresh-cut pine smell intensified our Christmas spirit and heightened our impatience. All of us helped decorate our Christmas tree with our school-project construction-paper ornaments, and whatever mismatched Christmas balls and lights we could find. Instead of using garland to decorate door frames, we hung two hundred or so holiday cards that friends and relatives sent to Mom in response to her hand-written Christmas greetings or photo cards such as this one from 1957.

Our family baked hundreds and hundreds of Christmas cookies. From one holiday season to the next we stored green, red, and yellow food coloring, green, red and yellow sugar sprinkles, at least four bottles of sugary dot decorations, red cinnamon candy hearts, and occasionally gum drops. By the time Christmas came, we'd have used a full bottle of each of these to make sure we had decorated enough festive cookies.

For Santa, Mom filled dates with peanuts and rolled them in sugar. My next younger sister, Lor, specialized in baking Russian teacakes;

I specialized in pressed butter cookies called Spritz, using both our metal and our new plastic cookie press. Janet made terrific rolled sugar cookies in a dozen Christmas shapes. Decorating rolled Christmas cookies became an annual ritual. The stars got white or yellow frosting sprinkled with yellow sugar, the Christmas trees were decorated with green frosting with cinnamon candy hearts as Christmas balls. We put chocolate chip eyes and buttons on the snowmen, and used a molasses recipe for gingerbread boys and girls, outlined in white icing.

Spritz: Waseca County Cookbook

2 c. butter [salted]

1 c. p. sugar

1 c. granulated sugar

3 egg yolks

up to five c. flour

vanilla

cream of tartar

pinch salt

[My notes from 1982: When I used 2 t vanilla, ¼ t c of tartar, and ½ t salt, it was too big a batch to keep cold and still have sufficient mixing; better to start with 3 2/3 c sifted flour so the sugar is still crunchy. It's more like a butter cookie with an aftertaste.]

Traditionally, we also made almond bark, Russian tea cakes, and homemade egg nog. When I think back on the happiest days of my life, baking Christmas cookies with Mom and my sisters while listening to Christmas music comes near the top of my list.

Grama Miller's annual Christmas party was one of our very favorite special occasions. Grama Miller served green Jell-O made in a rectangular cake pan with chopped celery and shredded carrots, and a square Tupperware filled with pressed ham slices, mayo, and curly-edge lettuce on Wonder bread. Because we usually ate homemade bread and wild game or farm-raised meat, we thought of ham sandwich meat and boughten bread as a fabulous treat! Grama's sandwiches and midget pickles served in her crystal pickle dish are still two of my family's favorite comfort foods.

Grama Miller made the world's best divinity, a fluffy candy made with egg whites and sugar. She said her secret was to beat it just until the gloss goes off, and spoon it onto wax paper as quickly as possible. Her other specialty was chocolate cookies made with bacon grease, topped with frosting and/or half a black walnut.

After each kid filled a plate, two kids sat side-by-side on one of Grama's stair steps to enjoy our

1956 The Sunday before Christmas, forty or so Miller first cousins (plus parents) partied at Grama and Grampa Miller's. While adults sat in chairs or stood in the kitchen, a couple dozen kids crowded into the living room and the rest played in the bedrooms.

Christmas meal. After we ate, we played in the upstairs bedrooms with old-fashioned wooden toys, most of which Grampa Miller had carved.

I lived with my 80-something-year-old Grama Miller during my junior and senior years of high school so that her eldest son, Uncle Francis, could stop worrying about her falling, and/or burning herself. Grama didn't like to get her hand-stitched hot pads dirty. All too often she would pick up an aluminum pan without using a potholder and yell, "Heiss!" (hot). German was Grama Miller's mother tongue. By the time Grama's youngest sister, Marie, was born, WWI had broken out and Germans living in the U.S. were supposed to speak English to show their allegiance, even when speaking with family in their own home. My grandmother spoke perfect English except when she was surprised; at those times, her childhood vocabulary slipped out.

Every single day of the year, Grama cooked oatmeal for breakfast, served with raisins and skim milk. She was very particular, and didn't want to put even an ounce of fat on her *skin-and-bones* hips. In the middle of the afternoon, she cooked me a tiny little hamburger, and tucked it in her fridge. After Walter Cronkite finished reporting the five o'clock news on her black and white TV, all she'd have to do was re-heat that shriveled burger in a pan on her gas stove; these over-cooked burgers were marginal, but I didn't mind. For dessert, we ate ice cream and Oreo cookies, so who cares about the rest?

The Farm Bureau organization sponsored the only secular Christmas party that our family attended. It took place at Blooming Grove Township's Town Hall, a vintage one-room school house, complete with an outhouse out back. It had about ten rows of wooden benches to sit on while each family's contingent took the stage and entertained the crowd with a Christmas song. In preparation for the talent show, us girls requested to sing Jingle Bells so that Mom would pin three jingle bells on the bottom of each girl's starched can-can slip. That was our favorite! After we finished a potluck supper, Santa surprised us with grab bag gifts.

Our family reserved store-bought food for special occasions. New Year's Eve marked the only occasion of the year for which Mom bought junk food. They say absence makes the heart grow fonder, but in this particular case, absence makes the *tummy* grow fonder! We stuffed ourselves with Bugles, Fritos, Lay's ripple chips, and store-bought garlic and French onion dips. We also celebrated by serving two quarts of pop to serve about a dozen and a half kids, and stretched it by mixing it with nectar. We hung mistletoe for New Year's Eve, but no one ever kissed under it. My father once said he had never seen anyone kiss until he was eighteen. I remember everyone kissing babies, but other than that, kissing was pretty rare.

We went to church on New Year's Day morning. We were oblivious to traditional New Year's Day TV programs. Without a TV, there were no football games, and no parades to watch on New Year's Day. We were thrilled to have a few more days off from school so we could play with our new Christmas toys.

CHAPTER 9:

Beyond the Farm

PEOPLE WHO GREW up during the Great Depression, including my parents, learned that to share food with others was to offer love. My parents lived their post-Depression lives with an attitude of abundance, and shared what they had with all who entered, ever grateful for their blessings. Mom used to say, "The way to a man's heart is through his stomach." She tried hard to please Dad by serving his favorite foods. If Mom served things that Dad didn't enjoy, he complained, "Let's have this again in twenty years." No wonder she stuck to foods he liked.

Although I grew up with plenty to eat, prior to earning my own money in high school, I had eaten at only three restaurants. When I was in third grade, I ate my first restaurant meal at the King Melody Inn in celebration of Mom and Dad's 25th anniversary. They treated us to an

all-you-can-eat smorgasbord. Us kids kept asking for more and more shrimp and more ham until Mom got so embarrassed she told us we couldn't ask for anything else. *"It was one of the many times through the years when you didn't know whether to laugh or cry."*

When my parents were in their 80's, I occasionally steamed lobster tails for them, and served them with a little lemon and lots of butter

Mom passed away. Whenever these two love-birds went out to eat for an anniversary celebration, they came home with tall tales of awesome food, quite often of shellfish. They both loved lobster, crab and shrimp. When a Dundas, MN restaurant started an all-you-can-eat crab special, I remember them traveling an hour to get there. That restaurant surely lost money on my parents that night!

Mom and Dad celebrated their April 16th wedding anniversary sixty-six times before

Sometimes on their anniversary, Mom and Dad waited for us kids to go to bed so they could boil lobster tails at home. The stench of boiling seafood wafted through the register and kept us

1967: Mom and Dad celebrating their 27th Anniversary with steak and sautéed morel mushrooms. Mom looks pretty darn good for having delivered 22 kids, the youngest only a year prior to this photo!

awake, and we anxiously strained to hear what they were whispering. If the weather was nice, Mom and Dad often took a thermos of coffee and found a nature park where they could grill steaks for their early-season anniversary picnic, and revel in their love for each other.

To celebrate the good price Dad had negotiated on buying Bixler Baker's farm, he treated the whole family to Happy Chef's sixty-nine-cent per person pancake special. Dad didn't realize that ordering milk with the pancake special cost extra, so he told us to just drink water to save money. We complained to Mom that we *always* drank milk with pancakes, and she talked him into springing for the extra cost. That poor Happy Chef waitress served up twenty people, at least four of whom were young and made a sticky mess, and got my frugal Dad's most generous tip: two dollars, not nearly enough for the incredible job she did that night.

As children, we missed out on all the Italian, Indian, Japanese, Korean, Greek, and Vietnamese food I came to love when I lived in New York. We had never heard of pizza, nachos, cheese sticks, yogurt, or pate' nor even individually wrapped packets of crackers or cookies. We had also never heard of eating veal, crab, eel, or lutefisk. We had never tried stir-fry, egg rolls, nor wontons, and had never seen chopsticks. We knew nothing about fresh mozzarella, tortellini, rigatoni, or any authentic Italian food, nor French bread, Indian spices, or Cajun anything. We never, ever went to McDonald's, nor Burger King, nor Wendy's. No Culvers, no Applebee's, no Perkins, or ANYTHING.

Between Mom's Irish roots (aversion to spice), and Dad's German meat and potatoes heritage, the only three savory spices I remember seeing as a child were garlic salt, celery salt, and sage. For baking, Mom had a dozen or more bottles including cinnamon, nutmeg, ginger, allspice, and cloves. The condiments in our refrigerator were limited to ketchup, mustard, mayo, pickles, olives, soy sauce, and two or three kinds of salad dressing.

We used up jelly and jam so fast we didn't need to keep it in the fridge. That left room for such surprises as Dad's flavor-of-the-week fishing bait. We never knew when a new container was more likely to contain leeches, night crawlers or grub worms instead of some unfamiliar-but-delicious treat. Open unfamiliar containers at your own risk!

My third restaurant experience came as a result of our family winning a radio contest for having the largest family in the United States. While our country engaged in the Tet offensive in Viet Nam and mourned the loss of Dr. King, (neither of which I internalized at the time) Hollywood was making a comedy about a big family. The producers of the 1968 film, "Yours, Mine and Ours," hoped to find a big family who would help them advertise Lucille Ball and Henry Fonda's performances depicting a combined family of twenty children.

We drove an hour and a half to Minneapolis for a free private screening of the new film in the elegant Orpheum theater. In order to get our reaction to the movie, the company personnel monitored us as we watched the extreme chaos of Henry Fonda and Lucille Ball raising their recently-combined big family. I found the film silly, but frankly, it was more puzzling than funny; I kept wondering why that family didn't get their act together and get organized to reduce the pandemonium.

Before the movie, each of us got fitted for a new pair of shoes. After the movie, we were treated to a dinner at a restaurant. Which restaurant and what we ate escaped my memory; it must not have been too impressive. We were completely pre-occupied with the thrill of getting brand-new shoes.

This 1968 Minneapolis Star and Tribune article marked the third time our family had been prominently featured in the press; the first was a Sunday Pictorial Magazine cover story when we had fifteen kids, and the second occurred when Damien was born. My sister who lived in San Francisco learned about Damien's birth from the morning newspaper!

Our family was invited to try out for television commercials on more than one occasion. Carnation instant milk filmed us on a chilly, blustery day, piling into the van as if we were going to Easter Sunday Mass. Us girls looked great in our Easter dresses, coats, and bonnets. The boys all wore suits and ties, including the pre-school boys sporting their cute little bow ties.

The crew filmed the same scene over and over, trying to capture just the right take. Dad would get in first, then the kids, and lastly, Mom carrying the baby in a bundle of blankets. For the first few takes, the cameraman could see the baby's face as Mom got in the car. After that, Mom slipped into the house and exchanged the baby for a doll so that our youngest sibling would not catch a cold in that wind. She came back with the same bundle of blankets, but this time you couldn't see a face quite as easily, and the cameraman said, "Open up the blankets a little so I can see the face." She did. He didn't know the difference. We all snickered in delight.

Minneapolis Star Tribune article 1968
The "Yours, Mine, and Ours" production company treated us to a free lunch, free movie, and a free pair of shoes. I remember the thrill of getting those new shoes as if it were yesterday.

We didn't get hired to do that commercial, nor did we really care. The repetition that was required to shoot a successful TV commercial did not appeal to us kids, at all. We were not familiar with TV, nor were we interested in becoming famous.

After the 22nd child was born, my parents got many congratulatory letters, but they also got hate mail for about six months. The country was becoming conscientious about zero-population growth, and many people were furious to hear that there were so many in our family. Even one of our neighbors called my mother "a big cow" when she didn't realize she was being overheard on the party line. For a while, my parents didn't let any of the children go to the mailbox; they needed to sort the mail before anyone saw it.

My siblings and I lived in an era of innocence where something as simple as a new song absolutely thrilled us. When Kathleen came home from working for "Movement for a Better World," she taught us the song, "Up with People" by Paul and Ralph Colwell. We loved this new song, and sang it with great enthusiasm. It perfectly captures my mothers' eternal optimism, the lens through which my siblings and I came to view the world:

"Up, up with people, you meet 'em wherever you go,

Up, up with people, they're the best kind of folks to know.

If more people were for people all people, everywhere

There'd be a lot less people to worry about and

A lot more people who care."

Another simple pleasure was trying a new recipe. One nice thing about having such a big family is that when you cook something new or different, it's not a matter of *whether* it will get eaten, it's just a matter of how *long* it will take. Back on the farm, we got pretty excited when anyone introduced us to any kind of new and different foods, and I clearly remember some of those meals and the specific occasion on which we first enjoyed them.

When Kathleen came home from college, she baked a pan of lasagna, our first introduction to Italian food. What a treat! We found out about two new kinds of cheese, Parmesan and mozzarella, both yummy and both outside our budget, except of course for special occasions. After Marylu came back from a summer in Hong Kong, she introduced us to the idea of

Asian stir-fry. That was the first time I had tasted Asian food other than chow mein. Not long after that, Janet perfected the art of making egg rolls.

Linda wrote away for cheesecake recipes in 1971, and I've been using that Kraft cheesecake recipe ever since. Fondue became a big kick in the late seventies. Mom received a green metal fondue pot and six forks for Christmas and each kid patiently waited to deep-fry our meat in oil. I don't remember ever having cheese or chocolate fondue, (not Dad's cup of tea).

I thought Patty *invented* marble cake for her sixteenth birthday party. The idea of having both white and chocolate cake combined made everybody happy. A couple years later, Patty learned about pizza at college, and for months we bought Jeno's pizza kits containing dry pizza dough mix, a four ounce can of pizza sauce, a tiny packet of spices, and an ounce of Parmesan cheese. Between adding flour to the dough, rolling it paper-thin, then adding hamburger and tomato sauce to the toppings, we stretched each costly kit into two cookie sheets worth, enough so that everyone could have a piece of pizza. We could not wait to try our newfound treat.

It seems strange to recall a time when fresh fruit and vegetables were virtually unavailable during the winter. I can remember when I was first introduced to baking using peaches; prior to that they were considered too expensive. After Marylu (nicknamed Peach), studied in Atlanta, peach pie and peach sauce "suddenly" came into our menu planning.

In a year when anti-war riots abounded and Martin Luther King called our own government "the greatest purveyor of violence in the world today," my siblings and I on the farm were oblivious to the mood of the country until Marylu came home from college with a black male friend and freaked my parents right out. Mom said that if Marylu ever bore a mixed-race child, that the child would not be well accepted; Mom's worry was not for my sister but rather for the potential child. After that, though, my parents mellowed and became completely comfortable with racial diversity. They were happy when, during the 1968-1969 school year, I was requested to tutor the daughter of the first black family to move to our all-white town.

About this same time, health food was "in." Mom roasted soybeans from our field and tried to get us to quit snitching Dad's salted peanuts (from the bottom of his sock drawer, where he hid his personal stash of peanuts, chocolate, and sugar-coated orange slice candy). No dice; we kept wanting *real* salted peanuts. Sometimes we were tempted to break off a piece of Dad's hidden Hershey's chocolate candy bar or his Christmas-gift almond bark, but getting caught would definitely NOT have been worth it.

Here's how we came to be introduced to Mexican food. Dad made a living farming, and also from buying and selling land. Somewhere in the seventies, Dad also made a little money in the soybean futures market. In the fall of 1975, Mom and Dad sold a farm he had bought after the tornado and for the next twenty years, he received an annual farm payment large enough to change the way our family lived. Dad started taking Mom on annual vacations to distant places. Mom and Dad discovered tacos and Margaritas in Mexico, and for months they tried to replicate them at home.

I was introduced to waffle cones the year that the Association for Retarded Children's (ARC) annual picnic took place on our front lawn. After it was learned that JFK's sister was mentally challenged, the notion of retardation carried less of a stigma, and people were willing to talk about it and work together to provide appropriate care for special needs children. Mom worked tirelessly to organize our county's ARC, and champion support for our county's first "group home."

Every summer, one of the ARC members would host a potluck picnic for families with mentally challenged children, including games and prizes. It was fascinating to meet other mentally challenged kids and observe the similarities amongst them, especially the Down syndrome children; they were adorably cute, and so very friendly. But the thing I remember best? The ARC bought ice cream in tall brown two and a half gallon containers, and box upon box of regular cones and waffle cones. Anyone who asked for another cone got it, no questions asked, and we could even ask for two scoops. Yippee!!

I need to give the reader some background on our family history with regard to mentally challenged offspring. Because my mother's father had four mentally challenged brothers, Mom grew up thinking of people suffering from developmental delays, mental challenges and even full intellectual disability as "normal." In the one-room school house where she attended class through eighth grade, each child was taught according to his or her ability, reinforcing Mom's view that everyone is normal. In the late forties, when the Sacred Heart grade school principal asked Mom to take Rose Ann home from school because she was unable to keep up, Mom cried and cried. She had trouble thinking of Rose Ann's learning difficulties as anything other than *normal*.

IOn Memorial Day, we marched in the local parade then visited the graves of our relatives. Ginny (in the navy dress) in front of our family's first blue van.

Mom taught us by example to have compassion for special needs children. She conceived her own version of "No Child Left Behind" long before that law was passed. Certain skills and privileges were offered sequentially, according to birth order; everyone waited their turn. For example, none of us could stay overnight at a friend's house 'til our elder siblings that wanted to attend a sleep-over had done so, and until they reached fourth grade. If someone had not been invited to a sleep-over, Mom was known to create an opportunity for that person to stay with Aunt Marg or Aunt Therese for a night so that the next younger one would be free to attend a sleepover.

Aunt Marg and Aunt Therese shared my mother's joie de vivre, her love of children, and her values, and were happy to help Mom in this regard.

Aunt Marg's house was our favorite because she always baked sweets for us, usually chocolate chip cookies or a cake. When she let us play with teeny lipstick samples from the Avon lady, we were in HEAVEN. Aunt Marg was good at styling hair. Instead of braids, she offered me the chance to have a "duck-tail" haircut. I didn't like the thought of looking like a duck, so I stayed with my long hair. I watched her cut the other girls' hair and was sure I could do this.

I asked Mom if I could cut Marcia' and Alice's hair. I must have been 11. Those poor girls had to walk around with choppy hair until it grew enough for Aunt Marg to straighten it up. It was immediately clear that cosmetology was not my natural calling!

Mom treated everyone fairly, regardless of ability. Mom wouldn't let us learn to ride bike until each of the elder siblings, even those who were developmentally delayed, could ride bike. We were taught to look out for those who needed a little extra help, and make sure they got the support they needed. Mom instilled in us the sense that everyone belonged, that we were all part of a whole.

Most of us kids had no trouble empathizing with Rosie, Bob and Marty, but sometimes struggled with other siblings who were on the lower end of the capability spectrum. Mom and Dad gave extra attention to those siblings. Craving validation, more gifted siblings strived all the harder. In this way, co-existing with mentally challenged siblings frustrated some of us, but at the same time strengthened us. We improved under the pressure, not unlike how pressure on coal creates diamonds, and we bonded more closely with one another because of our shared experience of being given responsibility for taking care of special needs siblings at a young age.

After Bob and Marty moved into a group home in the early 80's, they thrived on winning Special Olympic ribbons and medals for running and speed walking. In preparation for competition in the early eighties, all the athletes got a pro bono physical from a Mayo Clinic doctor who noticed that both my brothers had unusually large testicles, high foreheads, and narrow palates that over-crowded their teeth. The Mayo researched our family's genes in 1985 and diagnosed those with an inherited genetic condition.

Until well after I graduated from college, doctors didn't know what caused the type of retardation that affected our family. When I was in fifth grade, I was chosen to stand next to Mom in front of the ARC exhibit at the Waseca County Fair. The ARC posters had been designed to convince fair-goers that retardation was not inherited, that it was just random, and I was living proof, so to speak, that a mother of mentally challenged children should not hesitate to conceive another child.

In May of 1991, researchers identified the gene that causes a specific type of retardation known as Fragile X Syndrome (FXS): decreased or absent levels of fragile X mental retardation protein leading to intellectual disability. Technically, FXS results from excessive CGG repeats (cytosine, guanine and guanine) on one of the 23 pairs of chromosomes. Between 1 and 50 CGG repeats are within a normal range; 50 to 200 CGG repeats is termed a "pre-mutation" where a wide spectrum of learning disabilities is common. More than 200 CGG repeats is known as Fragile X Syndrome, and can cause physical symptoms, developmental delays and intellectual disability.

A mother like mine would likely have had one fragile X chromosome, and one healthy X, and any effects from a fragile X may or may not have been noticeable without genetic testing. Some children inherit the mother's healthy X while others inherit the fragile one. Because girls have two X chromosomes while boys have only one X, a boy is statistically more likely than a girl to exhibit symptoms from pre-mutation X chromosomes, and also statistically more likely to develop FXS. Since 1991, it has been possible for parents' CGG repeats to be tested to explore their odds of passing a fragile X to their offspring. It is also possible to have fetuses tested.

My mother advised at least one of my cousins to bear a child even if she found out her fetus exhibited Fragile X. As a Catholic, Mom did not believe in birth control nor in abortion. She believed all children are "God's children," and she gladly accepted all the children God gave her.

In retrospect, Mom's four challenged uncles exhibited symptoms recognizable as stemming from a fragile X: large ears, high forehead, uneven gait, and mental deficiencies. One of the four was confined to a state hospital before there was a good understanding of this condition. Mom would acknowledge that these four uncles were "a little slow," but since various symptoms resulting from a fragile X were so common in her experience, she viewed the entire spectrum as, may I say, a normal distribution.

Fragile X Syndrome and the spectrum of its pre-mutational symptoms are akin to an elephant in the family living room. In my opinion, the biggest downside of our parents raising such a huge family was dealing with the effects of this. The more kids Mom and Dad had, the more the anomaly showed itself. The result was that our parents' attention got increasingly diverted into care-giving special needs' children, and it necessitated that the more capable siblings share parenting duties and responsibilities.

My siblings were nearly finished having children prior to 1991; I'm unaware of the worry of passing on a fragile X affecting any of my siblings' choices on whether to bear children. I currently have three nephews and two great-nephews who live in group homes because of their special needs, and I am aware of other nieces and nephews getting genetic tests as part of their family planning.

After Bob and Marty moved to town, Waseca's Elm Homes group home staff did a marvelous job of helping my two brothers improve their skills, including their competitive athletic skills. Every year at Special Olympics, Bob won medals and ribbons. A couple years after moving in, Bob asked if he could travel to New York to visit me. He was learning to swim, and wanted to stay in a hotel in New York City with an Olympic size swimming pool. He insisted the pool had to have an underwater light at the end. The only New York hotel room I found meeting his criteria cost $1250 a night. There's no way I could afford that, so I booked him a room in the NY suburb of White Plains, reasoning that Bob would never know the difference. I picked him up from the airport, served dinner at my home, and then drove toward the hotel.

"This is not New York! This is White Plains!" he exclaimed. "White Plains is where my company is!"

I was too shocked to respond. When had he learned to read?? He had gotten a job and was earning a living moving cardboard cases of vegetables for Birds Eye General Foods. On every single Birds Eye box, it said *White Plains, NY.* I felt horrible. I had to eat crow, and fess up that his hotel room did indeed have an Olympic size pool with a light at the end, but he was not going to be staying in NYC.

Bob spent the following three days touring NYC with me and my brother Art. When I accompanied Bob back to Minnesota, we entered my parents' house at suppertime. Dad asked Bob, "Well, what did you do in New York?"

Bob proceeded to recite, in sequence, every single thing we had seen and done, including exactly what he had eaten. That's how I first learned what a terrific memory Bob has. My jaw nearly dropped to the floor. My brother had acquired new skills, bought many new clothes, and made a whole new life for himself at the group home. In short, he had "grown up." I was so proud of him! I gained a ton of respect for his group home caregivers, especially Kathy and Dennis.

Bob's first paid employment was to work as a carry-out boy for Wolf's grocery store. That assignment ended abruptly after my normally happy brother told off a particularly bitchy customer. From the way the store manager described the incident, my siblings and I quietly said to each other, "Go, Bob!" The rest of Bob's three-decade career was spent at the local Birds Eye factory where he got along just great.

My brother Marty is equally content living in the group home. In fact, he is one of the happiest people I know. None of us will ever forget when Marty went around the circle at our 2011 family reunion tearfully saying to each person, "Happy Linda! Happy Virginia," and so on down the line. While many of us strive to live in the moment, my challenged siblings seem to live in the present with no effort whatsoever.

CHAPTER 10:

Our Shrinking Household

OUR HOUSEHOLD GROWTH peaked in 1966-67 following the birth of Damien. Eighteen children lived at home. The house itself stayed the same size for a good many years until a plant room was added after Mom and Dad retired. However, as the years went by and children left the nest, one by one, beds began to disappear.

Just like when our family was growing, and Mom and Dad abruptly moved our assigned beds around in anticipation of a new sibling, now they adjusted sleeping arrangements after each high school graduate headed off to college. As our household shrank, Mom and Dad were once again challenged to balance the number of youngsters in each bedroom, and to again exchange boys versus girls' bedrooms, depending on how many beds were needed for a given school year.

It is impossible to remember all the permutations of who slept where in any given year. Often, one memorable childhood incident triggered a broader recollection of who slept where. For example, there's general agreement on when Janet moved to the big girls' room; it was just after Lu moved out. Not counting Mike Charlebois, seventeen of us lived at home at that time. Here's one story that anchors our shared recollection of who slept where when.

To build us a swing, Dad tied a sturdy hay rope to the branch next to our treehouse in the pig pasture just beyond our garden fence. When Janet jumped from the highest branch above that treehouse, the hay rope snapped and the fall knocked the wind out of her. I was standing on the tree house ledge; when she didn't move, I raced to find Mom, afraid Janet was dead. "After

I fell from the treehouse swing," Janet said, "I recuperated in the bottom bunk in the northwest room." Diane agreed: "Jan moved in when Lu moved out, and was still there when I graduated in '67, leaving sixteen Miller children at home." When Dad found out we broke that hay rope designed to carry hundreds of pounds of hay bales, all he could say was, "What in the sam hill were you doing?"

It is easy for me to remember where I slept in 1967. That's the year Mom and Dad attended the world's fair in Montreal and they brought me a maroon pennant as a souvenir. It became the largest of my pennant collection, and fit snuggly on the south-facing wall in the little girl's room, right over my bunk bed.

Ginny slept in the middle room during junior high when the cedar chest was in that room, "first bed on the right as you walk in." At that time, Mom wanted Charlebois to have his own room (not to sleep in the same room as Bob and Marty) so she moved him into John's old room when it became available. Whenever John was home on weekends from the Ag School, Charlebois moved his rollaway bed back into Bob and Marty's room.

Pauline recalls how Greg and Damien had bunk beds in the baby room with a ladder for

1975: Mom and Dad celebrated thirty-five years of marriage, as happy and in-love as the day they wed.

the top bunk; she slept on the floor there during Christmas break when the college kids came home. When Angi moved upstairs in 1968, one bed got removed from the baby room for the first time. Hurrah! We no longer needed bunk beds in the little room so John had built a platform bed and put his desk/stuff *under* it. How creative! The second sign of downsizing came when John left for college, leaving us with sixteen at home, counting Charlebois, who by this time was one of the family.

1975: All 22 children attended John and Sandy's wedding.
Back row: Diane, Marylu, Pat, Virginia, Alice, Linda, Lor, Pauline, Robert, Art.
Middle row: Pat, Alice, Rose Ann, Helen, Janet.
Seated: Al, Ramona, Dad, Mom, Kathleen, John.
Front: Marcia, Greg, Damien. Angi, and Marty.

In 1970, Janet left home to attend St. Ben's. In 1971, Linda chose to go to St. Mary's college. Now our household was down to fourteen. That's the same year Charlebois moved out and I started working from three to eleven PM at the local canning factory and moved to town to live with Grama Miller, leaving one more bed free on weekdays. Thirteen.

Dad removed the bunk beds from the little girls' room because only four people slept there! With no new babies to require that toddlers get bumped upstairs, the two youngest in the family, Greg and Damien, stayed downstairs until 1972, even though Greg was old enough to start kindergarten. One bunk bed migrated to the little room in anticipation of Greg moving up.

Damien recalled: "I was pretty spoiled my kindergarten year because I got to hang out with DAD in the afternoon. In the winter that meant chasing down fox with the snowmobile. Dad would put the 12 gauge [shotgun] along the foot rail so it would be handy when we caught up to the fox (at least that's how I remember it... He only threw me off once during the chase that I can remember, although I do remember clearing open water in the ditch running through the slough. That caused both of us enough of a scare that we had to head over to Uncle George's place to tell him the story and grab a few cookies from Aunt Marg."

Dad's recollection of that time: *"It was a special day in our lives that fall when Damien started school. Now the house was empty, and Ceil could relax for a few hours at a time every day, for the first time in thirty years."*

In 1972, Kathleen graduated from college and headed to Colorado to teach. Ginny graduated from Waseca High School that year, the first Miller kid to finish at public school after Sacred Heart parish closed the High School for lack of funding. John graduated from St. John's University; he returned home to build a phalaris binder and help Al cut phalaris grass prior to teaching in Puerto Rico that fall. We needed to subtract one girl's bed and find a place for one grown boy. Holding at twelve kids total but oh, oh! Need a boy's bed.

Greg reminisced about his move upstairs: "I took over the metal bunk bed Charlebois had slept in; Art saved me one drawer and exactly one hanger." Nice brother! Four years after John left, Art and Greg slept in the little room. The sign on the door still read "John Charles," so everyone continued calling it John's room long after John had left home.

Once Greg moved upstairs, Mom needed only one (not two) empty crib, so, for the first time since 1940, Mom and Dad slept without a crib in their bedroom... They had spent *thirty-two years* sleeping next to a baby crib. Amazingly, Pauline, although only six years younger than I, cannot remember the master bedroom EVER having a crib in it! Wow! Who could wrap their head around that?

By this time, Mom and Dad had lots of grandchildren, so they maintained a crib in the baby room. Damien remembers sleeping in the baby room until age five when he started kindergarten and moved upstairs. News flash! No more kids downstairs.

Damien recalled, "Whenever it stormed, Bob & Marty and I would plaster our faces against the southwest window to watch lightning as if it were fireworks... ooh! Ahh!" "...and does everyone else already know that Bob and Marty were super-light sleepers, and never actually *slept*?"

1983: Greg poses with Al's daughter Candice, the youngest of eight children.
Behind them stands the basketball hoop, the number one and number two brooder houses, the east henhouse, and the first pole barn.

In 1973, with only a guest crib left, the baby room once again became the piano room. Dad had made a rule that he would help pay for college only for those kids who attended a Catholic college in Minnesota. I wanted to go where the fewest siblings had graduated so that professors would have less pre-conceived expectations, an issue that had haunted me all the way through grade school and high school.

Whenever some teacher or other well-meaning adult would quiz one of us, "Do you play piano like Kathleen? Do you play violin like Marylu? Do you sew like Diane? Are you in Speech and Choir like Janet?" we sometimes wanted to jump out of our shoes and say, "Don't expect me to be that!" As Linda once said, "I'm not a Homecoming Queen nor a cheerleader. I just want to ride my horse!" Worse than an innocent adult's comparative questions was a sense of shame whenever Dad would ask an accusatory question, "Why can't you shoot a deer? Why can't you drive a stick-shift?"

I chose St. Ben's where only one sibling, Kathleen, had graduated. Upon arrival on campus I attended a welcoming reception. The President of the college took one look at me, immediately recognized me as a Miller, then innocently compared me to my big sister, and shared that he enjoyed having my sister as his student driver, and hoped I would be just as delightful an asset to the college. Ugh! I had no idea my sister was the college President's driver. As sincere and complimentary as it was, it was definitely *not* what I wanted to hear.

After I left for college in January of 1974, Art moved out to study airframe and power plant mechanics at Winona Vo Tech. That brought the count from twelve down to ten children at home. Greg was not allowed to have Art's room to himself, even though there was plenty of space to do so. Instead, Damien moved in and they slept in bunk beds.

Lor took my place living with Grama Miller. Then, in 1975, she spent her junior year of high school in Bolivia as a Rotary foreign exchange student. Time to subtract one more girl's bed, making it nine (five girls and four boys). Bob continued living at home while working at the local food factory.

In 1976, the little girls' and big girls' rooms again got renamed, this time to simply "the two girls' rooms." With what was considered *so few* kids living at home, and no babies to worry about, indoor pets were allowed for the first time. While Linda's friends traveled to Florida, our family took care of their dog and their gray house cat, Zelda. The cat sat in the window and would not let anyone near it. Our own dog got nervous, came untied, and chewed one of our pig's legs. After Dad unceremoniously killed that pig he declared, "No more dogs!"

In 1977, when Dolores graduated from high school, Linda and Helen graduated from college, and Art graduated from Vo Tech and also got his pilot's license. That same year John attended Mankato State to get his teaching certificate. Still only nine kids at home, but extra people coming home to celebrate required extra beds. Thus, sleeping bags and camping options started growing.

Alice and Angi both moved out to start high school at Good Counsel Academy in Mankato in 1978. Temporarily, three girls and four boys lived at home. After a year, Angi stayed. Alice returned home, recalling, "The big girls' room had Pauline, Marcia and me until Pauline moved out." "After that, Marcia moved in with me." Back to eight at home, but, OMG, no one slept in the big girls' room. Really? An empty bedroom at the Miller farm for the very first time?

Our house continued the process of emptying when Bob moved to Waseca's first group home, near Trowbridge Park, on 11/27/1979. Now there were seven. Alice graduated from Waseca High School in '81 and moved to St. Cloud to attend Vo Tech. Down to six. Angi graduated from Good Counsel Academy and was the first kid to choose an out-of-state university: Creighton U in Omaha, Nebraska. Sophomore year, she transferred to Notre Dame. Only five left, with three boys outnumbering the two girls for the first time ever. Linda got her master's in Psychology, and Jan finished her MBA from Indiana U. More celebrating. More sleeping bags, and more camping in tents in the back yard.

Rose Ann moved in to the co-ed group home near TrowBridge Park in 1982 leaving four, one girl and three boys, at home. Marcia became Mom's number one helper. In 1983, Marcia and Greg graduated from Waseca High School. Marcia moved to Mankato that year and lived with a family while doing job training. Only three left, all boys.

In 1983, Greg joined Art (who was the first to attend a state university), at the University of Minnesota. Sister Ramona got her Masters in Ministry. Only two kids remained at home: Marty was 25 years old, and Damien was 18. "For a while, I lived at home with Mom, Dad and Marty," said Damien. "We were a foursome."

Suddenly, the Miller household started *growing* again. Marcia moved home after her job training. Mom and Dad once again had three at home. Pauline moved back home prior to delivering a baby. Make that four... Mom had set up a baby crib, and was totally surprised when Pauline delivered the joy of her life on July 3, 1984, twin boys! Uh, oh, almost overnight six beds (four children's plus two grandchildren's) were needed. When Damien left home to attend St John's University, Marcia, Marty, Pauline and her developmentally delayed infant twins, Matthew and Michael, temporarily lived with Mom and Dad. Subtract one. That makes five.

Marty moved in to Bob's group home on January 3rd, 1985. Down to four again. By then, Waseca offered separate group homes for men and women. Because of Marty's speech impediment aggravated by congenital hearing loss, Marty affectionately calls Robert "Bobert." Marty was very happy to move to "Bobert's house."

Pauline and her twins moved to their first apartment, leaving one last child at home. Marcia moved to Mankato to start working. Party time: all twenty-two children have been launched into adulthood! The upstairs of our childhood home remained empty from then on.

Just in time for their 45th Anniversary, Mom and Dad officially become empty nesters.

Dad reminisced: *"January 13, 1987 was just another winter day to most people, but to Ceil and I it was a sort of bench mark. It was Damien's 21st birthday and he was home alone with us that evening for deer chops and birthday cake." "I think we went to more P.T.A. meetings over a longer period of time than any family around here. And I still can recall Ceil getting the kids clothes lined up for school every fall to say nothing about school supplies. It was a major part of her life for forty years."*

After all of us left home and Dad sold his farm equipment in preparation for his golden years, he and Mom decided it was time to upgrade the farm house one final time. The fourth extension became a four-season "plant room."

In her retirement, Mom raised a few canaries and lots and lots of flowers. When Dad retired, he removed some canned goods shelving and installed a lathe in the new part. He took up woodworking as his retirement hobby. After a couple months of having to trudge up one flight of stairs to use the master bathroom, he had a third toilet installed in his basement workshop. Holy Cow, do I (and my siblings!) wish our home had had a third toilet when all of us lived there!

Meanwhile, my siblings continued lots and lots of education. Angi graduated from Notre Dame and was commissioned as a Captain in the Army. In 1986, Marylu got her Masters in Gestalt Therapy and Art got an Engineering degree from the U of M. Greg also graduated from the U of M in 1987. Art finished his master's degree in the spring of 1990, the same year that Mom and Dad celebrated their 50th wedding anniversary and moved to their retirement home in town.

Dad completed "Memoirs" in 1989, and distributed about a hundred copies to family and friends. His mother had kept a diary for him as a child, and he kept a diary all his life; he was what Diane called "a natural writer, storyteller." *"I put this together,"* Dad wrote in his memoir, *"primarily so my children would have a sort of documented record of their dad's various escapades."*

At the end of his memoir he noted: *"It doesn't seem possible that it all really took place, that our family all grew up and moved away and we have our 11-room house to ourselves, except on weekends when we usually have some of the family dropping in for a few days."*

In 1991, Patty graduated as an LPN. Sister Ramona got her Masters in Franciscan Studies and John got his Master's degree in Computer Science in 1992. Diane was awarded her J.D. degree, and Art received his PhD in 2005. In 2007, the summer before I retired, I took a required Physical Education class so that I could finally qualify for a Bachelor of Arts degree from the College of St. Benedict. Ginny was posthumously awarded her Medical Administrative Assistant degree from the National American University in 2014, shortly after having suddenly passed away suddenly of a heart condition. No doubt I'm missing some of our family's many educational accomplishments, but you get the drift.

Mom finished her memoir, "My Career" in 1994, again just for family and friends. Linda had interviewed her at the time as to her motivation for writing. Linda recalled, "She wanted to pass on her family history to the next generation; she also knew that both the public and her offspring would be curious about her life, and she wanted to say: "I did it all and I had fun doing it."" As our parents aged, twenty-two healthy, happy children continued raising families, farming, working, studying, teaching, traveling, hunting, fishing, and enjoying music.

Mom and Dad did an unbelievable job of raising twenty-two children. They inspired us to get educated and to use our talents well. In her memoir, Mom wrote: *"Before my career*

ends I would like to see my children all happy and contented in whatever they have chosen for their lives, especially being at peace with their God. I would like my children to remember that God loves them and so do we. Never forget to thank God for his blessings. Remember all the good times we had together and do not dwell on any misfortunes you may have had." As the final line of her book she wrote, *"If I had my life to live over again... I would do it just the same."*

My parents led by example, living each day to the fullest. They encouraged us to pursue our passions. They taught us to be considerate of others. They gave us self-confidence such that each of us could become our own person, create our own family, flit around the world and still feel grounded, knowing the deep taproots from whence we came. Mom and Dad were never wavering, always there, steady and predictable, a mountain of faith.

CHAPTER 11:

Where are they Now?

MOM PASSED AWAY peacefully at age eighty-three, a few years after developing congestive heart failure. Dad died less than a year later on his 90th birthday, and, as my brother John said, "They are probably *still* getting high fives from all the angels and saints." As much as I dearly loved my parents, my brothers and sisters are just as close to me as Mom and Dad were; I am eternally grateful to be a part of the Miller Clan.

About half of my immediate family live in Minnesota. While I call Florida home, others of my siblings reside in Colorado, Iowa, Illinois, Oregon, and Washington state. In addition to those states, our nieces and nephews live in Alabama, Alaska, California, Idaho, Kansas, Montana, New Mexico, Nevada, Nebraska, and Wyoming. Our clan has seventeen states covered! We can't afford the time and money to visit all our siblings, so we have to settle for scheduling a get-together. After my parents passed, our family began a new tradition of getting together for a family reunion every three years.

Although our family has almost fifty nieces and nephews (depending on whether you count children born out of wedlock, children who were given up for adoption, step-children by marriage, etc.), we are all still close. We also have more than three dozen great-nieces and nephews.

People sometimes ask me how children raised in such a big family "turned out." Wonderfully, if I may say so! No one is in jail. No one has drug-addition problems. No one is

July 3, 2011 Family Reunion: the last time all 22 Miller siblings were together
Back row: Bob, Art, Marty, Al, Greg, Damien, John
Middle row: Alice, Angi, Lor, Diane, Ramona, Marylu, Jan Irene (Pat in front of her),
Ginny (Helen in front of her)
Seated: Linda, Marcia, Rose Ann, Kathleen, and Pauline

battling cancer. We are a healthy family, a happy clan, a well-educated group, and a well-traveled bunch. We each pursued our own likes and dislikes, and created our own life away from the legacy of our big family.

1. **Sister Ramona**: After serving in leadership for her Franciscan community and directing pilgrimages to Rome for many years, she now teaches High School religion part-time and serves on congregational committees as her retirement career.

2. **Al, Jr.**: Raised eight children with his wife, Donna. Farmed, worked as a mechanic, trained dogs to hunt coon, for hobbies plays cards, hunts, fishes, and plays fiddle.

3. **Rose Ann**: Enjoyed the peace and quiet of a group home, loved dolls and children's books. Passed away 9/28/2013 following a flu bug.

If they were still alive today, Alvin and Lucille would surely be proud of their forty something grandchildren as well as three dozen (and counting...) great-grandchildren. This photo was taken in July of 2011 at our first Miller Family Reunion without our parents.

4. **Kathleen**: Raised four children. Teaches piano lessons. Greatest joys are her children and their families, and being out-of-doors in the beauty of nature. Enjoys Sherlock Holmes and other detective novels.

5. **Bob**: won dozens of medals at Special Olympics, and loves to walk.

6. **Pat**: worked as a nurse and raised three children with her husband, Glen; enjoys scrapbooking.

7. **Marylu**: Taught, worked as a homeopath, raised four boys; loves flowers.

8. **Diane**: got her law degree and worked on legislation for health freedom, raised two daughters, likes music/dancing.

9. **John**: Directed the computer lab/taught computer science at St John's University and had four children with his wife, Sandy; family archivist who loves the woods.

10. **Jan Irene**: After managing technology project teams around the world for years, she now consults and coaches organizational leaders and applies her leadership skills to local wildlife habitat conservation and watershed restoration; raised one son, loves yoga, singing, swimming, and painting.

11. **Linda** : Self-employed; loves biking and bird watching.

12. **Ginny**: worked as a nurse and raised four sons; loved flowers, especially tulips, she passed away 5/8/2014.

13. **Helen**: sold information technology solutions and managed salespeople; loves to travel and to sew

14. **Art**: PhD research engineer for NIOSH, raised two daughters with his wife, Michelle; beer connoisseur who loves hunting.

15. **Lor**: does research for Northeast Iowa Community College, raised two children; loves singing, biking, and baking.

16. **Marty**: picks up the garbage in parks and along roadsides; loves visitors.

17. **Pauline**: works for Walmart, raised two boys; loves to cook and stay busy.

18. **Alice** : caretaker for an apartment building, loves gardening.

19. **Angi**: assistant to the dean of St Edward high school, raised five children with her husband, John; loves to cook and to read.

20. **Marcia**: works in the kitchen at Mankato State University; loves to spend time with siblings.

21. **Greg**: Along with wife Karen, raised five children; bought the farm from Mom and Dad and still owns a piece of it, loves staying young and fit. Self-employed agronomist. Catholic.

22. **Damien**: manages ten thousand acres of wildlife refuge; loves hunting, and all things outdoors.

Epilogue

In 1982, my career took me to New York, where I tried every ethnic food I could find. I'd have to write a whole separate book if I wanted to cover my NY dining experiences. But just to offer a quick glimpse, food in NY ranged from the bizarre to the fantastic. On the former end: the first time I flew to NY, some friends sent me on a scavenger hunt where I had to locate a duckling just about ready to hatch when that egg got hard-boiled. I had no trouble finding one in Chinatown; whatever the Chinese call hard-boiled, premature duckling was, I learned, a fairly common delicacy!

At the fantastic end of the spectrum, I happened upon a NY restaurant not far from Central Park that specialized in caviar, smoked salmon, and champagne. Through the display window, I noticed one bartender dedicating himself to three customers seated at his tiny four-person bar. When I saw a waitress serve smoked salmon and capers to a guest at one of the three two-person tables, I couldn't resist going in.

A caviar expert behind the refrigerated countertop educated each new customer on the subtle differences in top-quality caviar. I sat down and enjoyed a teensy fifty-dollar snack, just to find out how the rich and famous live. Then and there, I absolutely fell in love with caviar and smoked salmon. I learned that NY chefs and restaurateurs frequent this itsy-bitsy restaurant to taste the merchandise before they buy large quantities. Later, I realized that what I had just sampled cost twice that much in a nice restaurant, and that I had just gotten a bargain!

I lived in NY for over fifteen years. I came to love the fabulous food options in Manhattan, but I never lost my nostalgia for an era of innocence. In fact, life in NY intensified my joy of entertaining, my desire to spend time with family, and my love of Mom's home cooking. I hope you find yourself offering hospitality to an ever-growing body of family and friends who share my parents' zest for life, and that you take every opportunity to experiment with Mom's simple but tasty recipes.

ABOUT THE AUTHOR:

Miller spent her 31-year sales and management career with IBM and with ADP'S Brokerage Group. In retirement, she enjoys quilting, fishing, traveling, and playing tennis. She lives with her husband, Tom, in North Port, FL and welcomes feedback at helenrita.miller@gmail.com
Look for her family's recipe collection, "Cheaper by the Two Dozen: Recipes" as well as "The Perfect Courtship," 300 penny-postcard love-letters her parents exchanged between 1938 and 1940.

CPSIA information can be obtained
at www.ICGtesting.com
Printed in the USA
BVHW05s2124040418
512448BV00021B/1177/P